A CROWD
IS NOT
COMPANY

ROBERT KEE

CARDÍNAL

Dedication

To the memory of my friend Squadron Leader Ian Cross, D.F.C. and those 49 of his fellow prisoners who were shot with him by Hitler's orders on re-capture after escaping from Stalag Luft III in 1944.

A CARDINAL BOOK

First published in Great Britain by Eyre & Spottiswoode Ltd 1947
Second edition with an Introduction published by
Jonathan Cape Ltd 1982
Published in Cardinal by Sphere Books Ltd 1989

Reproduced, printed and bound in Great Britain by
The Guernsey Press Co. Ltd, Guernsey, Channel Islands.

Sphere Books Ltd
A Division of
Macdonald Group Ltd,
66/73 Shoe Lane, London EC4P 4AB

A member of Maxwell Pergamon Publishing Corporation plc

Contents

Introduction   7

Part One   11
Part Two   69
Part Three   123
Part Four   183

Introduction

For a crowd is not company and faces are
but a gallery of pictures and talk but a
tinkling cymbal, where there is no love.

FRANCIS BACON

Introduction

A Crowd Is Not Company was begun in the summer of 1945, almost as soon as I got back to England after three years and three months as a prisoner-of-war in Germany. It was finished late in 1946. Though a recollection in post-war tranquillity, it is also an immediate distillation of personal experience without the advantage or disadvantage of such hindsight, maturity or sophistication as may have come my way since. Re-reading it for the first time after nearly thirty-five years I am glad of this. Not only does the book reveal some details of my experience that I had forgotten but also some forgotten attitudes, so that for me at least it has a strange authenticity, almost as if it had been written by someone else.

I remember clearly the need to communicate authenticity at the time and it was this which led to some indecision about how to present the book. It had been begun as a 'novel', with 'him' and 'them' viewed from the outside in the traditional God-like stance of the fiction writer. But the very contrivance of fiction seemed to introduce a spurious note opposed to what I wanted to achieve. Another way of saying this, of course, is that my resources as a fiction writer were inadequate to the task. I am glad that in whatever way I recognised this and remember the sense of relief with which I finally decided to drop the structure of invention and stick to unashamed egocentric narrative. On the other hand the book was published both in Britain and the United States as a novel. Why?

There were two interdependent reasons. First, it was a matter of publishing history that the boom in books about the First World War had not occurred until some ten years after it had ended, and the time was thought to be not yet ripe for any more memoirs of the Second World War. Nevertheless publishers were on the look-out for new young writers to cultivate for the supplies of paper again becoming available. Novelists of the future were what they wanted, and if one wanted to be a novelist — which I think I then did — it seemed expedient to appear one.

Secondly, there was in fact an aspect of the book which could be used to validate the term 'novel'. Even though it was a true narrative of experience it was not always in every detail literally true. As people often do when telling stories, I had embellished it here and there to enhance what seemed the essence of situations and intensify the nature of the literal experience. Not only had the dialogue obviously not been remembered in such exact detail as here set down but I had made some sketchy composites of some of my fellow prisoners. The accounts of being taken prisoner, and of the escape between pages 127 and 187 are true in almost every detail (my companion on the escape was Squadron Leader T.D. Calnan, who has written his own account of a later escape we made together, and 'Willy Myers' was a future Chancellor of the Exchequer). On the other hand one or two events were embellished to the point at which embellishment began to take them over (the abortive attempt on the wire is an example). This did not worry me because so much detail of the three year experience was being left out that I wanted to strengthen the sense of the whole. It seemed to me that just as fiction can lay claim to larger more universal truths than fact, so, by embellishing fact in the interests of larger truth, I could lay some claim to fiction.

And so, when my publisher, the writer Graham Greene then working for Eyre and Spottiswoode, asked sympathetically if I wanted to call it a novel, I said 'Yes' rather readily. It was a measure of his talent for encouragement that he let me have my way. Reviewers were kind and none, I think, questioned in print the book's appearance as a 'novel', though one, Peter Quennell, did tell me at a literary party that he couldn't understand why I had called it one and I immediately wished I hadn't.

I am in no two minds about its category today. *A Crowd Is Not Company* is an autobiographical memoir, a self-centred account of how one Englishman of middle-class background in his early twenties saw and felt these war experiences at the time. For this reason nothing has been altered, added or removed. Only the four letter word of the famous Air Force song on page 123, which had to be bowdlerised for the publishing conventions of 1947, has had its manhood restored. If the language in the dialogue itself seems rather unrealistically lacking in such four letter words (which were used just as prolifically by young R.A.F. officers then as they are in almost all walks of life today) this presumably reflects self-censorship before those same publishing conventions; though even so the late Douglas Jerrold, the senior partner at Eyre and Spottiswoode complained in what I thought of at the time as a rather absurd 1914–18 anachronism, of 'the unnecessary language of the trenches'.

Today I feel some sympathy for the anachronism at least. Douglas Jerrold was then talking some twenty-eight years after the end of a war he had himself experienced in youth but that 'Great War' was still more strongly present at some level in his mind than the even greater Second World War he had just come through. The experience of war in youth is indelible and awesome, though it can appear to be forgotten for decades at a time. At an age when one is just beginning to take on life on one's own account a sense of the whole vast range of it is suddenly glimpsed in many startling aspects, including its remorseless indifference to the fate of the individual human being.

My own war experiences, a part of which are described here, were on a very small scale beside that of many combatants and particularly beside the horrific tragedy being played out in that very German-occupied Europe in which the scene is set. Meantime I have lived what would conventionally be regarded as a reasonably full life and enjoyed many important human emotions, happy and sad. And yet, re-reading this book, everything that has happened to me since seems somehow secondary to what happened then.

It is in this way, I think, that those who have been through a war are divided from those who have not: the most impressive thing in their life can seem already to have happened. Which is why there is some compulsion to reach across the divide and communicate it — perhaps in the hope of being rid of it.

London, 1981   ROBERT KEE

9

Part One

1

Part One

1

For the rest of the world it was one of the most unimportant nights of the war. I listened to the wireless early the next morning and heard that only one British aircraft had been shot down.

As it was a night which meant so much to me I have thought about it often and it is vivid in my memory.

It began with 'briefing', the familiar atmosphere unlike any that I ever saw filmed or described. It was only possible to understand the mixture of barbarism and sensibility, inanity and cunning, cowardice and courage which ran through members of an Air Force squadron in varying degrees if you had it inside you as well. And then you had neither wish nor time to think about it self-consciously at all. Before a trip it was necessary to develop a shell of indifference so that the conflicting emotions inside you might be kept out of the way and I suppose it was this that outsiders took for calm or nonchalance or determination and praised accordingly.

We were to lay a mine off the Frisian island of Terschelling. It was a straightforward task. The weather, which was fair at the time, was expected to deteriorate as we flew east. We were to start early and turn back if it got really bad.

Before going down to the hangar I sat on the lavatory in the Mess and had the feeling I had had before every trip that this was going to be my last. However, as I had already returned twenty-three times in spite of it, I was ceasing to pay it much attention.

For some reason which I forget the time of take-off was postponed twice. Twice we climbed into our clumsy puffed-up clothing. Twice we piled each other high with maps and pigeons and parachutes.

11

Twice we all wished each other good luck and twice we all returned to the dismal crew room. As always in Service life, the third time, when everybody was quite convinced that it would be another anti-climax, we went.

'Where's the pigeon?'

'It's all right: George has got it.'

'We should be back by midnight.'

'Yes. Piece of piss.'

In the lorry an air-gunner began to sing a song to the tune of 'I like to climb an apple-tree . . .':

'I like to fly o'er Germany
And let the Jerries shoot at me . . .'

Those who noticed were embarrassed.

I looked across at my wireless operator, born to be called 'Butch'. He made an appropriate face.

The lorry stopped at our aircraft.

'T for Tommy.'

Four of us struggled out. There was the clink of parachute harness on the tarmac.

'Well, good luck.'

'Good luck.'

'Good luck. Butch.'

As the lorry drove off again someone leant out of the back and shouted:

'Good luck, Butch.'

Butch said: 'I wish to God people would stop wishing me good luck. They make me think I'll be needing it.'

The rear-gunner seldom said anything but was a good rear-gunner and climbed in after him.

Of all the simple pleasures which together with periods of vexation, boredom and panic made up my flying experience I always enjoyed the take-off most. I took off well, getting the tail of the Hampden up early and keeping her straight as I developed speed. The power of the racing engines seemed to enter into my body through the contact of my fingers with stick and throttles and the pressure of my feet on the rudder-bar. With throttles fully opened and both hands free to hold the stick, the strength of the aircraft became my own and with it, as I eased the nose gently off the ground at the other end of the aerodrome, came the whole power of flight. I was God and as I swept over the little field on the other side of the road I noted contentedly that smoke was coming from the chimney of the cottage in the corner and that there was a light in an upstairs room.

At 2,000 feet where we set course above the aerodrome it was less exciting. There was nothing to do but keep the faintest corrective touch on stick and rudder. I always felt it was a waste of the power that was miraculously mine. I wanted to dive and twist and turn like a seal that has come up from the water and discovered the sunlight. But in the belly of the aircraft there was a large black cylinder and there was nothing to do but sit and suffer the restraints of this clumsy pregnancy.

There used to be magic in the line of the Lincolnshire coast in the late dusk. Though I had never walked there I loved it dearly. To fly dully across it towards the cold grey sea and the night was like leaving my mother to go to boarding school for the first time.

Unnoticed the night became complete.

As often happened the meteorological report was the opposite of the truth. The cloud above us began to thin out as we flew further east. Flying below it was too bumpy to be comfortable so I climbed to 3,000 feet. Then I remembered that we had to come down to 400 feet to drop the mine and that it would be dangerous to come down through cloud without knowing where we were. So I went below it again.

'For God's sake make up your mind,' said the navigator.

I said nothing. I was annoyed with him because he was right.

We flew for nearly two hours. Occasionally the navigator asked the rear-gunner to drop a flame-float on which he could check our drift.

'How are we doing, navigator?' I asked, mainly because it was expected of me.

'All right theoretically, but we'll be able to check our position when we see the Dutch coast.'

'Good,' I said. It was a sensible answer.

The cloud had thinned out into straying down. It was as if some-one on the enemy coast was blowing an enormous puffball. Through it I could see the dark blue sky pricked with stars like the ceiling of a dome I had once seen in Italy. The nose of the aircraft dipped rhythmically under the control of the automatic pilot. Below, the sea was flecked with phosphorous.

The pin-head voice of the navigator spoke in my ear-phones:

'There's something on the right.'

I cut out the automatic pilot.

'What sort of thing?'

'I don't quite know. Land or something.'

I looked over the side. The sea had turned white and in the distance the whiteness seemed to swell and expand.

This was my first operational trip for a long time and I had forgotten to expect snow. In England the snow had gone a fortnight ago.

'But we should find islands here, not the mainland,' I said.

'The sea's frozen, I think. It's bloody difficult to tell which is sea and which is land. The islands are all joined by ice to the mainland. It's impossible to tell their shapes.'

At this stage of the war navigation was uncertain and the technique of minelaying primitive. Navigation was carried out by 'dead reckoning', a calculation of position made on the basis of a theoretical wind forecast before take-off. Wireless aids were often untrustworthy and the only sure aid was the visual pin-pointing of a piece of ground on the map. In order to lay a mine at a chosen position in the sea it was necessary first to find the nearest land. The aircraft then had to be flown in the direction of the sea position for a number of minutes dependent on wind and air speed. The mine had to be dropped from a height of about 400 feet.

'What are you going to do?' asked the navigator.

This annoyed me.

'We must pin-point the nearest piece of land, of course.'

'But it's impossible to tell the shapes of the islands.'

'Well, we must try.'

I knew by his silence that he thought I was being a fool.

'What do you think we're over now?' I asked him. 'Sea or land?'

'Buggered if I know,' said the navigator.

The island answered.

Little clusters of stars appeared erratically behind us. Two searchlights were switched on. Like men turned out of bed they lurched sleepily around for a few seconds and then found us. In the cockpit it was like being the centre of a white fire. The stars appeared all round us. I could see their angry red centres as they burst and the straggling beard of smoke they left behind. The noise was like angry dogs barking. I banked the aircraft steeply and turned. Then I climbed and

14

turned again. The searchlights followed us easily and contemptuously. Other smaller guns were joining in now like little nations
securing their share of the spoils at the end of a major war.

I could hear the wireless operator shouting something which I
could not understand. Somebody else joined in.

'Weave! Weave!'

What the hell did they think I was doing?

I must not panic. I must not panic. Think.

It was like trying to think how to do a sum in the last moment of an
exam. with the invigilator about to say: 'Stop writing.'

'Weave! Weave! Weave!'

I took my intercommunication plug out of its socket and the
voices stopped abruptly.

If I fly due north I am bound to escape over the sea in a few
minutes. Stop twisting about and fly north. I turned the gyro onto 0
degrees and climbed hard. The stars trailed away. The smaller guns,
feeling that they were making fools of themselves, dropped out
again. We passed through the straggling cloud into the peace of 4,000
feet over the sea. It was difficult to believe that there could ever have
been noise and danger.

I pushed my intercommunication plug back into its socket.

'Everyone all right?' I asked.

'Yes.'

'Yes.'

'Yes.'

'Everything all right behind, Butch?'

'Yes.' His voice was soft and soothing. 'I don't think we were hit.'

'Hullo, navigator,' I said.

'Hullo, pilot.'

'We won't waste any more time trying to find out which that
island was. We'll glide down back to it and set course from it as if it
were the right one. Then we'll drop the mine and go home.'

'O.K.'

I shut off the engines, closed the radiator gills and began to glide.

We passed through the cloud. After a few minutes the sea became
white again.

'We're nearly there, navigator. What's the new course?'

'030 degrees.'

'Good.'

Some bumps appeared in the flat whiteness.

15

'O.K. — turning onto 030 degrees now.'

I opened the radiator gills and pushed the throttles forward. The noise of the engines was like the shouting of a drunkard in church.

The guns and the searchlights were onto us at once. One of the first shells hit the port engine.

I was trying to continue the turn so as to get away as soon as possible. For a moment I could not think why the turn seemed peculiar. Then, when I tried to straighten up, nothing happened. It was like trying to walk straight in a fit of giddiness. Before I had completely realized that the port engine was out of action, we had spun. Our height was about 800 feet.

I ceased to notice whether we were still being shot at or not. Out of the past a voice spoke clearly in my brain. 'You must push the stick well forward. It's a Hampden's only chance in a spin.' I pushed the heavy stick forward until it almost touched the instrument panel, pressed the full strength of my leg onto the rudder opposite the spin and waited. There could be no chance at this height. The snow and the frozen sea which had been waiting so patiently below came up to meet us.

There was no panic. I thought: 'This is Death. I am going to die.' Certainty brought calm. At the same time I felt that I had never lived so intensely before. Death was the climax, not the end, of life. This feeling was so strong that the force inside me seemed to overflow my personality. I thought that something from inside me that was not me would watch me die and would go on.

Then my ordinary little personality spoke:

'If you ever get out of this you'll have a story to tell in the Mess.'

But it was too late. Already through the perspex glass of the cockpit I could see the smoothness of the white beach and the powdered whiskers of the dunes racing towards us.

Butch's voice came clear and worried over the inter-com.:

'What the bloody hell are you doing now?'

I had no time to answer.

In a childish gesture of self-defence I pulled back the stick.

The darkness shattered all round me like a great black plate.

2

Before I threw up my hands to protect my head I felt a slight response on the controls. I afterwards decided that we were beginning to regain flying speed when I pulled back the stick. If we had had another 300 feet we might have recovered and flown away. As it was, we crashed in something like the landing position.

It can all be worked out quite simply and dully now but at the time I was not interested in the way it happened. It happened: that was all that mattered.

There was a grinding, sliding sensation and more noise than I had ever heard in my life. Flashes broke across my eyes. I waited for pain and fire.

There was only silence.

I uncovered my head. It was difficult to believe that the wreckage in which I was sitting had once been an aircraft. The wings seemed to have disappeared completely. The useless broken stick lay ridiculously across my legs. All round me blotches of metal were heaped upon the beach. The cockpit itself had disintegrated and I was sitting on the ice.

My clothes were soaked in petrol. I thought of the fire again. It used to be a joke among the ground-crews: 'The old Hampden burns beautifully.'

For the first time since I had made up my mind that I was going to die I panicked. I struggled to be free to run away.

I could not move.

Then I remembered that I was strapped in. 'Always strap yourself in,' an instructor had once said to me '— always. One day it may save your life.'

I pulled the release-pin, stepped over some wreckage and began to waddle across the ice with the seat-type parachute still clamped to my bottom. My left leg hurt slightly and I was bleeding from my left hand but I paid little attention to either. There was nothing inside me but fear: I had remembered the mine.

I waddled past a blotch on the ice which was not metal. It had a hand and a flying-boot. I thought only of the mine and waddled on. I had always known that I was not brave but I had never expected to find myself such a coward as this. I understood what a great thing brave men did.

I stopped and was ashamed of myself. I was dressing up an

ordinary obligation into bravery. I knew that it would worry me for the rest of my life if I did not do what was expected of me. So it was really cowardice which made me do even that. I shook myself out of the parachute harness and went back.

I turned over the blotch which was not metal. It groaned. The face was swollen and painted with blood. I recognized my navigator. I tried to pull him away. His face turned over again and I dragged it across the ice. He began to groan louder and moved. The pain seemed to bring him to consciousness. I decided that he was not very badly hurt and went to see what had happened to the other two.

There was enough left of both of them to tell me that they were dead. It looked as if their part of the aircraft had received the full impact of the crash. I remembered Butch saying one day with mock simplicity: 'It must be horrible to "buy it", mustn't it?'

Though I had found what I was looking for I could not believe that it had very much to do with the two men I had known. I went back to the navigator.

He was conscious but very dazed. With a great deal of help he was just able to walk. He seemed to have broken his leg, and one shoulder was very painful.

'I can't go on,' he moaned. 'Let me go.'

I shouted at him, trying to pierce his semi-consciousness:

'The mine! The mine's going off!'

I only succeeded in frightening myself.

It took us about twenty minutes to go two hundred yards. I wondered if I should try to go for help.

But my duty was supposed to be to escape.

This was my first hint of the mental confusion which awaits defeated men and defeated nations in war. The words 'honour' and 'duty' were no longer sufficient guides to action. What should I do? Escape and leave someone to bleed and freeze to death, or get the Germans to save him and thereby give myself up? Which did 'honour' and 'duty' demand? Both. Honour as a human being told me to save a man's life. Honour as a human being at war told me to escape. I had often heard talk about the futility and inadequacy of war but this was my first personal experience of it.

On this occasion however honour, in the end, had no say. I heard shouts and shots, and self-interest took control. I dropped the navigator, telling myself that he would be safe there if the mine went off and that the Germans would probably find him later, and began to run. I had no idea of the direction in which I was running. Unpleasant possibilities rose like ghosts in the night before me: I was running towards the sea; I was actually on the sea and the ice would break at any moment; there were land-mines on the beach — every shadow suddenly became a mine. But there were unpleasant realities too. I was falling over every few yards owing to the extreme unsuitability of flying-boots for running over the ice. And there were shots behind me. Already I was beginning to feel that my enterprise was a fatuous failure. This was not the sort of escape people made in films.

The shots continued and looking back I saw little flashes in the darkness like matches struck by a man looking for something in a cellar. For some time I had heard a soft sighing over the ice which I had taken for the wind. Now I realized that there was in fact very little wind and that the sighs I had heard were bullets. This was too much for me. I do not think I was exceptional among air-crew in having an amateurish terror of small arms fire on the ground. I gave up and fell on the ice. I waited, pressing my head idiotically close to the ground. I had never felt so miserable or ineffectual in my life.

After a time there were no more shots and I began to hear voices. Torches were being flashed on the ground. I thought it would be safer to speak first so I shouted: 'Kamerad.'

A little man came quite suddenly out of the darkness holding a rifle and stood about two yards from me.

I knew that my humiliation was complete but to save my pride I clung to a ridiculous hope.

'Wer sind Sie?' I asked. 'Sind Sie Holländer?'

'Nein.' It was almost apologetic.

He was obviously curious about me and a little afraid. But as I had by now exhausted my German our conversation went no further.

Other soldiers came up, all equally curious. I was superficially searched for arms.

'Englishman?'

I nodded.

'Engländer.' 'Engländer.'

It seemed to be a passport to friendship. Several of them smiled.

'Bad luck,' said one in English.

Another asked: 'Verwundet?'

I shook my head.

It was as if we had been engaged on a night exercise and it was over

19

now and we were waiting to go home. A great emotional warmth swept over me. They were being kind to me when I was miserable. These are the things which matter between people of different countries whatever the statesmen and historians say.

I tried to explain about the navigator, but I was not certain that they understood. We set off purposefully and spent the next half-hour trying to find the wreckage of my aircraft. The Germans became less attentive to me as they became more pre-occupied with the fact that they were lost. I expect I could have got away from them quite easily but I was already deciding that escape at any price was a foolish maxim. Once one of them turned to me and asked: 'Officer?' I said: 'Yes,' and it appeared to make some impression because I could hear them repeating the word among themselves.

At last we heard voices and the sound of a motor truck. We almost stumbled over the navigator who was lying as I had left him. When they picked him up he began to shout deliriously. He seemed to think that he was still in the aircraft and was blaming me for doing something foolish. I tried to help the Germans carry him, but they would not allow it.

'Offizier,' said a little man as if to remind me of my position.

I followed them towards the truck which had stopped with its engine running. There were lights and I could see the silhouettes of men and pieces of wrecked aircraft.

For the first time I understood the finality of what had happened to me. I could neither talk, think nor dream my way out of this. Enemy territory which I had always thought of as being a few hours flying away had suddenly become my world. I thought of people I knew and of what they would be doing at that moment: my father, turning off the news perhaps, and my mother knitting and saying: 'There doesn't seem to be much, does there?' Elizabeth, sitting at home and waiting for me to ring her up when I got back: George, waiting for his cue somewhere on tour: Dick, drinking port in the Senior Common Room. None of them had any idea of what had happened to me. All of them were still close to me, yet all had now become mere characters in the novel of my past.

The men moving among the lights were almost life-size now. One of our group shouted to them and there were shouts back. Because it was now all so certain and I knew there was no way out I resorted to the technique of the child which refuses to accept a situation it does not like. I stormed and stamped with despair. I tried to cry, but could only moan. I tried to swear but could only find the same words over and over again. None of the Germans took any notice.

I remembered that I had got some secret wireless information in my pocket. This was always printed on rice paper so that it could be eaten if there was any danger of it falling into enemy hands. I had thought this an absurdly dramatic precaution when I was with my squadron but now I snatched the flimsy paper from my pocket and stuffed it into my mouth. Somehow this seemed to compensate for my weak behaviour of a few moments before. But again none of the Germans took any notice.

A large man with spectacles under his tin hat came towards me. He had a tommy-gun slung across his chest. He seemed to have some authority and was more business-like than the others. But his first question was familiar:

'Are you an officer?' he asked in English with a schoolroom accent.

'Yes.'

He pointed towards the truck. I saw that this was an ambulance with the doors open at the back and a light inside.

'Please to enter,' he said.

I climbed in and as many Germans as could came after me.

They laid the navigator on a stretcher on the floor. He was talking continually of alterations of course and new winds found. In the light I saw that his face was now quite unrecognizable with bruises and blood. We drove away.

The Germans were looking at me with even greater curiosity than before now that they had me under the light.

'Pech gehabt', 'Pech gehabt', they kept saying, and smiled.

I shrugged my shoulders to show that I did not understand.

'They say that it is bad luck for you,' said a little man sitting next to me. He wore a peaked cap.

I noticed for the first time that I was beginning to feel warm after being cold.

I wanted to talk to the man in the peaked cap.

'Are you an officer?' I asked.

He seemed to think this so funny that he repeated it to the others who laughed with him.

'No,' he said, 'I learnt my English when I was a steward on the *Bremen* before the war. I was a steward for six years.'

'Were you really?' I said appreciatively as if making polite conversation at a party.

The ambulance was held up at a barrier for a few minutes. There was shouting and some tin-hats looked in from the back. Then we moved on again.

The man in the peaked cap pointed at the navigator.

'What is he saying?' he asked. 'I do not understand.'

'He doesn't know what he is saying: he's delirious.'

'Oh, he does not know what he is saying.' He repeated it in German to the others.

'Ah,' they said. They looked at the navigator and shook their heads.

The ambulance stopped. I was asked to get out, and found myself at the door of a dug-out built into the sand dunes.

'Please come in,' said a voice in English.

3

It was as if he had been waiting there for me all my life.

'Do sit down.'

The inside of the dug-out soon became familiar. I felt that I had known it for a long time. This was an appointment which I had repeatedly put off but which at last I was being forced to keep. A photograph of Hitler stared benignly over a table spread with a white cloth. There were plates of biscuits and sandwiches and little slices of sausage. Behind the table stood the tall middle-aged man who had spoken to me. He wore naval uniform. On either side of him were two younger officers who stood up when I was shown in. There was an un-English smell of cigar smoke.

I began to think quickly. This would be an interrogation. I must take no notice of their politeness or kindness which was designed to trap me into giving information. They might even try to make me drunk.

'I expect you would like some brandy.'

I longed for some.

'No, thank you very much.'

I found it impossible to answer brusquely as I had intended.

'Then perhaps some tea. I know all Englishmen like tea.'

'Well, yes, I would like some tea.'

He shouted and an orderly came in. He spoke to him in German.

The orderly went out.

'Although I do not speak English as well as I should, I did at one time know England well. I have always liked Englishmen.'

Be careful, I thought, this is the sort of thing you were warned against.

But again I found it difficult to be rude.

'What part of England did you know?' I asked.

'I was at Oxford after the last war. There I made many friends. I used to go and stay with them in their homes — in London, in Sussex, in Devonshire . . .'

He seemed to have forgotten about me in the middle of his sentence.

'. . . But it is now a very long time since I was there.'

He stared at the table as if he were talking to himself.

His voice had a soothing hypnotic effect. I remembered my original impression that this had all been prepared. The two other officers were staring at me with a curiosity which I had at first thought similar to the curiosity I had found among the soldiers. Now I began to suspect that there was something sinister about their observation of me.

'I am afraid that these two officers do not speak English, but as you can see they are very interested in you.'

I tried to smile politely but I was beginning to feel frightened. What was it they wanted from me? Perhaps there was someone behind me who was just about to hit me over the head.

I turned round quickly. There was no one there, only the little door by which I had entered.

'Is there anything you want?' he asked.

'No, thank you.'

The orderly came in with a pot of tea. I thought it might be drugged so I only pretended to drink it, putting the cup to my lips and setting it down again full after an interval.

The officer talked of Magdalen and Piccadilly and Haywards Heath.

'I and many like me in Germany think it is a tragedy that we are at war with you. What have we got to fight about? You are not like the French. You are the same family as us. And yet we are fighting each other, each with barbarous allies. The Germans and the English have plenty in common with each other, but what have you in common with the Russians or we with the Japanese?'

'It is not a question of races but of ideals.'

'But the Führer has always said that he has no ideological quarrel with England.'

'I don't care what he says,' I blustered. 'Anyone can say they have no quarrel with people so long as they always get their own way.'

We began a series of recriminations about the events leading up to the war. Occasionally he translated what I said for the benefit of the other two.

'You are not drinking your tea,' he said suddenly. 'Do you not like it? Perhaps it is not strong enough for you? Englishmen, I know, always like their tea very strong.'

'I'm sorry,' I said, wondering how I could save face, 'I suddenly don't feel very well.'

He jumped up.

'You are not wounded, I hope? They told me on the 'phone that you were not wounded. Would you like to see a doctor?'

He seemed concerned for me. But my hand had stopped bleeding some time ago and I could not reasonably pretend that I was wounded.

'No, thank you. I'm all right,' I said.

'Perhaps you are suffering a little from shock?'

I was grateful for this.

'Yes, I think perhaps I am.'

'In that case I will not keep you any longer than I can help.'

His manner changed. The others began to look bored.

'First of all your name, rank and number please.'

I gave them to him. He repeated the words after me and wrote them down.

'That is all I will say.'

He looked hurt.

'Of course, you don't have to say anything you don't want to.'

He began to write again.

'You were in a Hampden,' he said. 'You were shot down by flak. Two of your crew are dead. One is wounded.'

He looked up at me.

'Let's see, what was he, the navigator or one of the gunners?'

'I will only give my name, rank and number,' I said pompously.

He stared at me before writing again.

'It doesn't matter,' he said, 'I don't expect they will really want to know.'

24

I felt that I had been very clumsy.

'There,' he said, putting down his pencil, 'I think that will do.'

He reached for the telephone and when he was connected spoke down it briskly in German. I heard the word 'flak' repeated several times, but otherwise understood nothing at all. He hung up the receiver.

The two officers who had hardly spoken were beginning to fidget on their chairs. One of them asked him a question. He turned to me.

'I am afraid you will have to spend the night in the men's guard-room. It will not be very comfortable for you there, but we have nowhere else to put you. However there is a bed and I dare say you are quite ready for it.'

He stood up.

'Good-bye,' he said, 'and I hope we shall meet again one day in happier circumstances.'

'I hope so,' I said, because it was impossible to say anything else.

But I was distrustful and was still wondering what this was leading up to.

We all stood up.

'These two officers will lead you to the guard-room.'

I was very tired but I knew that I must look out for a trap.

As we were going out through the doorway he stopped us. He seemed embarrassed and stammered for the first time in his English.

'I'm afraid it is my duty to search you before you go. You see, you are my responsibility and I should get into trouble if you were not properly searched.'

This seemed reasonable. I could not understand what he was so worried about.

I held up my arms as I had seen German prisoners do in news-reels. He waved his hand.

'No, no,' he said, as embarrassed as before, 'I will take your word. Have you anything on you? Any arms?'

'No.'

'Anything you might be able to use for escaping?'

I had forgotten all about my escape equipment. This was a routine service issue collected by air-crews before every operation. It consisted of a map, a compass, a small rubber water bottle and some French, Dutch and German money, all packed into a little tin box which was then bulging in the breast pocket of my battle-dress.

'Any escaping materials?' he repeated.

For the first time his face became serious and severe.

I did not answer. For some reason it never occurred to me to lie or make any effort at all to save my invaluable little tin box.

'What have you got in your pockets? Please put everything on the table.'

A pencil. A handkerchief. A packet of barley sugar that had become very sticky.

'Nothing else?' he asked firmly.

The intolerable 'honour' system had won again. I pulled the tin box out of my battle-dress and put it on the table.

'Thank you,' he said. 'Good-night.'

It seemed to me that he was colder now, disappointed that I should have been found to have anything so hostile as escape equipment in my pockets.

We went out into the darkness. The clouds had cleared and the cold stars flashed little blue signals for people of all countries to pick up and decode as they liked.

'Komm,' said one of my escorts.

'Come please,' said the other, 'I learn English in school.'

We stamped in silence over the snow-covered dunes.

'Why do you fly so low?' asked the man who had learnt English in school. 'Why so low?'

I shook my head.

They had a short conversation in German and seemed to disagree about something.

All three of us became embarrassed and stared at our boots. Soon we were walking down a road between two rows of little sea-side villas. They looked empty and forlorn as if they had not yet adjusted themselves to their premature change of life.

Very deliberately, and as if it were giving him great pain, the German who had said little began to speak.

'Once,' he said, 'I was in Hamburg. I saw what you do there. All little houses. All such little houses.' He waved his hand up and down the road.

It was a great shock. Of course I knew that, in its practical effects, our bombing was no more confined to military objectives than was that of the Germans. I was even surprised to hear definite first hand evidence of any damage at all, military or not, for raids on Germany in those days usually seemed depressingly unsuccessful from the air. But it was a shock to hear the exact tone of bitter resentment that I

...ad heard so often in England and felt so often myself. I had always assumed that this sort of civilized dismay at barbarism was the monopoly of our cause. For the first time I realized the humiliating narrowness of mind with which one has to be equipped in time of war. A doubt grew into my mind: perhaps the whole certainty of purpose with which I was fighting the war was based on equally naïve assumptions.

'Why always the little houses?' asked the German.

I began to argue with him. I told him about Coventry and London and Plymouth and Bristol and the Polish towns and villages bombed without a declaration of war. I told him about our own lack of any real bomber force until the Germans made us build one. I told him about my sister who now had no legs.

'Yes,' he said, 'I know. But I still do not see why the little houses.'

It was a relief to find that the narrowness of mind was common to both sides. But it seemed to me that I had not properly answered his question and that he was really voicing the unthinking complaint of the people who lived in the little houses all over the world.

'Krieg ist Krieg,' said the other man. 'Immer schlecht.'

And that was the end of my first interrogation.

For by now we had arrived at a big army hut by the side of the road. There was a sentry in a steel helmet at the door. The windows were lighted. When the door opened a great smell of sweat and leather and stale cigar smoke rushed into the cold night air. In the haze I could see figures lying on mattresses on the floor. It reminded me of the London tubes during an air raid.

My entry caused a stir. Men who had been asleep and were woken up by the noise did not appear to resent it but sat up on one elbow and stared.

I was given into the charge of an N.C.O.

'Good-night,' said the two officers simultaneously.

After they had shut the door the atmosphere shook for a moment.

The N.C.O. stared at me.

'Pech gehabt,' he said suddenly and broke into a grin.

The phrase rumbled in repetition round the room.

Someone showed me a mattress on the top of a two-tier bed. Another gave me a slice of dark brown bread with a piece of sausage on the top which I ate because I did not want to hurt his feelings. They stared at me as I ate. The N.C.O. brought some blankets and I began to undress. When he noticed that my clothes were wet he took them and hung them in front of a large iron fire. He commented on the smell of petrol that came from them and made an elaborate joke of not putting them too close to the flames.

I climbed onto my bunk.

A man came out of the haze and stood alongside looking at me. He flashed the gold fillings in his teeth.

'For you the war is over,' he said and retired into the haze.

I lay on my back and tiredness came spinning towards me in widening circles as the white beach and whiskery grasses had come spinning towards me out of the night. Fixed in the centre was the naval officer who had interrogated me. He seemed to be very worried and he was stretching out his hands. 'It is no use,' I said to him, 'I will only give you my name, rank and number.' But as he came closer I saw that he was not asking a question. His face was agonized and he was trying to tell me something.

I fell asleep.

4

In the morning a little aeroplane came buzzing across the blue window-pane of sky and alighted on the sugary beach. We watched it from the guard-room.

'It has come to take you away,' said a German who spoke English.

I was glad. I had a headache from the stale stuffy atmosphere. I was bored with the arguments over the map. (They showed me how deep they had advanced into Russia and I showed them what we were going to do in the West. 'Aber, wann, wann, mein Lieber?' 'This year. Dieses Jahr.' 'Ach, Quatsch.' 'What does he say?' 'He says, he does not believe you.') My sense of shame was beginning to swell. I wanted to justify myself. On the journey I would escape.

Outside there was the sound of wheels crunching over the snow and the creaking of a cart. I was watching a card trick one of the soldiers was showing me and did not look up until the cart had almost passed the window. It was being driven by a German wearing little black pads over his ears to keep them warm. In the back of the cart were two long wooden boxes.

'Ihre Kameraden,' said a soldier who was sitting by the window.

I watched it disappear down the road. The room was suddenly quiet. I began to treasure its warmth on my cheek and the beat of the blood in my veins. I looked out over the empty white road to the sky and saw the morning sun sparkling. I knew the joy of the world and wondered at it like a child.

The telephone bell rang. The N.C.O. answered it and when he had hung up the receiver it rang again. Soldiers were beginning to look at the clock and fumble with equipment, apparently preparing for a guard change. Another routine day was beginning. By the time the N.C.O. had reached for his helmet and buckled on his belt the room was almost empty. He led me out into the snow and we crossed the island towards the beach.

'Fieseler Storch,' he said, pointing at the little aeroplane, but already my technical interest in such things had been packed into the past.

Two Luftwaffe officers in blue leather coats were standing beside it. There was a lot of saluting as we arrived and I tried to appear defiant when they looked at me. I had decided that I should take control of the aeroplane and try to fly it to England.

One of the officers showed me into the aeroplane and himself sat down in the pilot's seat. I looked round for something with which I could knock him out after we had taken off. A heavy iron bar lay on the floor beside my left hand. My stomach was moving with excitement but I tried to look bored. I should hit him across the back of the neck like a rabbit.

'I like very much to fly,' he said. 'It pleases me. I have done ten flights to England against ships.'

'Ten? Really?' I said, feeling silly. It was as if he had spoken a line from the wrong play.

The other officer climbed in and sat between me and the pilot. I had forgotten about him. I should have to knock him out too.

The propeller was swung. The engine leapt, shouted, and was tamed, and in less than a minute we had taken off from the little beach and were circling the island.

I will wait until we are clear of the island, I thought.

I suddenly noticed that we were diving down again. We were heading for a little cluster of figures round something on the beach. As we flew closer and lower they looked up and waved and I recognized the pathetic twisted wreckage of T for Tommy.

We climbed again. I should not be able to postpone my attempt much longer.

The man between me and the pilot loosened his belt and taking an

29

automatic from his holster turned round and sat facing me.

'No funny stuff,' he said in excellent American.

With a sense of relief I abandoned my idea of escape.

At the aerodrome in Holland they were expecting us. We taxied towards the buildings and a little party of figures came to meet us as if they were welcoming a foreign diplomat. But when we got out they stared and said nothing, and I followed the pilot up the lane they made. Someone came quietly out of the crowd and spoke to the other officer, looking at me. I felt as if I was a schoolboy who had done something wrong and was being taken to see the headmaster.

I had to wait in a corridor. Memories of long waits in countless English corridors made it familiar. Then the door opened and the headmaster was standing in front of me. He wore riding boots and a monocle and his face was made shapeless by duelling scars. His grey hair was cropped so short that at first I thought it was bald. He looked at me with confident contempt.

It was easy to be defiant. I put my hands in my pockets and leant back against the wall. This was very much more simple than dealing with the naval officer.

The German's face became distorted with rage and anger, but he did not move. We remained like this for about a quarter of a minute. Then he walked back to his desk in the room and turned to face me again. He yelled something so loudly that my ear-drums rang. I walked in with my hands still in my pockets. A clerk sat by the window.

I was beginning to think that the staring match would never stop when he suddenly sat down and began to finger some papers on the top of his desk.

'Hampden?' he asked, looking up at me again.

It was a tactical error.

'Sorry,' I said, 'Name, rank and number only.'

He must have realized that his dignity was in danger for he said something in German to the clerk and never spoke to me again.

The clerk came over to me. He was a gentle little man rather like the steward from the *Bremen* whom I had met the night before.

'The officer says, will you kindly oblige by filling in this form?'

It seemed very unlikely that the officer had said this.

'Sorry,' I said briskly, 'Name, rank and number only.'

'All right,' said the clerk wearily and showed me where these were placed on the form.

A few minutes later I was led away to a cell. I was glad when the door banged noisily behind me. For the first time since I had been shot down I was alone.

Now, I thought, I shall be able to think this out: to find out exactly what it is that has happened to me, to see what effect it is going to have on my life, and how I am going to deal with it.

I sat down on the wooden bed. There was a lot of straw in the mattress and it had been filled recently so that it was pleasantly responsive. It no longer seemed important to me to think about escape. Doubtless I should think out some plan later. At the moment I had more fundamental problems. This was the most overwhelming experience I had ever had and I wanted to understand it. I swung my boots up onto the bed and stretched out full length.

First of all, I was not dead. My turn to die had come and I had been inexplicably reprieved. I remembered a phrase I had once copied down out of *Don Quixote*:

'Julius Caesar, that valiant Roman Emperor, being asked what kind of death was best, "That which is sudden and unexpected," he replied; and though his answer has a relish of paganism, yet, with respect to human infirmities, it is very judicious.'

I remembered the queer mixture of fear and belief with which I had read this and afterwards written it down. Now I thought it was an equally good answer to what was the best kind of life.

I stretched with pleasure on the friendly straw. This, then, was my first thought: I was not dead and I was glad I was not dead. What next? What did I build on this foundation? Nothing. I realized suddenly that this was all. This thought contained all others. The only important thing about the rest of my life was that it was there.

High up on the wall of my cell I could see where somebody had written his name with a pencil.

'Flying Officer . . .'

I could not read the name but underneath, with a defiance which I found sympathetic, somebody else had written:

'V. R.A.F. V.'

I decided to sit up and read the name. But my body was reluctant to sit up. The straw was comfortable and the cell was warm and I was alive. Sleep covered me like an eiderdown which some invisible nurse had picked up from the floor and put back on the bed.

I awoke to see a German N.C.O. with a ginger moustache looking curiously round the open door of my cell. He grinned and blinked shyly when he saw that I was awake. He shut the door quickly behind him and came and sat on the small wooden chair in the corner. For a few seconds he stared at me, still grinning and blinking. I felt that I had to make some sort of social effort so I swung my legs off the bed and sat sheepishly on the edge. He removed his peaked cap. His bald head above the little blinking eyes and ginger moustache made him look pathetically unmilitary and friendly.

'Guten Morgen,' I said. It was already late afternoon, but it was the only German greeting I knew besides 'Heil Hitler'.

'So, Sie sprechen deutsch . . .'

He asked me a lot of questions which I did not understand.

'Ich verstehe nicht,' I said pedantically.

He resumed grinning and blinking.

'Engländer?'

'Ja.'

For the first time he stopped grinning, and, resting his elbows on his knees and his head on his hands, began to shake his head from side to side. He apparently forgot that I could not understand German or else decided that what he wanted to say could not be left unsaid, for he began to talk fast and seriously. I understood almost nothing of what he said. He was obviously very depressed about something, even disillusioned, and I got the impression that this something was the war. He was speaking very much more quietly than when he first came in and occasionally looked reproachfully at the door as if the thing which had depressed him was just the other side of it. Sometimes I understood a few words or phrases ('Japaner nicht gut', 'Demokratie') but on the whole it was a hopeless conversation just because he so badly wanted to get his meaning across to me. Sometimes he grunted at me as if trying to get me to say something, but always I had to give him the same classroom answer: 'Ich verstehe nicht.'

Eventually he gave it up, stood up and put on his hat.

'Essen kommt,' he said in his former hearty voice, and slowly rubbed his stomach with one hand.

'Guten Appetit,' he said and left the cell.

I wanted to shout after him that I had made a mistake and that I had really understood him very well.

It was a very good meal. The enormous steak was dominated by waves of potatoes, carrots and onions. During the next three and a half years I often thought of this meal and of the amount I had to leave on my plate because I could not eat any more.

About an hour later I was taken to the railway station in a closed van by another N.C.O. and a soldier with a rifle. Except to tell me to stop or to go on neither of them spoke throughout the whole hour of the journey to Amsterdam. Once or twice I caught the N.C.O. staring at me with an expression of hate and disgust but he never maintained it when I stared back, and would look suddenly out of the window or at the papers in the portfolio he was carrying. The soldier looked very simple. He was the sort of man who was aware of his simplicity and of the advantage which people continually took of it. He was quite determined that I was going to try and escape, and followed so close behind me on the railway stations that I could smell his breath. In the train he sat opposite me with his rifle across his knees and his steel helmet drowning his face. He looked half determined, half afraid, as if I was a lion which he as assistant keeper was helping to escort from one zoo to another.

I had neither intention nor wish to escape. Outside the window it looked as if the few farm houses we passed were floating in a sea of snow. There was so much snow that it seemed impossible that this was not the natural surface of the earth. Reason and conscience both told me that if I were ever to have any chance of escaping successfully this was that chance. I was in a friendly country and was less effectively guarded than I ever would be in a prison camp. But I thought of the snow, the speed of the train, and the rifle, and decided that I still had no intention of trying to escape.

To satisfy my pride I tried to give the soldier some grounds for his suspicions. I walked suddenly faster on the railway station as if I was testing how closely he kept up with me. On the train I looked furtively at the lock on the carriage door and watched the railway embankment carefully as if assessing the effect of falling out onto it at speed. By the time we reached Amsterdam the man was in a frenzy of preparedness and anxiety, and followed me down the platform with his rifle in my back. This frightened me but seemed to make me a hero in the eyes of the Dutch who broke out into a fever of winks and jerked-up thumbs and V-signs all round me. Their genuine spirit made me feel bogus and cowardly.

At the entrance to the station a big Mercedes with two men in Luftwaffe uniform and a driver inside was waiting for us. The N.C.O. handed over the papers he had brought and after clicking his heels and saluting went back into the station without looking at me. The soldier, obviously relieved by his loss of responsibility, slung his rifle and followed after him.

5

One of the Luftwaffe men was an officer and the other a Feldwebel. (The rank of Feldwebel in the German forces nominally corresponded to the British rank of sergeant, but a Feldwebel enjoyed greater prestige than a British sergeant and slightly more responsibility.) The Feldwebel sat in front with the driver, and the officer, who undid the flap of his holster and swivelled his belt round so that his automatic was more accessible, sat in the back with me. The Mercedes began to purr softly and then swept powerfully away into the streets of Amsterdam.

It was already nearly dusk and I supposed the Dutch people whom I saw on the pavements and on bicycles were hurrying to get home before the curfew. I asked the officer who was looking out of the window if there was a curfew. For about half a minute he did not reply and I thought that he either did not understand English or was trying to humiliate me. Without looking back into the car he suddenly drawled in good English:

'Yes, there is a curfew.'

I soon noticed that the car was being driven very dangerously. The driver seemed as concerned to show off his excessive acceleration as if we had been prospective buyers and he a salesman. Once when he swung across the road to frighten a cyclist by passing within inches of him at forty miles an hour I expected the Feldwebel or the officer to be angry. But the officer continued to look out of the window, while the Feldwebel slapped his knee with enthusiasm and, pointing to a group of civilians on a corner of the pavement, nudged the driver in the ribs. The driver headed the car towards them and accelerated.

When we were about twenty yards away from them an old woman turned and saw us. I just had time to see the panic on her face before the driver applied the brakes. With the scream of a falling bomb the car mounted the pavement and crossed it onto the road the other side. The group disintegrated. I never had a chance to see if anyone had been hurt or not because we were already accelerating up the next stretch of road. The Feldwebel bounced up and down with laughter so that his hat fell off the back of his head and even the officer allowed himself a smile. But neither of them looked back.

I was so angry that I could feel the scorched marks which the blood made on my cheeks. I tried to think of something dignified and contemptuous to say to the officer but could find nothing. Meanwhile the Feldwebel was talking excitedly to the driver like a school-boy egging on an accomplice to do something which he is fortunately not in a position to do himself. The driver seemed pleased by the idea and the Feldwebel sat back in luxurious anticipation.

We were approaching a big road junction where there was a controlled pedestrian crossing. I could see a few figures strung out across it in the gloom. The driver surprisingly began to slow down. We were about thirty yards from the crossing and travelling at about fifteen miles an hour when a middle-aged man stepped off the pavement into the road. The driver immediately accelerated towards him. The man decided to run further across the road rather than go back. The driver again headed the car towards him. By this time we were only a few yards from him and the car had almost stopped. The man was standing undecided in the middle of the road like a rabbit caught in headlights at night. Every time he began to move the driver jerked the car a little further towards him. We were so close that I could see the unhappy mixture of terror and subservience in his face. The Feldwebel was choking with laughter. As there was now no room left for the driver's game, he suddenly accelerated past the man and we were again moving down the street at forty miles an hour. We had passed so close to the Dutchman that I thought we must have run over his foot. I looked back and saw him grovelling in the road for his hat.

A few minutes later we drew up at a big concrete building which the officer told me was the town jail but which seemed to be a large Luftwaffe barracks. The Feldwebel stepped out of the car and opened the door for me. I tried to stare my dislike into him but I must have been unsuccessful for he merely said with a primitive accent: 'Good in auto, yes?' and grinned. I pretended to ignore this and he said something in German after me which I took to mean: 'You must be a very dull fellow if you don't think that sort of thing funny.'

We went into the building. Long empty corridors echoed boots and voices and slammed doors. I felt cold and tired. We passed along some of the corridors and slammed some of the doors. A man with a great bunch of keys joined us and led us down some steps to a doorway marked 'Luftschutzraum'. I tried to work this out in terms of 'Der Freischütz' but failed. I looked forward to reaching my cell, because I was beginning to feel miserable and wanted to be alone and warm. But when the door was locked behind me the cell was dark for there was neither window nor electric light. I felt my way over to the bed. It was an iron bed with two folded blankets on it and a thin straw mattress. I sat down and began to cry.

It seemed impossible that only a few hours before I had been happy in my cell at the aerodrome. Now I felt only shame and hopelessness. I realized with a shock that this was the first time I had been really unhappy since I had been taken prisoner. It seemed to me that my personal disaster was so great that hitherto I had not allowed myself to understand it. That was why I had been quite happy all day.

In the afternoon I had thought that the only important thing was that I was alive, now I wished that I was dead. 'Killed in action' was at least a positive end, but 'Prisoner of war' — waiting for two or three years for other people to win the war for you — was just ineffectual and pitiable, an end which was also not an end. I thought of the two members of my crew who were dead and remembered that if any of us had deserved to die it was I, who was responsible for the disaster. I thought, as most people probably think once or twice a year, that I should never be the same person again.

There was only one redemption from this shame and misery: I must escape back to England. I should wait until I had got to the prison camp and then escape. I knew that I should succeed. I should be in England by the summer of that year at the latest. My pride suddenly felt better. I stood up and began to walk impatiently up and down the cell in the darkness.

The lights were obviously controlled from some master switch for they went on without a sound. The bulb was in a little ventilation window above the door. There was no other window. I saw that the cell was clean but that several English names had been written in pencil on the wall. Some people had written dates under their names and sometimes there were short messages.

'Don't sign the Red Cross form — it's bogus', 'Look out for that little shit Elbing' and 'No bloody marge again'.

Hanging on the wall by a nail was a notice printed in English:

'It is forbidden to defile the walls with names.

Signed   Oberst.'

Underneath 'Oberst' somebody had written 'Oh balls'. All this made me feel very much better and I immediately wrote my name up on the wall.

Soon I heard a noise in the passage outside: boots, voices, keys and doors. It stopped just outside my cell. Something flashed in the centre of the cell door like a lens in an old-fashioned camera. I noticed for the first time that there was a little hole in the door. I was just going to look through it to find out what was happening in the passage when I saw a fishy eye fixed in the centre. It stared at me for a few seconds, then the lens flashed again, a key was put into the lock, bolts were drawn and the door was opened.

He was so tall that his steel helmet grated gently against the top of the door when he came in. He looked down at me as if he were a giant and I had just climbed a beanstalk. Then he shook his head.

'Wie alt?' he asked.

I understood this.

'Twenty-two,' I said in English.

He shrugged his shoulders and smiled as if deprecating his lack of education.

I wrote it down on the top of the table with my pencil.

'So jung,' he said in astonishment, and I noticed that he had not got the face of a giant at all but that of a very old and reliable nanny.

We looked at each other.

'So jung,' he repeated. Then: 'Krieg ist Krieg,' and he shrugged his shoulders again and opened his hands. 'Sheisse,' he added explosively as if he had at last allowed himself to be convinced of something which he had wanted to believe for a long time.

He ducked out of the cell into the passage leaving the door open. There was the sound of a knife being put onto a plate. He came back with two slices of dark brown bread and a semi-transparent lump of fat on the top. Then he fetched a mug and a can of hot coffee.

His face lit up encouragingly.

'Essen,' he said, 'Guten Appetit.'

I smiled. It didn't look much of a meal.

'England – nix Essen?' he asked.

'England — viel Essen,' I said.

He shook his head doubtfully as if he did not believe me but didn't want to be harsh about saying so.

I remembered the little N.C.O. in the cell at the aerodrome and rubbed my stomach appreciatively.

'England — viel Essen,' I said.

He ducked out of the cell, looked both ways along the passage and ducked back again. He put a finger to his lips and brought his face close to mine.

'Im Krieg,' he whispered, 'Alles Propaganda.'

'No,' I said, 'not Propaganda.'

But he had already left the cell and, with a parting wink of his fat kindly face, shut the door. For a moment I sensed his eye staring at me through the hole in the door but as soon as I looked at it the lens flashed and the cover on the other side swung quickly to rest.

I drank some of the coffee, which tasted of acorns, and looked at my meal. I wondered if it was the usual supper for prisoners. I spread a little of the peculiar fat on a piece of bread and put it into my mouth. Its complete lack of any taste was so nauseating that I spat it out and decided to eat the rest of the bread by itself. I was finishing this when there was the sound of boots in the passage again. My door was opened and a very young-looking man in a peaked cap was shown in. The giant nanny had unlocked the door for him but kept in the background and gave me no sign of recognition.

'Do you mind if I sit down?' asked the young man in effete, accented English. He sat down on the wooden chair and I sat on the bed.

'My name is Elbing,' he began. 'Quite easy for you to remember, you know. Just the river Elbe with an "-ing" on the end. You have heard of the river Elbe, I expect.'

I looked to see if he was trying to be unpleasant but he was obviously making an effort to be polite.

'I am sorry you did not have a very good meal,' he said, looking at my plate. 'You see, it is rather bad luck for you that you happened to come here on one of our meatless days.'

'Oh, I see.'

It was good to know that supper would not always be like this.

'Now to business,' said Elbing. 'I want you to trust me. You see I am only a Feldwebel and I have no ulterior motives at all. I always get on very well with English prisoners of the R.A.F. I worked for some time at the prison camp where you'll be going tomorrow, and there I made many good English friends, especially –' he stopped and looked blankly at my battle-dress, 'Are you an officer?' he asked quickly. 'Yes,' I said. '– especially among the officers,' he continued. 'Yes, many friends and no bull-shit.'

He watched me for the effect of this slang. It was impossible not to be slightly surprised and impressed. He was pleased.

'The fact that I say "bull-shit" shows that I am not bull-shitting yes?'

'Perhaps.'

'Good, now I just want you to save me and yourself a lot of trouble by filling in this form for the Red Cross.'

He produced a form from the inside of his greatcoat.

'I will only give you my name, rank and number.'

'Oh, come on, what are you afraid of? You don't think I'm trying to get information from you, do you? We have all we want to know about that sort of thing and anyway it is not my job. You see although I wear the German uniform, you might really say that I am more neutral than anything else. I am only interested in getting your name back to the Red Cross as soon as possible so that your mother and father will be saved unnecessary worry. Come on now, just fill in the form.'

I looked at it: 'Name . . . Address . . . Station . . . Squadron . . . Group . . . Command . . . Name of Station Commander . . .'

I filled in my name, rank and number.

'That's all,' I said, grateful for the sacred formula.

'Look here, old boy,' he said, suddenly confidential. 'You will land me right in the shit if you don't fill this up. You see it is only a routine matter and they will not be able to understand why I couldn't get you to fill it in. They will think I have been collaborating with you or something.'

He looked so genuinely worried, that I began to doubt myself. Perhaps I was just being a ridiculous prig, behaving quite differently from anyone else who had ever been taken prisoner.

'Look here,' said Elbing. 'Do you know Wing Commander Fender, or Squadron Leader James or Pilot Officer Summers?'

'What if I do?'

It was the first news I had heard that Robin Summers, shot down over Brest a few weeks before, was alive.

'Well, if you do, do you think any of them would have signed this

39

form if it had not been all in order and above board?'

'Did they sign this form?' I was astonished. I just could not imagine Robin, who used to throw Verey cartridges onto the ante-room fire behind the Group Captain's back, falling for this sort of thing.

'I don't know which one of these you knew, but all of them were shot down recently and all signed the form without a murmur. Summers, for instance, said to me "Elbing, old boy, I can see there is nothing phoney about you."'

This settled it. If there was one thing Robin could not stand, it was people calling each other 'old boy'.

I suddenly felt angry and stood up.

'Look here,' I said, 'I have given you my name, rank and number and that's all you're going to get. Now get out because you bore me.'

The giant nanny must have understood the tone of my voice because he strolled into sight through the open doorway and looked at me reproachfully.

Elbing stood up.

'You little fool,' he shouted. 'You'll hear more about this.'

He went out.

The door was shut and bolted. The cell still echoed my voice. Left alone with it, my self-confidence began to fade. Perhaps I had made a ridiculous fuss about nothing. It was disconcerting how the desire not to appear a fool followed one into captivity. I lay down on my bed.

It was written on the wall just above my head:

'Look out for that little shit Elbing.'

My self-confidence returned like blood.

'Thank you,' I said aloud.

There were boots outside again and the door was unbolted. It was the giant nanny.

'Essen fertig?' he asked, staring at the plate and the rejected lump of fat.

'Ja.'

He picked up the plate and concentrated on the lump of fat.

'Nicht gut?' he asked in astonishment.

'Nein.'

He set down the plate and taking a piece of newspaper out of his pocket wrapped the fat up and put it in his pocket.

'Gut für Kinder,' he said unconvincingly and hurriedly left the cell.

6

The next morning, after I had drunk some coffee and sat for an hour with the first suggestions of boredom stirring inside me, the Feldwebel who had enjoyed the ride in the Mercedes so much came to the door.

'Nach Frankfurt,' he said gaily as if he anticipated a journey packed with thrills and amusement. He gave me a friendly smile.

He was aware that I had disliked him the day before and seemed anxious to make me change my opinion. The car which took us to the station drove as sedately as a Daimler in a royal procession although the people of Amsterdam were on their way to work and provided admirable subjects for baiting. Sometimes I caught the Feldwebel looking wistfully out of the window at a dilapidated horse and cart or an old man on a bicycle but he controlled himself and tried to make polite conversation. This was at first very difficult because he knew as little English as I knew German. Gradually, however, we evolved a pidgin language based on English, German and the telepathy of tone.

I wondered why he should bother to try and establish contact with me. It was a characteristic I had noticed in most of the Germans I had met since being shot down. If I had ever thought of the possibility of being taken prisoner while I was in England, I should have expected all Germans to be like the officer who had tried to interrogate me at the aerodrome or the two soldiers who had brought me from the aerodrome to Amsterdam. I had not yet recovered from the simple shock of finding that many of them talked and behaved exactly like us. It was even more of a shock to discover that these believed just as firmly in the Nazi cause as those who shouted and sneered. Their talk and behaviour took a slightly different form from ours just as their uniforms did and for the same reason but their major premises seemed to be the same. They thought that they were right about the war; they did not like awkward gaps in conversation; they wanted to be friendly to people they felt sorry for; they felt the natural human contempt for the way in which the Almighty ran the universe and yet their full share of human resignation towards it.

It is easy now to regard this wonder at an enemy's humanity as naïve, but as it is the business of war to foster the naïveté on which it thrives, so there can have been few people in England during the isolation years of 1940–42 who did not take the impersonal nature of their enemy for granted. We felt as different from them as from enemies from Mars. The Germans were the bombs which smashed the towns and villages of England or they were the words in the newspapers which told of defeat. They were a ridiculous race which was all Gestapo and people sticking out their arms at a villain-clown with a tooth-brush moustache. They weren't human beings like you or me.

When we arrived at the station an enormous suitcase was taken out of the car.

'Is that ours?' I asked.

The Feldwebel nodded.

I remembered seeing pictures of German prisoners carrying what was described as their emergency Red Cross clothing in Tate and Lyle sugar boxes through London.

'What's in it?' I asked.

He smiled and said vigorously: 'For you.'

I had to admit that the German service for prisoners seemed better than our own.

While the Feldwebel was talking to the driver of the car, the little soldier who was coming as an additional escort stood by the suitcase. He was a mousy man: long thin strands of hair protruded erratically from under his steel helmet. He wore his militarism apologetically.

The car drove away.

The Feldwebel pointed to the entrance to the station and the mousy man signed to me to pick up the case. For a moment I felt an instinctive resentment, but remembering that it contained things 'for me', I picked it up. The Feldwebel saw this and for some reason it worried him. He made me put it down and began a long, fast conversation with the soldier. I caught the word 'Offizier' several times and occasionally they looked from the suitcase to me and back again. Eventually the soldier shrugged his shoulders and picked it up himself. Its weight seemed to drag him out of sight into his enormous greatcoat. I offered to carry it. He shrugged his shoulders again, muttered 'Offizier', and staggered on. We went into the station.

We took a first-class carriage to ourselves. The soldier bolted the door which gave onto the platform and sat down opposite me. He put his rifle and his steel helmet up on the rack and was soon asleep. The Feldwebel stood at the entrance to the corridor turning away people who wanted to come in. I sat in a corner looking at the Dutchmen who smiled surreptitiously from the platform.

When the train started the Feldwebel sat down and put his feet up on the seat opposite.

'Prima,' he said.

He opened the suitcase. It was very full although I could not see properly what was in it because he kept the opening away from me.

He produced two numbers of *Colliers Magazine* which he handed to me. When I opened one of them and saw English words I could feel the tears pricking at the back of my eyes. I spent a long time reading the advertisements.

As we drew nearer to the German frontier I began to wonder exactly what 'frontier' meant in a frontierless continent. It was much as I had expected. The train stopped for about two minutes. A man looking classically like a detective passed down the corridor but did not come into our carriage. The train moved on. I was in Germany.

The fields and clouds were the same as those I had seen for the last half hour. There were the same farm houses and the same people on bicycles moving along the roads. But it was the enemy's country, an enemy whom we had fought so far as one might fight an armed man in a dark room. For three years now we had moved stealthily through the darkness, sometimes absurdly confident, sometimes terrified, but always wondering just what sort of man it was that we heard creeping along the wall towards us and what sort of weapon he had in his hand. Now for me at least the light had been turned on.

I stared out of the window at this country about which I had wondered for so long. My past curiosity gave a sharpness to the outlines of the trees and the houses and a magic quality to the people I saw moving about.

For me the mystery of the enemy's identity had been increased by the peculiar sort of war I had fought. Sometimes I had caught glimpses of his shadow on the wall. Flying over the country at fifteen thousand feet at night, I had seen strange toy woods and towns and the eiderdown pattern of the fields. Only once it had looked real: when we flew back one night from a blazing Hamm at twenty feet in the moonlight. It had looked exactly like England: bicycles propped against hedges, trim gardens in housing estates, A.R.P. men running about the streets of the towns. But the experience had been short and isolated and the moonlight had given it a sufficient touch of unreality for me to be able to fire my machine gun at everything I saw without scruple. Now this was to be the country in which I should eat and sleep, read books and write letters for the rest of the war. It was even just possible that I should have to spend more of the war in this country than I had done in my own.

I wondered just how long the war would last. I did not think we could invade this year. We should leave it until next year and make certain. But even then the war would be only just beginning.

The Feldwebel had not moved and I looked all the way up his black leather jack-boots and the thin grey greatcoat with its cheap tin buttons looking as if they had come out of a Christmas pudding before I noticed that his eyes were slightly open and that he was watching me with an uncle's amusement.

'For you the war is over,' he said.

Somebody else had said this to me and now I disliked it.

'No it's not,' I said feebly, although I couldn't think why it wasn't. Then I said: 'It won't be over for me until it's over for everybody.'

'But how not over for you?' asked the Feldwebel. 'What can you do now?'

I knew there was nothing I could do but that didn't seem to be the point.

'I can escape,' I said.

He made a sound of disappointment.

'In camp the escape is impossible. There is wire and machine guns. And why escape? There is sport and lessons. Here if you try I shoot.'

He looked out of the window.

It suddenly became very important for me to explain why my war was not over. I knew that he would not understand what I was going to say but it was as if there was an invisible person in the carriage before whom I had to justify myself.

'You don't know what people in England think about this war,' I said. 'It isn't the same thing to us as it is to you. We haven't any ambitions and we don't want any great changes, so we all hate war. And it's just because we hate it that we'll beat you. This is a personal war for each one of us and it's going on inside us all the time. It won't be over for any of us until the people who make war have been destroyed.'

I was out of breath with excitement and anxiety. I knew this was muddled and that it was not quite what I wanted to say, but I felt better for saying it.

44

I had surprised the Feldwebel. He was leaning forward staring at me with his hands on his knees. Even the mousy man was awake.

I struggled on.

'We're fighting for simple ordinary things: the right to grumble whenever you feel like it; the right to be wrong and stupid, and the right to become less wrong and stupid if you want to; the right not to suffer bodily pain. . . . All negative things, but that's the point. Without these simple things as a foundation you would never build anything positive at all.'

It all sounded very silly in a stuffy railway carriage spoken to two German soldiers who did not understand English.

The mousy man went to sleep again.

I was disappointed in myself. If this was really all we were fighting for, it seemed very feeble. I felt that I should have talked about Habeas Corpus, intellectual liberty and social security. I was angry with myself. I had failed in front of the invisible person in the carriage. I had failed in everything. I wasn't fit to fight the war. For me the war was over.

7

The cold grey suburbs of the town we were entering reflected my misery. I looked out of the window for air raid damage but could see none and decided that this was one of the minor Ruhr towns which had not yet been attacked. Once I noticed the familiar gap in a row of houses like the space left by a drawn tooth, but I could not be certain that it was the result of bombing and if it was it had happened a long time ago.

The Feldwebel was watching me.

'Nix kaput,' he said. 'Alles Propaganda.'

A few minutes later the train arrived in Duisburg and we got out. We had to wait for an hour for our connection to Frankfurt.

The Feldwebel took us to a German Red Cross canteen. It was nearly two o'clock and there were few soldiers drinking the hot soup and ersatz coffee. The women who were working there looked at me in a kind curious way at first and then took me for granted. The Feldwebel drank his soup straight out of the bowl and baited the mousy man because he wouldn't do the same. Then he put his feet up on the bench and snored for ten minutes.

When we got back to the platform the train was not yet in. We waited on the platform. The mousy man sat on the suitcase panting dismally. The Feldwebel looked disappointed at having to endure a situation which he couldn't control.

It was very cold and the grey gloom of Paddington and Euston was in the faces of the people who stood near us and of the soldiers who dragged their rifles and kit-bags from one platform to another. The Feldwebel said he was going to the lavatory.

A civilian came up to the mousy man and asked him a question. I heard the word 'Engländer' and saw from the corner of my eye that they were looking at me. I had an idea that I should make a show of dignity and tried to do this by looking straight ahead, as if the crowds moving up and down the platform were beneath my notice. It must have looked very silly.

The first suggestion that something was wrong came from the silence. I was suddenly aware of the station undertones: the wheels and the steam and a distant whistle. There were no voices.

I looked around. The faces were packed white and sullen all round me. There was a small space between me and them but the mousy man and the suitcase had disappeared. I could not understand how it had all happened so quickly.

I was very frightened. I remembered how once when I had been in a crowd teasing an awkward boy at school I had noticed his terror and been glad I was not him.

I tried to concentrate my attention on one face. I thought it would make me feel less helpless if I was opposed by something definite. But it was impossible. The faces seemed to shift as I looked at them. I could not see exactly what was in them but it was more than curiosity. They were all pale.

A woman suddenly shouted from the back of the crowd. It was like the scream of a solitary parrot. Then a man stepped forward into the space around me. The whole crowd seemed to move forward a little with him. He was well dressed but had no hat and I noticed that his hair was thin. His face was grey with hatred and I wondered if he was going to hit me. He strutted all round me, his upper lip shaking loosely. Then he stopped in front of me and put his face very close to mine. He shouted and wagged his finger. It was absurd but unpleasant and frightening, like someone making a scene in a 'bus. I stepped back to avoid the overpowering closeness of his face and a little man on the inner circle of the crowd startled me with a friendly smile, but

I could not find him again when I looked for him. The man with the thin hair continued to shout and wag his finger.

Suddenly something strange happened to the crowd. It was as if its backbone had been removed. The mass wobbled shapelessly and disintegrated. There was a swelling of human voices. A peaked cap was cutting its way through the crowd towards me and I recognized the Feldwebel. He was shouting and people were breaking away from him on both sides. When he reached the empty space in which I was standing I saw that he had drawn an automatic.

The crowd had dissolved. Nobody paid any attention to me. It was once more a typical scene on any war-time station in Europe. The mousy man reappeared struggling with his suitcase and sat down on it again.

I glowed with relief. I wanted to go up to the Feldwebel and shake his hand. I felt absurdly that we three were on the same side fighting the rest of the world.

'Thanks very much,' I said.

He said nothing. As he looked down to put his pistol away in its holster I noticed that his face had changed. It was difficult to remember that I had ever thought of him as a schoolboy.

A few minutes later our train came in and we established ourselves in a first class carriage. This time, when people tried to force their way in, the Feldwebel shouted at them abruptly. Once, when an officer questioned his right to keep the carriage empty, he produced papers to prove his case and the officer left to fight for a seat somewhere else.

As the train drew out I became very lonely. It was not just that I was alone in the middle of the enemy. After the agony of the scene on the station I felt that there was no-one in the world on my side. The pale faces on the station and the millions of identical ones behind them were all that was left of the world.

I was cheered by some superficial damage to the station at Cologne. I pointed it out to the Feldwebel.

He was angry.

'Yes,' he said. 'A little damage but elsewhere none at all.'

And moving out through the suburbs it looked as if he was right.

It was not until we were running beside the Rhine that the Feldwebel thawed. The mousy man had gone to sleep and a jolt from the train knocked his steel helmet off the rack onto his knees. He awoke with a mousy oath. The Feldwebel bounced up and down on his seat with laughter as he had done in the car at Amsterdam. He picked the hat up off the floor and put it on his own head.

'Better than English Stahlhelm,' he said.

Ever since I had been taken prisoner I had found the presence of German helmets fascinating. They were continual concrete evidence of the sleight of hand which had conjured me from one world to another. Now it was the English helmet which belonged to the world of the news reel.

The Feldwebel suddenly pulled the helmet sideways over one eye and began to sing in English:

'We're going to hang up the washing on the Siegfried Line . . .'

He choked with laughter. I remembered the fatuous winter of 1939–40 and laughed too.

He pointed at a rock on the other side of the Rhine.

'Die Lorelei,' he said and began to sing again.

'Ich weiss nicht was soll es bedeuten

Das ich so traurig bin,

Ein Märchen aus alten Zeiten

Das kommt mir nicht aus dem Sinn . . .'

'Heine,' I said.

'Yes.'

'A Jew.'

He shrugged his shoulders and, whistling the Lorelei, stared out of the window at the castles on the Rhine.

It was night when we arrived at Frankfurt. There were big crowds on the station and the Feldwebel and the mousy man kept very close to me. Soon the mousy man became exhausted by struggling with the suitcase and for the first time the Feldwebel carried it for him. Our connection for the prison camp did not leave until 11 o'clock and the Feldwebel was wondering what to do for the next two hours when the air raid siren blew. It sounded the same as the English siren except that it was slower. We went down into the station shelter and I experienced the familiar claustrophobic sensation of waiting for something to happen. The shelter was clean and well built. Civilians sat on benches joking and playing cards and rocking screaming babies to sleep. It was obvious that the air raid siren had never been much more to them than a bore. Some of them stared at me and a woman asked the Feldwebel who I was but there was no sign of hostility. When the sound of high-flying aircraft began to soak into the atmosphere people stopped talking but looked more interested than afraid. Some guns were fired. I wondered whether the flak was accurate and thought of the people fifteen thousand feet above us in Wellingtons, Stirlings and Hampdens, eating chocolate and plotting their track or weaving desperately and praying like tiny panic-stricken children.

No bombs were dropped and the sound of engines died away. People began to discuss where the aircraft were going to. The Feldwebel thought Mannheim.

The 'all clear' blew, identical to ours.

We went up onto the station again. There was still an hour to wait so the Feldwebel suggested that we should have some coffee. We went to the restaurant where there was a special room marked 'Für englische Kriegsgefangenen'. A woman came in and said perhaps we would rather have soup. The Feldwebel agreed and she came back with three large bowls of hot pea soup. The mousy man pulled out some bread and sausage, wrapped up in a copy of the *Völkischer Beobachter*. There was a large black headline on the front page, thickly underlined in red:

'Gegen den judisch-bolschewistischen Feind zum Sieg!'

Somebody had made a speech. It didn't seem to have much to do with us as we sat there making heavy sucking noises over our soup.

8

On the walk from the village station to the camp itself the mousy man finally collapsed. He stood in the middle of the deserted snow-packed road and raised his eyes towards the Feldwebel with the expression of a dying dog towards its master.

'I'll carry it,' I said.

The Feldwebel hesitated. Then he shrugged his shoulders.

'All right.'

It was a cold night and I had no overcoat but I was soon sweating with the effort of carrying the suitcase. I shifted it from one hand to the other in an attempt to ease the pain in my back and shoulders. I could not think what it was that could be for me and yet so heavy.

'How much farther?' I asked.

'Not far,' he said and pointed vaguely into the night.

For the first time I began to wonder about the camp and the people I should find inside it.

A searchlight suddenly lit up the white road and played around us. The Feldwebel shouted in German. He sounded nervous. The searchlight remained fixed on us and a heavily muffled figure in a long overcoat and a steel helmet came towards us. He spoke to the Feldwebel and looked at me. He had the face of a very old man. When he had gone the Feldwebel imitated his accent which he said was a thick Austrian one which he could hardly understand. The searchlight was switched out and I saw that there was a wall of barbed wire running parallel with the road on one side. It was too dark to see what lay behind it but we came to a corner where a tall wooden tower rose suddenly towards the stars. There was the sound of someone trying to keep his feet warm above us.

I was surprised when we went on past this, because the camp seemed to have ended. But after walking for about fifty yards we came to another thinner wall of barbed wire with a gate in it. A sentry let us in after looking at the Feldwebel's papers with a torch and we walked up a garden path towards a sort of suburban villa.

Just inside the door there were two Germans in the grey uniform of the Luftwaffe sitting at a table. A stove in the corner of the little room was giving out great waves of heat and there was the smell of leather, sweat and cigar smoke which seemed to hang in all German guard-rooms.

It was a relief to be able to put down the suitcase. The Feldwebel took it into a corner and pulled out a large envelope which he threw onto the table. One of the other Germans emptied it and I recognized among the papers the interrogation form which the naval officer on the island had filled in. There was also my escape equipment. The man began to fill in a new form. The Feldwebel went out of the room.

I was very curious about the other contents of the suitcase which was now lying on the floor near me. I raised the lid with my foot.

I was astonished by what I saw. There were civilian suits and shirts, handkerchiefs and shoes. There were also several tins of corned beef, some packets of American cigarettes and two bottles of Black and White whisky. It was a reassuring sight. I let the lid fall again.

The Feldwebel came back, and the man who had been filling in the new form turned round in his chair and looked at me.

'For you the war is over,' he said.

This time I did not feel so angry, but I shook my head. I thought of the contents of the suitcase and decided that there was something in what he said.

He stood up and I noticed for the first time a bunch of keys at his belt. They jangled when he moved. He said something to the Feldwebel and went out of the room.

'He has gone to find you a room,' said the Feldwebel, sitting down in front of the fire and stretching his legs.

I was suddenly infuriated at the thought of what we had believed about the Germans in England. 'Correct' treatment of prisoners had always been acknowledged, but there had never been any mention of civilian suits or bottles of whisky. Apparently one even had a room to oneself. It occurred to me that we might have been equally misinformed about other things the Germans did.

The man with the keys came back.

'Komm,' he said.

I stood up and looked at the Feldwebel.

'Well, good-bye,' I said. 'And thanks very much for everything.' I looked towards the suitcase.

'Do I take this now?'

The Feldwebel stared at me blankly, his farewell smile still stuck on his face like an old label on a trunk.

'Nix verstehen,' he said.

'My things,' I said, a little surprised. 'When do I get them?'

He looked from me to the suitcase and back again in amazement.

'Yours?' he said. He shook his head. A new slow, sly smile appeared over the old one.

'No,' he said. 'All mine. There are yours,' and he pointed at the papers and my escape equipment on the table.

I still could not understand.

'But what's all that for then?' I asked, pointing at the suitcase.

He shrugged his shoulders.

'Frankfurt is my home,' he said. 'I bring some presents: food,' – his eyes twinkled – 'and whisky. English whisky. Left behind with the washing on the Siegfried Line.'

'But you said . . .' I understood completely. 'My God, you bloody swine and you made me carry . . .'

The Feldwebel waved impatiently to the man with the keys.

'Komm,' said the man roughly and pushed me out of the door.

He led me into a corridor. I was beginning to feel suspicious about my room, but when he opened a door with a key and turned on the light I saw a small clean room with a bed, a table and a chair. It looked a pleasant enough place in which to spend a period of compulsory leisure and I was glad I did not have to share it with anyone.

I was a little surprised that there was no sign of any other English people.

'This is the camp, isn't it?'

'Certainly.'

'Where are the other Englishmen?'

'In the camp.'

I thought that I was being stupid, so I gave it up.

'When can I get hold of some books?'

'Morgen früh.'

'I beg your pardon?'

'Tomorrow.'

'Oh, thanks.'

'Now you must surrender your clothes.'

'What?'

'Please to undress. Another uniform will be brought to you.'

He closed the door and locked it. I felt confused and dismayed. There seemed to be something which I had not properly understood. I took off my battle-dress jacket. The door was opened again and the German put a foreign khaki uniform onto the bed. He stood in the room while I changed. It was much too big and I wondered if I should always have to wear these clothes. He went out with my battle-dress and locked the door again.

I could not understand why the door had been locked. Surely one did not spend one's time locked in like a criminal. I listened for some sound of other prisoners in the building but although I thought I heard the locking and unlocking of other doors the only voices were those of the guards. I was very tired. Sleep fell like an anaesthetic.

In the morning the sun was shining and I felt better. I was excited at the thought of the unknown. Very soon I should be talking to English people again, people who were on my side after all. I should hear talk of 'prangs' and 'piss-ups' and 'good types' who 'put up blacks' in Lincoln and Nottingham. I shouldn't think this boring as I had sometimes done before. It would be the most friendly talk in the world. I should be able to consider seriously the idea of escape, and talk over problems of disguise and frontier crossings with other people for whom the war was not yet over. I wondered if there would be anyone I knew there.

I began to reckon up the people whom I knew to be prisoners. I remembered how in England I had pitied them all tucked away in oblivion: Feathers, the first man of my course to go missing; Johnny Soames whose aircraft I had watched skidding away from the formation on one of the early daylight raids over northern France. But these people had been shot down some months ago and as the Feldwebel had told me that this was only a transit camp I knew that I was not likely to meet them here. Robin Summers was the most recent casualty from my squadron, and I had heard from the German at Amsterdam that he was a prisoner. But, although I hoped very much that he would be here, it seemed to me that it mattered little whether one knew anybody in the camp or not. They would all seem like old friends after the last few days.

I looked out of the window at the sun flashing on a field of snow. A little boy came out of the woods opposite and began skiing down the slope towards the road. The window was barred on the outside but this did not seem unreasonable as there was only one thin wall of barbed wire as defence for the whole camp. I wondered what the place with towers and searchlights had been that we passed in the night. The only thing that worried me was that the door to my room had not yet been unlocked.

I heard a voice just outside my window. It spoke very quietly.

'Smoky! Hey, Smoky!' it said.

I pressed my head close against one corner of the barred window trying to see who was speaking, but I could see no-one. Whoever it was must have been very close to the wall. I waited.

'Smoky? Are you there Smoky?'

There was no doubt about the Canadian accent. I had heard it in barrack rooms and Officers' Messes all over England. I was excited. I longed to speak, but found absurdly that I was shy.

'Hey, Smoky!' said the voice again. 'Wake up, Smoky.'

There was a groan in reply. It seemed to come from above me.

'What's the matter, Smoky? Haven't you got rid of those squits yet?' The Canadian still spoke quietly and with a sort of urgency.

This time the groan above me was louder. Then somebody spoke in a strong New Zealand accent.

'It's about all I haven't got rid of.' He paused. There was a bump on the ceiling above me. 'Coo! Ain't it lovely to see the sun?'

I realized that the voices were coming from different rooms in the building. The Canadian was obviously in the room next to me. I found the courage to speak.

'How long have you been here?' I asked.

There was complete silence. Just as I was about to say it again, the Canadian spoke.

'Hey, Smoky! Did you hear that? There's some other guy here.'

'Yes, I heard it.'

'How long have you been here?' I asked again.

'Are you next door to me?' asked the Canadian.

'I think so.'

'I'll bang on the wall.'

He banged several times.

'Yes, that's me.'

'You English?'

'Yes.'

There was a shout from outside the wire and the sound of heavy boots running over packed snow.

'Keine Unterhaltung! Keine Unterhaltung!'

The sentry appeared on the outside of the wire opposite my window. He was an old man like the guard who had stopped us in the road the night before.

'Zurück da! Zurück!' he shouted.

I had not yet learnt that a German is not necessarily angry because he is shouting, and so was surprised when he added in a gentle cooing voice:

'Es ist verboten. Please . . .'

Half an hour later the Canadian banged on the wall again.

'Hallo,' I said cautiously out of the window.

'What did you think of the breakfast?' he asked.

'Not much.'

'You'll get used to it.'

'Oh.'

I asked him about the meatless days which the man at Amsterdam had mentioned.

'What sort of days?'

'Meatless. He said that sometimes the supper was small because it

54

was a meatless day.'

'Sounds like a German joke to me.'

'What do you mean?'

'You're in the Third Reich now. It's a meatless century as far as prisoners are concerned.'

'Oh.'

'When were you shot down?' he asked.

'Three days ago.'

He whistled.

'Hey, Smoky!' he called. 'There's a guy here who's only been down three days. We'll get all the gen.'

'Why, when were you shot down?' I asked.

'Four months ago.'

'And they still lock you in? When are we let out of these rooms?'

'Oh, we've only been here a couple of days. We were on the loose in France for a couple of months. Then the f——ing Gestapo picked us up. God knows what happened to the family they found us with, but they took us to a place called Fresnes gaol, Paris. We were there for two months. I can tell you this place is a bloody paradise compared with Fresnes. Eh, Smoky?'

The New Zealander spoke slowly from above.

'I used to lie on my bed all day thinking about every bloody meal I'd ever had in my life. At the end of each day my pillow was so soaked in saliva that I had to wring it out on the floor.'

'At nights,' said the Canadian, 'it was so cold that you couldn't sleep at all, and about dawn you'd hear the shots as they knocked off that day's quota of Frenchmen out in the yard.'

'Christ that used to give me the shits,' said the New Zealander. 'They'd told me that as I was caught in civilian clothes I was going to be treated as a spy, and every time I heard those shots I thought "My turn tomorrow".'

I could not think of anything to say. I was angry and ashamed of myself. All this had been done and was being done every day all over Europe by the people whom I had found so pleasant and human ever since I had been shot down. I could not understand this and only knew that I was angry. I should have liked to trample on the face of the first German I could find and kick him over and over again in the stomach.

'Hey, look out!' called the Canadian suddenly.

The old guard who had stopped us talking before ambled past the

55

wire on the outside. When he saw me looking out of the window he smiled, and, looking up at the sun, said:

'Schön, was?'

He began to sing.

Go on, I said to myself, trample on his face, kick him in the stomach. I knew that I could never have done it. As I lay back on my bed I tried to work out the connection between him and the British Empire and Fresnes gaol, but could make nothing of it.

Later in the day I learnt from the Canadian that we were not in the main part of the camp at all, but in the cells or 'cooler' awaiting interrogation.

This place had been the first German prison camp built specifically for British air-crew. The first prisoners had come here in the days when the state of war between England and Germany was still largely theoretical. The rooms had been comfortable and not over-crowded. Some of the prisoners had been to parties in the German Kommandantur. I once saw a copy of the German illustrated weekly *Der Adler* in which there were photographs of individual prisoners posing goodnaturedly. There had been a superficial state of friendli-ness and good will between the Germans and the British in the camp.

When the 'phoney war' ended and British aircraft were shot down in larger numbers, the camp became too small to hold all aircrew prisoners. Other special Air Force camps were built in different parts of Germany and it was in these that I eventually spent my time as a prisoner. But prisoners still came here first for interrogation and waited here until the camp was full, when they were 'purged' to other camps. A 'permanent staff', consisting largely of the original prisoners, remained to run the camp. The members of this permanent staff had adjusted themselves to captivity, but prisoners passing through had only just been shot down and were still unsure and bewildered. In addition to this the men who were passing through the camp after the first year often had a different view of the war from those who had been there since before the fall of France. Some of the early prisoners had regarded the Germans much as, afterwards in the pavilion, one might regard the football team to whom one had lost the match. The newer prisoners had seen English towns and villages burning. As a result of such differences there was sometimes friction between those waiting to be purged and the permanent staff. Charges of selfishness and even unjust charges of collaboration were

56

sometimes made against members of the permanent staff. The main camps too, where conditions and supplies of Red Cross food and clothing were not so good, were full of distrust and contempt for them. For their part the permanent staff thought all new prisoners childish, ill-mannered and unbalanced.

Some time before my arrival the permanent staff had surprised all the other R.A.F. prisoners in Germany by escaping from the camp by a tunnel. About eighteen people escaped from this tunnel and they were not all recaptured until four days later. The tunnel had taken several months to build and some of the accusations which had been made against these same people now looked rather silly. Those who had escaped were immediately purged to other camps. Those who had not escaped remained as a nucleus permanent staff to which a few of the prisoners passing through were added.

But the division between the permanent staff and new prisoners persisted. Most of the old prisoners were there because they personally had no wish to escape, and although their reasons for not wishing to were usually quite sensible and not always selfish it was difficult for a new prisoner to grasp them. In addition to this, all members of the permanent staff were comfortably installed and were certain of receiving Red Cross food supplies, while the others were passing through to the unknown. Finally they were resented as any established clique is resented by newcomers, and for their part, put on little airs and gave themselves privileges in return.

Such had been the history of this camp up to the time I arrived there. A garbled version of it had somehow reached England. In this the camp was run as a luxury camp by the Germans in order to lull people into a sense of false security while they were pumped for information. The pumping was said to be done by Germans, faultlessly disguised as British officers, or even, it had been whispered, by genuine British officers who had fallen for German propaganda. It was not until one had made oneself ridiculous by days of suspicion and over-cautiousness in the camp that one realized how hopelessly less dramatic was the truth.

Later in the war, with the increase in the size of our bombing attacks against Germany and the corresponding increase in the number of prisoners, the camp's character changed again. The permanent staff was gradually purged to other camps until there were none of the original 'old people' left. The Germans intensified and brutalized their methods of interrogation until it was quite usual for a prisoner who refused to talk to be kept in solitary confinement under intentionally unpleasant conditions for weeks. Prisoners passed through the place so fast that it ceased to be a camp in the true sense altogether.

It was not until I had been in the camp some days that I learnt the full story of the past. The Canadian in the next cell knew only that we would be moved into the camp itself when we had been interrogated. He said that an English sergeant who acted as orderly in the 'cooler' had told him this, and that he had promised to come back later in the day with some cigarettes for us.

I spent most of the day staring at the walls and ceiling and wondering when the next meal would come. Each time a guard arrived, either with food or to let me out to the lavatory, I asked for a book, and each time he said 'Yes' and didn't bring one. Once I banged on the wall for the Canadian's attention and got no reply. I felt very lonely, but half an hour later I heard his voice calling to me through the window.

'You silly clot,' he said. 'I was being interrogated when you knocked on the wall. The chap was furious and said he'd put me in a cell without anyone on either side of me if I talked to you again.'

'What was he like?'

'A nasty piece of work. Talked with an Oxford accent and produced that bogus Red Cross form the Air Ministry warns you about.'

'What did you say to him?'

'I told him he knew where he could put it!'

'Did he mind?'

'He didn't understand, but he laughed to show his sense of humour.'

I watched the dusk coming across the snow from the edge of the wood like smoke from a newly-lit bonfire. A figure walking along the path on the outside of the wire came into the corner of my vision. The guard, I thought, and paid no more attention to it until it stopped opposite my window and spoke.

'It's your own fault, chum,' it said. 'You ought never to have joined up.'

I saw that he had no hat and was wearing British battle-dress.

'Cheer up,' he went on, 'I'll bring you a few cigarettes in a minute when Arthur's opened the gate.'

'Who's Arthur?' I asked. There didn't seem much point in asking about himself. I had met him every day of my life in England: punching my ticket on a 'bus, cutting my hair, selling me an evening newspaper or looking after the engine of my aeroplane.

'Oh, Arthur's all right,' he said. 'Just a bit stupid, but you mean well, don't you Arthur?'

The silhouette of a small man in German uniform came shambling along the wire.

'Komm, Arthur. Guter Kamerad im Cooler. Zigaretten geben.'

It was the first time I had heard orderly's German: a rich hybrid language spoken with any English local accent which often achieved wonders when the phrases of classroom or grammar book produced only a blank expression and a shrug of the shoulders.

The German turned round obediently and the orderly followed him down the wire. A minute later I heard the orderly's voice inside the compound as he passed cigarettes to the Canadian through the window of the cell next door.

'And there are some for your pal upstairs,' he added and moved along the wall to my window.

He pushed two packets of Players and a box of matches through the bars while the German stood miserably in the background looking furtively up and down the wire.

'Schnell, schnell,' he mumbled.

'All right, Arthur. Don't panic,' said the orderly. 'He's scared the Gestapo'll get him,' he added to me, 'Christ, they would too if they searched his quarters. He must have got enough Nescafé there to make brews for the whole of Frankfurt. He sends regular food parcels to his family in Hamburg, don't you Arthur? Schwarzmarkt nicht, Arthur?'

The German winced.

'Schnell,' he muttered, "Posten kommt.'

'Still, he's worth it,' continued the orderly.

'Well, thanks very much,' I said. 'I suppose there's no chance of your bringing any food some time is there?'

His manner changed.

'We're all pretty short of that, I'm afraid sir, but I'll see what I can do.'

'Thanks,' I said. 'And there's one more thing.' I lowered my voice.

'Schnell,' whined the German.

'Yes?'

'What about escape? Is there any chance?'

'Absolutely none at all, sir, from here. You'd do better to wait.'

'Thanks.' I was secretly relieved.

He stepped back from the window and rejoined the German.

'So long,' he said. 'See you tomorrow if Arthur hasn't been sent to the Ostfront by then. Eh, Arthur? Ostfront?'

The German growled.

'He's scared stiff of it,' said the orderly. 'Well, so long. Vorwärts, Arthur.'

They disappeared into the dusk which had now reached the square of my window.

The next morning I banged on the wall to attract the Canadian's attention but there was no answer. I waited another half hour and banged again. There was still no answer. But there was a sound of boots in the passage outside and my door was unlocked. A man in Luftwaffe officer's uniform put his head inside.

'It's no use trying to talk to him, old man,' he said. 'He's been moved across to the main camp.'

'Oh, I see,' I said sheepishly. It was like being caught 'talking in the dorm.'

'I expect you're pretty keen to get across, aren't you?' he asked, without coming any further in.

'Well, yes, I am.'

'Good show, then I'll try and get you through as soon as possible. Expect me some time this afternoon. In the meantime is there anything else you'd like?'

'I'd rather like something to read.'

'I'll do what I can. Well, so long for now.'

He shut the door.

But the only person I saw for the rest of that day, besides the German who brought my food and took me to the lavatory, was the English orderly. He came just as it was getting dark again.

'They've moved the chap next door to another cell,' he said, as he handed a crust of bread and some cigarettes through the bars. 'It's because he was found talking to you. Still, I expect you'll all be out in a couple of days. No-one's ever in for much longer than four days altogether.'

'Thank God for that,' I said. The staleness of blood and brain which comes from solitary confinement was already maturing inside me.

'Sorry about the bread. It was the best I could do.'

'But it's wonderful.'

'Oh, don't thank me. I stole it out of one of the Posten's haversacks when I was cleaning out the guard-room. It's good for these buggers to have to go hungry. Good practice for after the war.' He changed his tone. 'I was caught at Dunkirk when they thought they'd won the bloody war. I shan't forget what they were like then. Marched us back into Germany the whole bloody way. Bullets for those that couldn't keep up and a fifth of a loaf a day for those that could. I shan't forget that.'

He turned and looked at his guard who was waiting tamely behind him and keeping an occasional look-out along the wire.

'Christ,' he said, 'I'm looking forward to watching these buggers starve.'

I laughed. The possibility of anything like that happening to the Germans seemed a long way off in those days.

'Well, I must be off,' he said. 'Come on, Arthur. So long.'

They moved out of sight.

The next day I was interrogated twice. It was a tedious business. Both the interrogators had been doing their job for so long that they no longer thought much about what they were saying. They were as familiar with their patter as music-hall comedians.

'Perhaps you can just let me have a few details . . . Nothing important, of course . . . We respect your status as a prisoner of war and don't ask you for military information . . . But you want to be sure that your parents get to hear as soon as possible that you are safe, don't you? . . . Good . . . Now what did you say was the number of your squadron? . . .'

The first interrogator was not the officer who had looked in the day before but a wizened little old man who seemed half afraid of me. He also wore uniform but explained that he only held an honorary rank. At the time his Jewish appearance did not strike me as peculiar because I had not yet got used to the idea of people thinking racially, but I learnt later that he was half Jewish and that he did this job to keep his Jewish wife out of trouble.

'What did you say was the number of your squadron?'

'I didn't.'

He looked out of the window towards the wood.

'No,' he said. 'None of them do.'

There was a silence in which I almost began to feel sorry for him.

'You know all about this form, I suppose,' he said.

He had the bogus Red Cross form which I had seen at Amsterdam on his lap.

I nodded.

'Yes,' he said. 'They all do.'

Eventually he persuaded me to give him the name and address of my parents. It was like giving a button to a blind beggar. I wrote to my parents at that address for the next three years.

The second interrogator was the hearty man of the day before.

'Hullo, old man. Quite comfortable? . . . Now then, perhaps you can let me have a few details . . . Red Cross . . . formality . . . number of your squadron?'

His reaction to my replies was more vigorous than the other man's and once he even pretended to get angry.

'Well, if that's your attitude, and I call it bloody unco-operative, there's nothing more to say.'

But it was obvious that he was used to it all. Soon we slipped into an argument about the war.

This time I remembered all the things I had forgotten to say in the railway carriage.

'We stand for the liberty of the individual − Habeas Corpus.'

'What about India, then?'

'We aim at social security.'

'What about the slums? There are no slums in Germany.'

'We uphold the rights of free nations.'

'How was the British Empire built?'

Something was going wrong. I became angry and confused.

'Well, anyway, the fact that the whole of Europe is against you shows that we're fighting for something worth-while.'

'But my dear old boy, what can have put the idea into your head that Europe is against us? You must have been listening to the B.B.C. or something.'

When he left I had a sense of futility and frustration. I had not yet learnt that every German soldier from private upwards had had an elementary political education which made this sort of argument child's play for him. It was a fact that quite easily became disheartening during the first few months of captivity. So he left me in a stew of doubt. I determined to spend the first part of my prison leisure working out my reasons for knowing I was right. But it annoyed me that I had not got them worked out already. And to my annoyance was added the realization that perhaps he had not been such a bad interrogator after all.

9

The wood opposite was smoking with dusk again and I was looking forward to seeing the orderly, when my door was opened and I was told that I would be moved across to the main camp at once. This excited me and while I was being photographed and having my particulars taken — 'Hairs: black . . . Nose: straight . . . Knowledge of German . . . little . . .' — I was thinking of the pleasure of being once again among my own people. We went out of the building.

The air was cold and the snow crunched as we walked. It was a relief to be able to look at objects in depth again after the hypnotic closeness of the walls and the limited view from my room. I saw a range of hills behind us. Something inside me stretched as I walked so that at the same time I was walking on the top of those hills.

The camp came into sight at the bottom of the road. I saw the massed coils of barbed wire, the tall wooden towers and the muffled sentries that we had passed on the night I arrived. I was astonished at the smallness of the area which these enclosed. It was about 100 yards long and 70 yards wide. Inside there were some long wooden huts which occupied almost all the space. It was like a large man inside a suit that was too small for him. A few figures in battle-dress were walking round the perimeter. Two were throwing a ball about. The ball came over the wire as we passed and the German who was escorting me threw it back.

'Danker,' said the man in battle-dress, and to me: 'Hullo, old boy' as if it was inevitable that I should have come there some time or other, and went on throwing the ball about.

We arrived at the gate. It was a double one and the man on duty smiled as he let me in.

'For you the war is over,' he said and locked the gates behind me.

I was alone in the camp. For a moment I had a ridiculous sense of anti-climax. All the emotional turmoil and excitement of the out-break of war, all the long drawn out details of my training, the thrills of flying and the fear of death, all the bustle and anticipation of the last few days had ended in this, in my standing alone on a slushy path in the late afternoon with absolutely nothing whatever to do.

One of the couples walking round the camp was approaching.

'Hullo, old chap, you just arrived?'

'Yes.'

'Good show, well I'm the clothing officer. If you're short of any clothes just come and see me, and I'll try and fix you up.'

'Thanks. I haven't got any clothes at all except what I've got on.'

The little eyes sharpened at the top of the thin nose.

'Of course I'm not promising anything, old chap. There are a lot of people here in your position and we've got to try and please everybody, which isn't an easy job in this place I can tell you.' He smiled at his companion who said rather sadly:

'It certainly isn't.'

'I should very much like a change of underclothes at least,' I said.

'Yes, all right, old chap,' said the clothing officer rather testily. 'Well, just come and see me.'

'Thanks very much.'

'Not that I'm promising anything, mind you.'

They walked on.

There was no-one else in sight. A German came out of one of the huts. He was unarmed and I hoped that he might be one of the interpreters.

'Can you tell me where I can see about getting a bed?' I asked him.

'You are new, yes?'

'Yes.'

He led me into the hut he had just come out of.

'I will take you to Flight-Lieutenant Sutton, the accommodation officer.'

We walked up the wooden passage. There were doors on either side and pinned to some of these were pieces of paper on which the occupants of the rooms had written their names. Steam came from underneath one of the doors and there was the sound of a shower running. Somebody inside sang:

'Now's the time to roll the barrel,
For the gang's — all — here.'

The German stopped outside a door at the top of the passage and knocked. The door opened. A Flight-Lieutenant in faded blue uniform came out.

'Hullo? Ah, Karl.'

He didn't notice me, but lapsed heavily into what even I could recognize as elementary German.

'Ich denke, Karl, dass Sie haben meines Buch.'

'Oh, that is terrible, Mr. Sutton,' said the German. 'Your German is worse and worse. And I haven't got your book.'

The Flight-Lieutenant became suddenly petulant, like a child that has lost its toy.

'Oh confound it, then where is the bloody thing?'

He turned back into the room and started rummaging among books and papers.

'Mr. Sutton, there is a new officer here.'

'What? Oh wait a minute, I must try and find this wretched book. I want to do Lesson Twelve tonight for our hour tomorrow afternoon.'

'Here, you can borrow mine, Mr. Sutton, until tomorrow.'

He produced a book from under his arm.

'Oh thanks, Karl, very much. Now what did you say?'

He saw me for the first time.

'I'm sorry to keep you waiting. Come in and have a cup of tea. Buzz off, Karl, no tea for you today.'

We sat down at a table and he poured me out some tea.

'It's a good thing to do something to keep your mind occupied, you know. That's why I do German. Can't say I've learnt much although I've started it again and again in the last two years. Still, it gives you something to do.'

'I suppose there are plenty of other books too, besides Grammars?'

'Oh yes, there are books.' He said it as if books were some terrible bore which everybody had to put up with but which weren't of the slightest use. 'But what you need is something to do. Take my tip: keep yourself occupied. If you don't want to learn a language, there are plenty of other ways of doing it. For instance, a very good way is to make everything you do take twice as long as it would normally take you. If it normally takes you a quarter of an hour to shave, make it take you half an hour. If you normally spend ten minutes making your bed, spend twenty minutes on it. You'll find you soon get through the day that way, and you're occupied all the time which is the important thing.'

'Thanks for the tip,' I said. 'Now do you think I could have a bed somewhere?' I suddenly wanted very badly to get out of that room.

'There's a chap called Summers came in the other day. You can go in with him if you like.'

'I'd like to very much. He was on my squadron.'

'All the people that were on my squadron are either dead or Group Captains by now.'

He told me where to go and I left the room with relief.

There was a man walking up and down the corridor outside. He came up to me as I shut the door.

'Are you the man that's just arrived?'

'Yes.'

'Oh good show. At least I don't mean that — not a good show for you, I know — but frankly when you've been down a long time it is a good show to see someone from home and get all the news. My name's Lomas. I wondered if you'd care to come along and have a cup of tea in my room. We're all rather keen to hear what you've got to say about the war.'

He spoke energetically and his words tripped over one another as they tumbled out.

'Thanks very much. I'd love to.'

There was only one other man in his room and he introduced him as George Apsley.

They were as shy as I was and the effort they made to be friendly was the most heartening thing I had experienced since I had been taken prisoner. They asked me questions about myself and my squadron and the way I was shot down. They made me feel of some value again and the warmth was flooding through me long before the kettle had boiled on the iron stove in the corner. There was a pause and I sensed a slight tension as Lomas spoke.

'And the war?' he said. 'How's it going on?'

'Oh, it's going on,' I said. 'That's about all you can say for it.'

'But it's going pretty well really, isn't it? You see, we only get the German news in this place, and of course that doesn't mean a thing.'

I thought for a moment.

'I don't think you could honestly say it was going well just now, but it will do soon and that's all that matters.'

'Any idea how soon?' asked George Apsley slowly. He had been shot down in September, 1940.

'No, but next year some time, I should think.'

'But we'll invade this year, surely?' said Lomas.

'I shouldn't think so. We're only just beginning to think about it.'

'Oh, I think there'll be an invasion this year, you know,' said Lomas confidentially.

'Yes, but which way?' said Apsley mournfully through his moustaches.

'Don't take any notice of George,' said Lomas to me. 'He's been a prisoner too long.'

'Oh no,' said Apsley. 'Only five hundred days the day after tomorrow.'

'Anyway,' persisted Lomas. 'What is happening?'

'Well, the Germans are pretty badly stuck in Russia.'

'Oh yes, they've had it there all right. Have the Russians retaken Smolensk yet?'

Smolensk, Smolensk. I had heard something about it once or seen it on a map, but I could remember nothing definite.

'I'm not quite sure,' I said.

'I think you'll find they have,' said Lomas. 'What about the Far East?'

'You heard about Singapore, I suppose?'

'The German news said it had fallen, but we don't believe that.'

'It's fallen all right, I'm afraid.'

'Good God!'

They were both astonished and Lomas stopped for a moment to stare at the floor.

'I bet they put up a bloody good fight,' he said.

'I don't know,' I said. 'There were 70,000 prisoners.'

They asked about the escape through the Channel of the German battleships *Scharnhorst* and *Gneisenau*.

'They didn't get clean away, did they?' asked Lomas.

'I'm afraid they got away,' I said. 'A destroyer claimed to have damaged one, I think.'

'The Germans said they shot down forty-one aircraft. How many were actually missing?'

'Thirty-seven, I think.'

There was another silence.

'Still, you think we're going to invade this year?' said Lomas.

'No, next year.'

'This year, next year, sometime, never,' said Apsley. Then surprisingly: 'Don't think I'm a pessimist, I'm not. The Germans have lost the war all right. It's just going to take rather a long time making them admit it.'

Later in the evening I asked him what life in a prison camp was like.

'I wish I could think of a slick answer to that one,' he said. 'But I never can. It seems to me that the only possible way of finding out what it is like is to live it. You see, all the things which at the moment seem strange to you about it become every day normality after a bit, so that it's untrue to give you an answer in terms of the lack of space or the lack of change or the lack of food or any of the other things which make this so different from ordinary life.'

He pulled at his moustaches.

'Nor is there any advice which an old prisoner can reasonably give to a new one except: don't worry. Everyone finds something congenial about this life. People are like chameleons: they can adjust themselves to any environment so long as they've no alternative. Lomas, for instance, finds his pleasure in wishful thinking about the war; Sutton in continually starting a language which he's physically incapable of learning; I paint — shockingly.'

He frowned.

'Even analysing it like this somehow makes it unreal, because in fact the whole thing is so un-selfconscious. Actually, I can think of an answer to your question, but you'll think it very silly.'

'No, I won't,' I said.

'Well, it's just that life here is exactly like life anywhere else. Of course the environment is very much more simple and unpleasant than the environment from which you've just come. But as I said, I've decided that human beings adjust themselves to any environment to which there is no alternative, and human life in here is the same as in the world outside, for which also there is no alternative. Viewed from the standards of the outside world, the main trends in human life are perhaps shown up rather more clearly here: selfishness, courage, the desire for escape, self-fulfilment etc., but then once you're here you don't think about the standards of the outside world very much.'

As I lay in bed that night, watching the flash of the searchlights on the darkened wall, I asked Robin Summers the same question. He had been there a few weeks, suffering most of the time from frostbite after thirty hours in a dinghy in the Atlantic. He still had moments of extreme pain and walked only with difficulty.

'What's this life like?' I asked.

'Bloody awful,' he said. Then he gave a great roar of pain and kicked furiously underneath the blankets. 'Bloody funny of course, too,' he added.

Part Two

1

I cannot write fully about the years that followed. Although at the time they were made up of an apparently infinite chain of familiar days, I can think of them now only as a whole. The only real characteristic of each day was that it was the same as the day before and to give any account of such days in strict sequence would make as tedious reading as it made tedious living. Now it is possible to summarize the main features of that life in a single chapter.

Apsley was right: you adjusted yourself to prison life. Unnatural conditions became natural and as time passed it was more and more difficult to believe that there was any other life beyond that which went on inside the wire. Certainly it was an adjustment which you fought against. It was claustrophobic to feel that the outside world, which reason told you was still there, was in fact disappearing. But adjustment went on all the same because it was the only way of making yourself tolerate a condition which you loathed. So the outside world faded.

Of course you could never forget about it. Sometimes you would see people who lived in it walking past the camp. News of public events poured in ceaselessly through the German loudspeaker and the secret wireless. Letters arrived from home. But all these things somehow had their centre inside the wire. It was as if they were all specially created to be viewed from there.

The pale women in black who walked along the dusty road beside the wire on Sundays, and the unguarded French prisoners who returned to their camps from work every evening might have been extras walking across a film set. It was difficult to believe that they had a life to the left or right of that stretch of wire.

The battles in Russia, Africa and Normandy became mere words, to be heard punctually from the loudspeaker at three or four o'clock, from the English news-reader if German security was sufficiently relaxed, or from anybody who thought he knew what the next allotment of words was going to be about. Rommel arrived at Alamein, the Russians drove the Germans out of Russia, English and American troops landed on the continent, whole German cities were razed to the ground in one night: I heard it all from the same patch of sand, four hundred yards long by a hundred wide in the middle of a Silesian pine forest. And in the forest there was nothing to show for it. The wire was still there and the bored guards and the roll-call, morning and evening, and the hundreds of faces you grew to hate just because they were a part of the unaltering surroundings. For three years the war was just a large scale Radio thriller. Sometimes it frightened us, sometimes it had us madly excited and always some-body listened.

Letters were fantastic tricks of the imagination, tangible messages received from the world of day dreams. As with all good day dreams you were confident that one day this world would materialize and yet at the same time it seemed as unattainable as another planet. So letters were unearthly and invaluable, even if they only came from Barclays Bank.

Of course reason struggled hard to maintain its accustomed position and simultaneously you knew that the people passing the wire slept somewhere and that the news on the wireless meant friendly troops nearer or further away. Sometimes you even wrote back to Barclays Bank. But the odds were weighted against reason, and other parts of the mind, like some Resistance movement long held down in an oppressed country, came out into the open.

Whether you lived eight men to a room in partitioned huts or ninety men to a cold stone barn, this remoteness of the outside world was the conditioning factor of prison life. Variations in standards of treatment and comfort made little difference relative to the permanence of this one condition. In some camps Red Cross parcels arrived less regularly than in others and when they failed altogether people talked about food all the time instead of, as usually, about food or football or politics or the theatre. But always the world in which you could go into a shop and buy as much bread and potatoes as you liked was remote. In some camps the lavatories were so bad that white slugs bred in the depths. You could see the filth heaving with them as you peered through the crudely cut holes in the wood which served for seats, and sometimes they would crawl out through these holes and invade the neighbouring parts of the camp. In other camps rats lived under the seats and bit people as they sat there naked. In others there was merely an overpowering smell when the wind blew in your direction. But always it seemed impossible that you would ever sit on the polished seat of a flushing lavatory again.

You took for granted the presence of the Germans and the wire as ordinary citizens take for granted the law of gravity. The morning and evening roll-calls ('appel') were complementary to sunrise and sunset. If there was an air raid at night and the lights on the camp boundary were turned out you missed the flickering of the search-lights as you miss the light of the moon when it goes behind a cloud.

So four hundred square yards became an everyday world. And, as in the greater everyday world, the majority of people were superficially happy. Each man had his everyday business in which he could feel he had his niche and even at times his indispensability. Almost every activity of the outside world was reproduced there and provided the same outlets, fatuous and valuable, for human energy.

For the bureaucratic minded there was camp administration, and there were good and bad bureaucrats. For readers there were books and rooms set apart as libraries, and there were people who learnt a great deal and people who read furiously and learnt nothing. For actors and producers and carpenters there was a theatre and for people who liked seeing plays there was an auditorium. For those who liked cleaning their buttons there was button polish and a British parade once a year on the King's Birthday. For those 'liked a job to do' there was the distribution of food and clothing and fuel, and there were some who did it honestly and others who were suspected of turning it into a 'racket'. For those who liked to go to church there were padres of several denominations and candles and a camp-built altar. And for those who liked to go to the office every morning by the 8.15 there were class rooms and classes where nobody learnt very much but where everybody thought they were doing something. Games players cleared areas of sand or dusty rubble. Strategists pinned up maps. Gardeners dug gardens. And people who liked to walk and talk walked round and round the perimeter track in endless identical circles.

As soon as prisoners had been poured into the particular patch of ground which was to be their camp, all this activity materialized from nothing; and it materialized in every camp regardless of the nationality of the prisoners. It was quite spontaneous, for the Germans instigated nothing although they would sometimes co-operate in an elementary way by allowing wood for goalposts or permitting the construction of a theatre. The ceaseless thrust and bustle came from something deep and primaeval in man. The restless indifferent force of human energy, responsible alike for beauty and ugliness, comedy and tragedy, saintliness and crime, had to find its own level inside the wire.

But if the determining force in human existence was unaltered, the peculiarities of environment — shortage of food, absence of women, lack of space, remoteness of the outside world — did produce corresponding peculiarities of behaviour. Some tendencies in human behaviour were encouraged, others repressed, and the results were both pleasant and unpleasant. Strange twists were given to the normal body of human nature, revealing that such freak developments are potentially in all of us all the time.

The only beneficial peculiarity of environment was the sense of detachment from the outside world. In the first place people developed a greater objectiveness than they had ever done while they were living in it. The formation of liberal thought by those who normally might have taken a pride in never bothering to think at all was remarkable. But more significant than this was the general increase in sensibility. There were no cinemas or pubs or dances so that we were forced to find pleasure in the ordinary things which surrounded us, the sky and books and the changing seasons. Many people seemed to become aware of such things for the first time in their lives. 'I never realized that sunsets could be so lovely.' 'This classical music has much better tunes than dance music and I don't seem to get tired of them nearly so easily.' 'At home you hardly know whether it's raining from one day to the next but here you feel better every time the sun comes out.' 'I never used to read poetry at all but I've just found out that it says all the things I've often felt but never been able to express.' 'I didn't realize Dickens was so funny.' Naïve unsophisticated statements such as these marked a regeneration which perhaps must be experienced by more than a handful of

72

prisoners if we are to care enough about civilization to want to save it.

As people became more intensely aware of the pleasures of beauty they wanted to create it for themselves and another new source of happiness was discovered. Commercial travellers began to paint, stockbrokers to act and footballers to write poetry. Perhaps none of it was very good, but it was at least the beginning of something true in the lives of people who had been educated to falsity. Certainly not everybody in the camp found pleasure in books or music or poetry or nature but many people who normally would never have had anything to do with such things were forced by their environment to look into them and found there greater wealth than they had ever known before.

I often used to wonder whether we should carry these new springs of happiness away with us when we emerged. I certainly intended to. If we could find a heightened sense of beauty in the world of a prison camp, I thought, surely we could find it in the great free world of which we dreamed? I cursed myself for having made such a feeble thing of life before being shot down. I determined that it should not happen again and it seemed impossible that it should for this time I should carry with me the foundation of happiness which I had found behind the wire. I used to despise the people who wrote me letters from England showing that they found the world drab and depressing. They seemed silly and childish and so much less wise than us who really did live in a drab and depressing world and yet found happiness in it. I laughed when I read of the things which they considered important: political creeds, literary cliques, careerist intrigues.

Looking back now I wonder only at my arrogance. The very fact that I had only properly discovered a foundation of happiness when separated from the world should have shown me that the tendency of the world was to flood and destroy such a thing. I should have known that no amount of understanding can carry any individual for long against the swirling crowds of social existence, and that soon after rejoining them I too should be stampeding with them. The fact that I was in a prison camp at all should have made clear to me the ruthlessness and irresistibility of the stampede.

All the other peculiar effects of camp environment were bad. In so far as material conditions were more unpleasant, so human beings were more unpleasant. It is not my experience that physical hardship 'brings out the best in a man'. Changes of character brought about by the fluctuation of material conditions were so marked that they were noticeable even at the time from within the camp. As the weekly parcel issue decreased from one to a half you began to notice who took more than his share of the butter or the jam and though you felt mean for noticing it you went on being mean. You were glad when someone suggested that the butter or the jam should be cut up into rations even though you did see the hard selfishness in his eyes as he said it and felt sick because you knew that normally he was neither hard nor selfish. When there were no Red Cross parcels at all you began to notice that people sized up the rations of margarine before they helped themselves, and though you despised them for it you were none the less sharp to do it yourself. A roster for crusts had to be started as these contained more bread than the average thin slice. After some weeks without Red Cross parcels, people began to arrive early at meals so that they could size up and take the largest of the scrupulously rationed helpings of potatoes, or the thickest of the apparently identical slices of bread. Though the differences were minute they were capable of calling forth the highest passions: great content if you did well, or jealousy and despair if you did badly. You loathed it when you saw other people behaving like this and yet you could no more control it in yourself than you could any other automatic physical reflex. And it was small compensation to be able to loathe yourself.

Life was not quite a state of nature or a question of the survival of the fittest, but in times of no food parcels the partition separating us from that state was unpleasantly thin and even at the best of times it was thin enough to be able to hear most of what went on on the other side. The general shortage of comforts and of everything which kept us just above the lowest level of life was sufficiently great to make individuals cling to what they had with something like fanaticism. Improvised cooking utensils, the contents of the three-monthly clothing parcel, a few nails, bits of wood for shelves, were objects around which a sacred ring was drawn. There was an unspoken religious respect for another man's possessions far stronger than the respect for property in normal society and correspondingly more unpleasant. If you wished to borrow such things you instinctively made it clear that you intended no blasphemy.

The effect of overcrowding was the disastrous one of turning you against all humanity. Your mind became numbed to everything about human beings except that they pressed close around you all the time, that they slept above or below you, that you could never turn your head without seeing some evidence of their closeness — their clothes or their books or their photographs — that they made it impossible for you ever to be alone. Although this was no fault of theirs you hated them for it. Certainly you did not quarrel with them all the time. Superficially you were usually on good terms with them as individuals and sometimes there was even an elementary sense of comradeship. But underneath you did not think of them as individuals. They were the crowd whose heads you could not see over. And the crowd was not company.

Of all the various forms of starvation and near starvation at work, sex starvation was the most complete. Officers did not go out of the camp to work and they had no contact with women. Some were prisoners for four or five years. 'What did you do about sex?' It is the question everybody asks and it is difficult to give a satisfactory answer because everybody wants a definite or even a sensational one. I think most prisoners would say that the sex problem worried them less than they had expected it to, but that is not to say that it did not worry most people some of the time and some people all the time. A restraining factor was undoubtedly the poorness of the food. But there was sufficient sex feeling left over to need an outlet and this was often more than could be successfully sublimated into a mere exuberance of energy in reading or games or any other form of camp activity.

I think there was very little practised homosexuality. The reason for this was a simple one: that it was highly impractical. The natural British attitude to sex made any open homosexual conduct such as was supposed to exist at the French Stalags inconceivable, while the lack of any privacy made public school secrecy impossible. As a result such homosexuality as there was usually took a repressed form. There were a few couples whose friendship was of long standing and who were always seen about together. There were a few people who 'took an interest' first in one young man and then another. There were a few young men who developed female characteristics, unconsciously perhaps at first but certainly consciously when they became aware of the power that these gave them. (There was a long correspondence in a camp newspaper about the

75

evil effects which female parts in a play had on such people.) There was a good deal of schoolboy teasing and even bullying which probably had its origins in sex. But it is useless to start deciding which aspects of behaviour did or did not have their origin in sex. Even in normal society it is boring and, after a while, meaningless to trace everything to a common source, especially when the detail is elaborate. It was just that in camp the link between sex and behaviour was often cruder and more obvious than in ordinary life. As with all the other special effects of camp environment, those produced by sex starvation were not organically different but merely the ordinary trends aggravated and emphasized.

All these twists given to human character by the conditions of camp life were noticeable in varying degrees throughout the years. And in normal life too they stand always within call. 'Is man no more than this?' says Lear, standing on the heath with his two companions and watching the madman. 'Consider him well . . . Here's three on's are sophisticated; thou art the thing itself; unaccommodated man is no more but such a poor, bare, forked animal as thou art.' It is a truth which I can never now forget as I go about a world in which human beings apparently have themselves under control. The smooth-phrased B.B.C. announcer, the amusing don, the self-confident politician, the jargon-perfect critic, the editor of the literary magazine — all are reducible within a few months to a bewildered defensive creature with hollow cheeks and desperate eyes whose only cares will be to see that he gets his fair share of the potato ration, that nobody steals his bed boards, and that he exchanges his cigarette ends for food or vice versa at the best possible price. Whenever I hear a man being witty or sensible or kindly or civilized I think: the qualities which now seem so much a part of this man could be stripped away at any time, and there would be left just a man who suffered and who fought with his suffering like an animal.

Such thoughts need not be pessimistic. But they should make us modest. They should also make us determined to prevent the conditions which bring out this aspect of our nature.

There was one practical advantage which our miniature world had over the world outside the wire. It was possible to escape from it. Those who spend their lives looking for some practical escape from the ordinary world eventually have to accept the fact that there is no

76

escape except through death or the imagination. In a prison-camp the world you wanted to get to was visible all the time and, although you did not live in it, you knew that it was only a matter of some barbed wire and a few yards away. Of course there were some people who, as in the ordinary world, were content with their lives and therefore had no wish to escape. Others realized that it was only a matter of patience to wait for the guaranteed escape which would be provided by the end of the war, and as the war dragged on more and more people became converted to this view. But the lust for escape was a powerful one and the fact that escape was possible made the idea a great stimulus whether you got away or not.

Not only was the world into which you wanted to escape there for you to see but you also knew that it was a practical possibility to reach it. There was nothing magic or even electric about the barbed wire. It could be cut or climbed or dug under. So satisfactory was this knowledge that many people were content with nothing else. It was possible to spend all day wandering happily round and round the camp musing on the possibility of a hole cut in the wire here, a tunnel dug there, or an assault with scaling ladders somewhere else. And all the time you knew that you would never take the risk of getting shot which this involved or have the necessary patience to carry it out.

Many people took this game of make-believe to fantastic lengths and went through the whole elaborate business of a preparation for escape without the slightest real intention of ever carrying it out.

Impractical plans absorbed imaginative people for weeks. There was the chemist who toyed with the possibilities of making synthetic gas for a balloon, the aerodynamic expert who planned to construct a glider out of bed boards, and the dog-lover who wanted to make himself a dog-skin out of an Irvin flying suit and crawl out as one of the guards' Alsatians. The orthodox visualized themselves cutting through the wire or bringing off some unprecedented bluff at the main gate. All schemes involved weeks and sometimes months of furtive planning, decisions on route and disguise, invention of a suitable story for travelling purposes and sometimes even the learning of a new language. Generally speaking, the longer the period of planning for an escape the more satisfactory it was for the prospective escaper. For weeks he would live in a world by himself conscious as he watched the humdrum routine of his fellow prisoners that he was destined for higher things and happy in the knowledge that he was not as other men. Each night as he lay in bed he would

77

imagine himself catching the train from the local station — such reveries usually assumed the initial achievement of getting outside the camp — or stalking the frontier guards among the mountains with Switzerland a few hundred yards away across the snow . . . Then the welcome at the British Embassy, the flight back to England, the smiles and the cheering and the medals, the pressing of Button A in the telephone box: 'Hullo, I'm back.' And at some point it would all become as real as it was ever to become again, as the happy escaper slid into dreams until morning. For weeks it would go on like this and then suddenly one day you would notice him just lying in the sun instead of studying his map, or reading a novel instead of his German grammar. 'How's that scheme of yours coming on?' you might ask him and he would reply with just a little too much nonchalance to sound natural: 'Oh, I had to give it up; we had good reason for thinking that the goons were on to it.' or 'It's too late now really: the mountains are impassable at this time of year . . . perhaps next spring . . .' And you would know that at last he had called his own bluff.

It is difficult to assess the amount of self-deceit involved in such unreal escapes. It was often obvious from the start that they would never lead to anything and this made those who were more settled openly contemptuous. They regarded such activity as a schoolboy game of cloaks and daggers. So it was, but that in itself was no real explanation. The state of mind of day-dream escapers was not simple and they both believed in their plans and knew quite well that they would never carry them out at the same time. Certainly there would have been no satisfaction in such behaviour if the would-be escaper had not for a time at any rate believed in himself.

Of course not all escape schemes were unreal. Many hundreds of successful escapes were made by prisoners during the war. But even in the most matter-of-fact and determined plans there was always an element of unreality. Everyone engaged on an escape scheme enjoyed the furtiveness necessary for good security: the concealment of tell-tale evidence under coats a few feet away from unsuspecting sentries, the private knowledge kept from other members of the hut. They enjoyed too the almost unlimited scope for invention and strategy, and the personal romanticizing in bed at night. It was the schoolboy's dream come true. Here were all the ingredients of an exciting life and nothing to pay. If you played spies or conspirators anywhere else your life was at stake. But here, if you were caught preparing an escape, the worst that could happen to you was fourteen days solitary confinement with books and writing materials, and it was often a pleasant change to spend a fortnight by yourself after months of compulsory association.

It was this element of unreality which made tunnelling the most popular scheme for escape. It gave easily the best value. While a wire or a gate scheme might take a few weeks if spun out to the maximum, tunnels were sometimes under construction for six months. During that time the pleasures of furtiveness were open to all concerned, and to these was added the satisfaction of hard physical work and the stimulus of a mild sense of danger while actually working under the earth. There was even one tunnel which, after it had reached its original destination outside the wire, was continued twenty or thirty yards to further cover. There it was saved further prolongation by discovery by the Germans before anyone had escaped at all. Several tunnels were completed but discovered before they could be used because the escapers were 'waiting for the thaw' or 'for the berries to appear on the hedgerows', and sometimes individuals would fail to go through with attempts (which others carried out) because 'their boots were being mended' or 'they had sprained an ankle playing basketball'.

It was only at the last moment that the real or unreal nature of an escape project was finally determined. Then of course it seemed to have been predetermined all the time. 'I knew he'd never try it: he never really wanted to get out.' 'It was a commonsense scheme and he wanted to get out: it was bound to work.' But it was not as simple as that. It was just that at the moment of climax when the escape had to be attempted or abandoned, it became if attempted something quite different from what it had been in the planning. It became a decisive and dangerous piece of initiative and the escaper got the credit of it having been that all the time.

So, year after year, abnormal influences jostled with the normal and all were considered normal. Sometimes rain lashed the tarred roofs of the huts until they glistened like the skin of a seal. Sometimes all life seemed stilled in the aquarium silence of a July sun. Always, outside the wire, the bored guards relieved each other at two hourly intervals while, inside, prisoners did the washing-up or quarrelled or went to sleep. And always, inside and outside, people dreamed of the end of the war.

2

Moments and impressions from this great desert of time remain with me but I have long forgotten in which part of it they occurred.

I remember a day in late spring when people looked anxiously towards the sky for signs of warmth. The dominating colours of the camp — grey, brown and dusty green — were strongly accentuated by the cold. People ran from the blocks to the lavatories and back with pinched faces and sat in their rooms wishing they had saved a little coal. Somebody said that it was a colder day than any we had had during the winter and it didn't sound ridiculous. During the morning I read Houghton's *Life of Keats* and copied out some passages from Keats' letters. After the familiar ladle-full of soup and two thin slices of bread, the afternoon moved orthodoxly towards the German communiqué and tea. I culled the German newspapers for new words and idioms and felt a little smug for having done 'something useful'.

Suddenly I remembered my weekly shower and hurried to join the ragged party which was forming outside. The German guard ran up and down beside us like a good natured sheep dog, counting and getting the numbers wrong and counting again. Eventually we moved off through the main gate of the camp to the Vorlager, or front camp, where the showers were situated.

This part of the camp was in itself no more attractive than the part in which we lived, but the very fact that we did not live there, that we did not know every inch of its dusty ground, that normally we only saw it from the distance, gave it a charm of its own. It was a pleasure to walk through it, to see differently arranged buildings, different sentry's towers, a different stretch of wire and a road running in a different direction beyond it.

I had dressed after my shower and was sitting on the steps of the shower room staring dully through the wire. Suddenly I awoke to the fact that I was staring at a tree on the other side of the road and that this tree was green and delicate. For a few moments I was intensely conscious of the tree and saw nothing else. Then I thought of all the trees I had taken for granted in the past — beside the Cherwell at Oxford or on the pavements of a Surrey suburb. Always I had regarded them as only incidental to the main theme, the real great things that were to happen to me. At the time I had wondered why this main theme somehow always eluded me, why the great events never materialized. Now as I looked at the tree I saw that the great things had been there all the time but I had mistaken them for the background.

Some Australians came out of the shower room and began arguing with the merry sub-human guard:

'Deutschland kaput!'

'Nein, England kaput!'

'Nach dem Krieg . . .'

I wondered what would happen to all of us 'after the war'.

I remember a dream.

I dreamt that my mind was ending. Order dropped from my memory as a sticky substance melted in the sun might drop from a table and spread on the floor. I cried desperately for recognition at people whose identities I had confused. I committed myself to a series of disjointed actions which at the moment of decision all seemed reasonable but which immediately afterwards were as terrifying as they were irrevocable. There was a fluid pain at the back of my neck and my own voice was strange to me. Somehow this all happened in the darkened room in which in fact I lay asleep. And although there were many dreams and faces I remained all the time in my bed. As a result when I awoke there was no positive proof that all this had not in fact happened, and that it did not belong to a mental lapse from which I had recovered. A remark which someone had once made to me about a man who had gone mad in the camp came clearly out of the darkness:

'. . . and the pathetic thing was that he thought he had just recovered from a long period of madness.'

I was relieved when the daylight came and I could surrender to the exhaustion in my brain.

New prisoners.

They arrived at ever decreasing intervals, always the same pale bewildered collection of strangers, always with new and astonishing stories of battle and the day-dream world. As they gathered outside the wire waiting for their guard to open the gate into the camp, they were suspended for a few moments in a sort of limbo. They did not yet belong to our world and they certainly belonged to no other. Inquisitive old prisoners collected on the inside of the wire to scan the incoming group for friends. They seldom found anyone they knew. Some of the men who came in late in the war had not joined up until after the older prisoners had been shot down. But the inquisitive crowd always collected inside the wire to outnumber the newcomers and to stare. I don't really know why I always went unless it was to remind myself that I too had once come from some other world than the one in which I lived. Certainly I always tried to remember the shocking effect which the sight of so many old prisoners, some of them bearded, all of them strangely dressed, had had on me the first time I arrived in a main camp.

In the slightly embarrassed silence that lasted while the two groups stared at each other through the wire, there were occasional calls of recognition.

'Hullo, Pranger, I've been waiting for you for years.'

'Hullo, George.'

'My God, it's Sammy.'

'Well, if it isn't old Pissy.'

Later there would be the questions and answers about the war, the old familiar stories of the way in which people had been shot down. It must have been heartbreaking for people who had been through sensational experiences to have to recount them to politely tepid audiences and to discover that their stories conformed to an orthodox pattern.

'. . . a burst of cannon shell in the cockpit: it was the first thing I knew . . .'

'. . . a piece of flak must have hit the elevators as we went straight into a dive . . .'

'. . . a 110 on its second attack . . .'

'. . . I think we must have collided or something . . .'

'. . . I think we must have hit the sea . . .'

'. . . my harness slipped and I dropped ten thousand feet hanging by one leg. Fortunately I landed in a river . . .'

They would be noticeable for a few days after passing into the camp, unfamiliar faces asking the way to the lavatories, or being excused washing-up by the people in whose rooms they had been placed. They used to look especially pathetic in summer. Then, in addition to their normal strained lost appearance, they had white bodies which contrasted unpleasantly with the strongly browned nakedness of everyone else. But soon they too would be absorbed by the world of the camp, know their way about it in their sleep, do the washing-up and water-carrying once a week, or walk about like negroes in G-strings made out of a towel. And in a fortnight or three weeks time they too would be found with the inquisitive crowd on the inside of the gate staring at the prisoners who had just arrived.

One autumn evening in 1944, twenty new prisoners arrived in the compound unexpectedly. Their closely cropped hair and the drawn pale look of hunger in their faces gave them that terrifying animal uniformity which falls over all human beings in permanent physical distress. For a time after D-Day the stories of incoming prisoners had developed a new excitement. They contained fresh and astonishing details of underground movements and midnight rendezvous. Now even these, by reason of their frequency, were beginning to pall. But the stories told by these twenty prisoners of the camp from which they had come, stirred the most lethargic and bore-minded five year man. We heard of daily torture, public hangings, guards who walked about with whips, gas chambers, castrated children and prisoners who lay dead for hours in the communal beds.

It was almost impossible to believe. Next morning the German camp Feldwebel would come round calling us 'Gentlemen', and the officer who counted us on appel would salute us and talk of German honour. The irreconcilability of two such extremes in one group of human beings could only be explained as part of the great mystery of human personality. Even at the time it seemed to me that it was pointless to be vindictive or even to allot responsibility for such happenings. It all seemed too important for that: a warning of what was inside us all as human beings and of what we must avoid at all costs.

But as I listened to the stories of these prisoners it was difficult not to be overwhelmed with feelings of hate and revenge. The camp and many others like it had been in existence for years. I felt ashamed for having loathed my own life for so long. None of us had ever heard the name of the camp before. It was called Buchenwald.

I remember an autumn afternoon when I was walking alone round the perimeter track which in Air Force camps was known as 'the circuit'. It had rained heavily earlier and the exhausted trodden ground seemed refreshed and cleansed. The flat Polish landscape stretched away into the marshes to the south-east, and I stopped for a moment and stared towards them. If only I could be out there, I used to think, just that far away, alone in the useless marshes . . . Great shafts of white after-rain light poured down from the edges of the clouds and soon the sun shone alone in a patch of blue, a weakening autumn sun. At a junction in the road outside the wire there was a yellow sign-post:

'BROMBERG 22 KM.'

If it had said 22,000 KM. it would have been all the same to me. The sun went in again and I walked on.

Three quarters of the way round the circuit I was surprised to find a small party of Germans erecting a barbed wire barricade across the path. They seemed to be cutting off a great slice of the camp. I was learning German and found pleasure in talking to the guards on any subject.

'Can't I go through?'

'Nein, verboten.'

Guards were either abruptly mistrustful or effusively friendly when they discovered that you could speak their language.

Some of the others came closer.

'Your comrades shouldn't try so many escapes, then life would be much pleasanter for you.'

'You are silly, you Englishmen. When the French were here they had much freedom in the camp because they were sensible and did not try to escape. They went to the cinema twice a week.'

It was a strange fact that the Germans who so admired soldierly qualities could never understand soldierly integrity in a prisoner of war, whereas the British, least military of all nations, were probably the most spirited prisoners.

I pressed home the usual arguments about duty and not fighting the war for the privilege of going to the cinema. One reacted in this way not because one had thought about it much but because some instinct demanded it. Often, in private, one thought it a pretty silly instinct.

'If you go on in this way, half the camp will be out of bounds before long.'

It was, before we left.

'You're all mad,' said a red-nosed Bardolphian Gefreiter, 'I wish I could be a prisoner: you wouldn't catch me trying to get back to the war.'

'When we heard that the French were going and the British were coming, we were glad,' said another. 'The French were a dirty lot. They walked round all day with their heads slumped between their shoulders like this' — he took up the appropriate attitude — 'instead of like this, as the British do.'

Here he stuck out his chest and strutted about like a professional walker setting out on a long distance race. 'The British are a military people.'

I looked at the faces of the other soldiers to see if he was trying to make a fool of me. It was obvious however not only that he was being quite serious, but also that they all agreed with him. I did not tell him that his imitation of the French was far more like what I had been seeing for the past year. Only a peacock or a P.T. instructor could have walked round a camp in the way he admired.

'And now that you have come, you disappoint us all like this,' he concluded.

I had neither the patience nor the German to point out the contradiction in his argument.

'So I can't go out through the garden?'

The man who had originally told me that it was 'verboten' and who had stood a little apart while the others talked, now came forward again.

'The garden is out of bounds from now on,' he said.

The fact that he was so self-consciously different from the other soldiers annoyed me.

'Be careful they don't send you to the Eastern Front,' I said. It was a favourite prisoners' jeer at the guards, though unfair in view of the relative safety of the prisoners' position.

He spoke a little louder but otherwise kept his temper.

'The Eastern front?' he sneered. 'The war in the East is almost over. In a few days you will hear that Stalingrad is completely in German hands.'

The others smiled and nodded.

'That's right,' they said.

'Stalingrad will never fall,' I said.

They all roared with laughter except for the sneering man who suddenly grew fish-coloured and shouted and wagged his finger. I looked at my watch to maintain a show of dignity and began to move.

'Stalingrad will never fall,' I repeated slowly and walked away.

It was an absurd remark. I could hear them laughing behind me.

The sun had disappeared and it was beginning to rain again. In a flower bed close to one of the lavatories, people were crouching like

85

tramps over roughly built brick fire-places, warming a little stew in smoky tins for the evening meal. Already the flames showed up vividly though there was no other indication of the failing light. In the blocks, I thought, a sort of interior fog will be creeping out from the corners of the ceilings and under the beds.

A man I knew came out of the block next to mine.

'Heard the news?' he asked, worried.

'No.'

'It was on the communiqué: the goons have taken another big factory in Stalingrad.'

'Oh, is that all?'

I had expected to hear that the whole city had fallen.

So many small rivalries existed between different cliques in the camp and so many of them seemed synthetic that it looked sometimes as if antagonism was essential to human beings as a form of self-expression. There were the people who were in favour of 'baiting the goons' and those who for various reasons thought this was 'bad policy'. There were those who wanted to escape and thought that everyone else ought to want to, and there were those who didn't want to escape and who didn't want anyone else to want to either. There were rival theatrical cliques, and rifts and vendettas among the games people over alleged unsporting behaviour. Some of the great controversies were so trivial that it seemed as if people had positively to search for something to quarrel about.

One of the most farcical rivalries was that which existed for a time between two groups of prisoners who earlier had been in different Oflags. They behaved towards each other like boys who had been educated at rival private schools. A new R.A.F. camp, to which I was duly sent, had just been opened and was still partly empty when one day a new batch of prisoners was announced. Everyone put on their coats and crowded to the gate with that mixture of patronage and curiosity reserved by old prisoners for those who had just been shot down. But when a crowd of equally hardened bearded old prisoners from another Oflag appeared on the other side of the gate, the inmates of the camp felt rebuffed and even a little concerned. Of course they welcomed them in and exchanged news and questions. ('Good God, I never knew you were down!' — 'Remember old Johnny Johnston? Well, he's here.' — 'Any idea what the squadron's doing now?') but from that moment there was a clear cut division between the sheep and the goats.

The goats were allotted a whole hut to themselves and the trouble soon started.

'These sheep are a dead-beat lot. They've got no spirit. They ought to stand up to the goons.'

'These goats are just like a lot of prep. school kids. They don't realize that you need to use finesse when dealing with the goons.'

'Do you realize how many people escaped from our place in six months?' asked the goats. 'Twenty-four!'

'Ah, but the only R.A.F. people to get back to England came from our place,' said the sheep.

'Our S.B.O. was much better than this man.'

'Impossible — Wings Balsdon's got the goons just where he wants them.'

'We could bust this place wide open.'

'All right then, try.'

So the goats dug tunnels all over the place while the sheep sat apart and disapproved. And when the Germans bust the tunnels wide open, both parties thought they had justified themselves.

A football match was arranged between the two groups. Tension ran high and fighting broke out among the spectators as well as among the players.

One day a German officer came in to the camp to supervise work that was being done on some primitive drains by Polish forced labour. He propped his bicycle against the brick wall of the wash-room. Unfortunately for him the work was being done close to the room where one of the most lively goats lived. When the German officer began to shout abuse at the Poles, this goat leant out of his window and shouted abuse at the German officer. The German officer switched his abuse onto the goat and a crowd soon collected.

'Come on chaps, we'll have some fun here,' shouted the goat and bounded out of the window.

Some of the German soldiers who were acting as escort for the Poles, began to unsling their rifles apprehensively. The crowd expanded.

'Someone go and let the air out of his bicycle tyres while I hold his attention,' shouted the goat.

The German officer, who thought that this was more abuse, shouted back. A figure crawled round the back of the crowd towards the bicycle.

'You lousy rotten Hun,' shouted the goat, and the crowd cheered or muttered: 'the bloody fool', according to their political line-up.

The Poles in the trench waited and smiled appreciatively.

'Wenn Sie alle nicht sofort zurücktreten, gebe ich den Schiessbefehl!'

There was a sharp pop as the valves of both tyres were unscrewed simultaneously, a swift rush of air and a dying sigh. The bicycle subsided wearily into the sand. The crowd cheered, the chief goat danced for joy and the German officer ran screaming and gesticulating to his bicycle. As he bent tenderly over it to examine the flattened tyres, a hand stuck a length of rubber piping out of the wash-room window and directed a jet of water down his neck. At this even the boldest goat fled to the nearest hut for fear of reprisal, and from the cover of the walls watched the frustrated officer screaming at sentries, Poles, hut and bicycle in turn. Then he took hold of the handle-bars and accepting defeat, pushed his bicycle painstakingly through the sand to the main gate.

Later in the day it was said that the Germans had refused to issue any more food parcels for the rest of the week.

'There you are, you see,' said the sheep. 'Now it'll take all Wings Balsdon's tact to get any parcels issued before next Monday.'

'It was bloody well worth going hungry for,' said the goats.

It was about twelve o'clock in the morning. The great cloud of dust raised inside the block by the morning's sweeping of the floor had not yet settled down again. But only the occasional shafts of sunlight gave it away as it worked slowly downwards, making the most of its daily exercise. It was that point in the morning when people usually began to think about the soup and potatoes that were expected shortly, rather than about the books they were reading. Little groups stood about talking of the war or Brighton or what they were going to cook for supper. There was the sound of empty bowls being put onto tables to receive the daily ladle-full of soup.

Nothing could have sounded more incongruous than the shot which stopped it all.

'That was a shot.' The little groups looked anxiously at one another. A man ran to the window.

'Yes, they've shot someone,' he shouted.

Everyone ran for the door to see what had happened.

In the carefully raked stretch of earth between the warning wire

88

and the barbed wire itself, a man was sitting in a queer hunched position. There seemed to be no blood but his legs were strangely wide apart. His face was like wax and his eyes stared like a doll's.

At the warning wire everyone was talking at once.

'Quick, get a doctor someone.' 'What's happened?' 'Ask the goon if you can get over and help him.' 'Who is it?' 'Anyone here speak German?' 'My God, it's Johnny Soames.'

I stared at the sitting figure. It was a man I knew quite well. On the other side of the double row of barbed wire a guard was standing still holding his rifle at the ready. Someone shouted to him asking if they could step over to help.

'Nein. Zurück! Zurück!'

He was a small man and it looked as if his rifle was much too heavy for him as he waved it threateningly at the crowd inside the camp. There were shouts of anger and he became still more excited.

'Look out, here comes the doctor.'

The crowd parted and an English doctor stepped over the warning wire and knelt down beside the man. Everyone stopped talking. The deliberate action seemed to pacify the German too.

The wounded man spoke suddenly in a quiet normal voice.

'Give me a cigarette, please, Doc.'

He sat there for a few moments inhaling the smoke. The doctor was cutting away the top part of his khaki trousers, and spoke to him reassuringly.

'Can I function on one all right, do you think Doc.?'

A new wave of talking spread through the crowd. A small party of soldiers with fixed bayonets was marching across the football ground.

'Everyone back into barrack! Everyone back into barrack!'

The crowd began to disperse. As I turned away I saw a small patch of khaki material caught on the very top of the wire.

A Feldwebel passed me with a drawn revolver. I wanted to express the anger inside me.

'What a brave sentry — shooting a defenceless man from two yards like that,' I said. It was pompous but it satisfied me.

He turned and came after me waving his revolver, but I easily lost him in the crowd.

In the block somebody said that he had seen the whole incident.

'What happened then?'

'How could he hope to get away like that?'

'He didn't. He waited until the guard was opposite him then he stepped deliberately over the warning rail and climbed slowly up the wire. The guard shouted to him three times but he took no notice at all. He shot him when he was right at the top.'

Several people were listening but nobody said anything at first. Then someone said:

'He must have gone off his head.'

I remembered how I had walked with him only a few days before.

'It's difficult sometimes to remember that you've had any other life,' he had said. 'Not that this is too bad, of course.'

I thought of the hundreds of others of us who said something like that once or twice a week.

During my first year as a prisoner some of us were moved for a time from Silesia to a camp in the Polish corridor. I was in the first party to leave and there were about fifty of us altogether. In fifty different variations of British uniform, with cooking pots, cardboard boxes and bundles of clothing slung about us, we shuffled out of the camp to a railway siding with an escort of thirty-six guards and three dogs.

After we had sat by the track for two hours the train came in. It was like a toy. Two old-fashioned third class carriages with close wooden seats were pulled by an engine that puffed bulbs of black smoke. When the guards had surrounded the train we were allowed to get in. We sat for an hour wondering if any soup would be issued. Then an interpreter came into the carriage and said:

'One moment please, gentlemen. I have some mail for you and will call out the names.'

So with our legs and bottoms already aching from the lack of space and the hard seats, we read about the party someone had given in Christ Church, or how well so-and-so was doing at the Ministry of Information, or what little Nicolette had said to her grandmother.

After we had read about these things several times over we started wondering again if there would be any soup. Quite suddenly all the guards jumped in, their tommy-guns banging against the sides of the carriage and their leather harness creaking, and the train chugged off at about fifteen miles an hour towards Bromberg.

We had only about a hundred miles to go but the journey was to take twenty-four hours. 'Räder müssen rollen für den Sieg,' screamed the notices in the little Polish stations where we sometimes waited for hours on end. But for the bony discomfort of the seats and the pressure of other people's legs it was quite pleasant to take our time. None of us had been outside the camp for many months and every field seemed infinite and exciting. It was as if our vision was a piece of elastic which was being stretched for the first time after a long period in a drawer.

When it grew dark the Feldwebel in charge began to get restive about escaping.

'Take off your boots please, gentlemen — it's healthier to sleep with your boots off.'

There were some protests:

'Hey, you can't do that, Glemnitz.'

'How shall we know our own boots again?'

Personally I should have been quite glad to get someone else's boots. Mine had been letting in sand and water for some time.

'Another atrocity, gentlemens,' said the Feldwebel, walking up and down the corridor. 'Boots off, please.'

He was a good-humoured Feldwebel really, although he had a tendency to panic and a tendency to be self-consciously patriotic. When the two combined the results were sometimes unpleasant.

When the great pile of boots had been collected at one end of the carriage, he spoke again:

'Listen, please. If anyone tries to escape the guards will shoot and they are all very good shots; also I shall take away the trousers of those who have not escaped.'

An ironical cheer went up at this and we settled down for the night. Before I went to sleep I heard Glemnitz talking quite amiably to someone about rugger:

'Yes, it's a very good game, but there is no culture in it.'

I awoke in the middle of the night with a pain in the back of my neck and a beating headache. People were asleep all over the carriage: on the floor, in the narrow luggage racks, in the lavatory. The windows which had been nailed up as an anti-escape measure were thick with steam, and water was pouring down the panes. I could still just see where someone had written: 'DEUTSCHLAND KAPUT' with his finger, but it had melted and the letters had grown tails like tadpoles. There was a strong smell of feet and breath. The guards were yawning and leaning against the wood-work. Occasionally they gave a perfunctory look up and down the carriage, but they had obviously wilted with the tedium of the journey and the foul air.

Suddenly I noticed that although the prisoner opposite me had thrown back his head and was snoring loudly, he was not asleep. He was fumbling with something close to his left side. There was a sharp click and he remained quite still. The guards still yawned and leaned. Snoring louder than ever he fumbled again and I saw him insert a small blade into the side of the carriage. My first feeling was one of excitement: I was getting all the pleasure of being in a conspiracy without having to take any of the responsibility for it. Then I thought that if this man succeeded in cutting a hole in the side of the carriage and escaping through it, there would be an obligation on me to go out after him. And I didn't want to jump out into the fast-moving darkness without any boots and within range of fifty tommy-guns.

Without moving his head from its sleeping position the man opposite said quietly: 'Snore, please.' I started a stage snore and I thought that together we must drown any other noise he could make, but when he began to use his saw it seemed to be the only noise in the carriage. I looked at the nearest guard through half-closed eyes. His eyes were half-closed too. Once his head began to fall onto his chest but he jerked it up again. Once he looked at his watch to see how long it would be before he was relieved. Once he lifted his cap and scratched the top of his head. Then he heard the noise.

At first he was like a man who thinks he smells gas or a fire, his body alert and his head held high as he looked quickly round the carriage. Then with a great shout he began to plunge over bodies and kit-bags down the gangway towards us. The man opposite me scuffled hopelessly with his tools, but it was much too late. Shouting and grey in the face the guard took them from him while everybody in the carriage woke up.

'What the bloody hell?'

'Shut up.'

'Good God, don't the goons even stop shouting in their sleep?'

Glemnitz, the Feldwebel, arrived.

'Oh, Mr. Winser, I'm ashamed of you.'

He took out a pencil and note-book like a policeman at a road accident.

'I shall have to report this.'

Winser was looking disgusted with himself for being caught.

'Oh bugger off, Glemnitz.'

The Feldwebel's voice rose a key.

'Now then, Mr. Winser, don't start any of that.'

'Oh all right, Glemnitz. I know. Orders are orders and Krieg ist Krieg and you're only doing your duty.'

'Exactly, Mr. Winser.'

'Well, now let us all get some sleep.'

'Bad luck, George,' somebody shouted.

Slowly the fuss subsided. Glemnitz closed his note-book and left the carriage. The guards were changed and the prisoners settled back onto the luggage racks or the floor or the upright wooden seats to sleep.

Soon there again seemed no-one awake except Winser and me.

'Bad luck,' I said, although for my own sake I was glad that he had failed.

'Oh, that's just what comes of being a prisoner too long: you make a fool of yourself like that.'

He too, closed his eyes.

Beside him in the thin inner wall of the carriage there was a pathetic rectangular hole like the slot of a small letter-box.

The lawn.

This was a patch of sand, stone and grass, about twelve feet by six, outside the window of a room in which I lived. The grass, grown from seed, just held its own against the weeds. But the green smell used to be there and it was strong enough to make me think of English summers when I looked at the sky. I could think that I was at school again, lying in the long grass waiting to bat, or walking over Berkshire downs or along a Devon valley. If I pressed my eye flat to the ground and looked into the next garden, the big bushes there with thick tall stems and flat leaves seemed part of a mysterious tropical forest.

A thunderstorm.

It came rolling towards us from the west. Lightning, deep in the clouds, flashed orange over whole quarters of the sky at a time. Occasionally a thin savage streak of wiry blue hinted at what the storm could really do if it tried. It moved over to the north before it reached the camp, so that we never heard much of the thunder. It was as if some giant electrician was just rehearsing effects in the sky.

When we were locked in we played the gramophone. A Beethoven Sonata and the Pastoral. We turned out the lights and opened the shutters and the windows. The searchlights from the guards' boxes competed feebly with the storm still sizzling blue in the distance. When someone who was putting on the records said: 'Fourth movement, called The Storm,' I wondered how the music would compare with the storm outside. A few seconds later I was despising myself for having been in any doubt. The music triumphed completely.

At first I could not understand how Beethoven could triumph over God. Then I realized that that was not what was happening. It was just Beethoven's sense of what was going on outside triumphing over our own.

Thoughts on my twenty-fifth birthday, which was to be my last in a prison-camp. I can remember them clearly because they were so much more optimistic than those I was to have a year later.

'Almost for the first time since I was a child,' I thought, 'I am glad that it is my birthday. I know now that there is every reason for joy at the thought of the day on which I was given life. I have learnt that the sun and the stars are eternally good, and that my body leaps in contact with this sparkling world and everything that it contains from the minds of Beethoven and Shakespeare to food and drink and a soft night's sleep. I see now that a child knows these things intuitively, including those things which are at first beyond its own experience. So that perhaps all I have done in twenty-five years is to find out something which I have known all the time. But a man can be content to know nothing more.

And the pain and the misery? I know that these things too are real, and yet I know that they too have helped me to find beauty. This is something I cannot understand: the wonder of sadness, the glory of pain.

When I look back over the years I see impatience as the great sin of life. The thrust and strain which has dominated these twenty-five years now seems quite irrelevant.'

But it is the tragedy of life that you cannot help thrusting and straining. Something inside me which I cannot stop is whirling me faster and faster past beauty into oblivion.

Six of us were sitting at a table. Closed copies of Hugo's Russian grammar lay in front of us and the lecturer was asking questions.

'Have you a brother?'

One of us translated it into Russian.

'Where is the meat and the butter?'

'Is this gentleman's luggage at the station?'

The double-tiered beds were close round us, making 'rooms' in the long brick barrack. On one of these beds a man lay asleep on his back, his arms by his sides and his feet together, like a lain-out corpse. From the other rooms came the sounds of hammering, quarrelling and playing bridge.

'Is there a telephone in this hotel?'

From the door came a familiar cry:

'Goon approaching!'

There was a change in the rhythm of the hammering and a scuffle in the corridor, but the quarrelling and the bridge went on as before. People who were doing nothing in particular took up the cry and chanted it down the block, like priests in some strange pagan mass:

'Goon approaching!'

'Goon approaching!'

The chant changed:

'Goon in the block!'

'Goon in the block!'

Through the gap between two lockers which was the 'door', I saw a bored German private wandering dutifully down the corridor.

'Are there stooges on in this block?'

At first I thought it was just another question for translation.

'Because if there are it's hopeless: we'll get no peace at all.'

A very tired gramophone in another room started playing a tune called 'Kalamazoo'.

'These bloody escaping people make life impossible. I'm not going on with the lecture if they're going to play their childish little games in here.'

The outburst seemed a little unbalanced but nobody questioned it. We had all been prisoners long enough to know that you must allow people to be unbalanced if they felt like it. We began to collect our books from the table.

'Well, thanks very much.'

'Thanks.'

'Thank you.'

'All clear!'

'All clear! All clear!' sang the priests.

'There you are again, you see. It's impossible. Quite impossible.'

95

He strode out of the door, the buckles jingling on his highly polished flying boots.

When I got out into the corridor I saw that a piece of wire had been strung between two beams on either side of the block and that a sort of ladder was leaning against it. At the top of this ladder there was a flat portion parallel to the ground. At the end of the flat portion there was a gap big enough for a man's body to drop through, and then a single rung like a short parallel bar in a gym. A queue of about ten people wearing gym shoes was lined up in front of the ladder.

'All clear, Charles?' shouted the man at the head of the queue to someone at the door.

'All clear!'

'All clear!'

'O.K. then, chaps. Let's go. Have you got the stop watch, Pakenham? Right then. Lights fused: go.'

He dashed up the ladder, clambered along the horizontal part, dropped through the gap and swung himself clear from the final rung onto the ground. The rest of the queue followed close behind him so that there were at least six people on the ladder at the same time.

'Bloody good show, chaps,' he said when they were all over. 'How long did that take, Pakenham?'

'I'm afraid something seems to have gone wrong with the watch.'

'Oh Christ.'

'Perhaps I just pushed the wrong knob.'

'Oh Christ. Somebody else take it. Tommy, you do it. Come on now, chaps, once again, and let's see if we can't break thirty seconds.'

'Goon approaching!'

The people in gym shoes dispersed quickly into different rooms while special dismantling personnel leapt out from behind lockers and took charge of the ladder. On my way out of the block, I passed a Feldwebel.

When I got back to my room I waited for my friend Malleson. I had noticed him near the end of the queue as it swarmed over the ladder.

'When's it coming off?'

'Too bloody soon.'

'Why, aren't you ready yet? You all seemed to be going over pretty smoothly.'

'Look here: that was in broad daylight over a single strand of wire, not under fire from any machine guns, and with no patrolling goon with a gun to meet us on the other side. Quite apart from that, and even if the lights are fused properly, it will take double the time on the night itself. In the block we start running from just in front of the ladder, but on the night we've first of all got to run from the block to the wire, which is twenty yards away in the nearest place and then put the ladder up. Even the dimmest goon is going to realize there's something queer going on in all that time. It's murder.'

I saw his point. Still, I envied him. I had already been a prisoner nearly a year and had not yet escaped. It was like being an undergraduate a year without having been drunk. It was not so much the escape itself that mattered but being able to say you had done it.

'It's all right for old Ryan,' Malleson went on. ' "Bags of chaps will get over, chaps." Well, maybe the first four or five will, and he's the first of the five. But after that the goon with the machine guns is going to get the range. No sir, I'm getting out of it.'

That afternoon I walked round the circuit alone and thought about it. After all it would have a great element of surprise in its favour and although there might be some shooting it was doubtful if the Germans would know what they were shooting at, especially if good diversions were laid on. The same scheme had been tried at another camp with four ladders. Thirty-two men had got over and the only people hurt had been two patrolling guards hit by stray bullets.

At tea I made one of the mistakes of my life.

'Any chance of getting in at the end of that scheme?' I asked Malleson.

He stopped thinking about the amount of jam he was taking and leant back in his chair.

'You're not considering . . .'

'Yes.'

'You must be mad.'

He took some jam.

'I'm sorry,' he said. 'You may be right, and you may get away with it. But I'm just not going to take the risk.'

'I think you're very sensible if you feel like that about it. But what are my chances of getting onto it?'

'Fairly good, I should say. There's a waiting list of three after the first ten and I don't see why you shouldn't persuade Ryan to let you be No. 4 on that. That'll make you No. 14 on the whole thing. Of course people are talking pretty big at the moment but half of them are as ready to drop off as I am.'

After tea I went out and saw Ryan. He had been playing football and lines of dust and sweat were pouring down his strained red face.

'Sure,' he said, in answer to my question, 'and if one or two of the chaps drop out, you'll have your chance. Good man.'

I went away wondering if I was being a fool. Still, there was no getting out of it now. I was only on the waiting list anyway and it wasn't very likely that four people would drop out.

But my uneasiness increased throughout the evening, and the words repeated themselves in my head:

'There's no getting out of it now.'

By the next morning I was feeling definitely unhappy. Malleson had said that half the people were as ready to drop out as he was and he had already dropped out. I tried to forget about it and to go about my routine day as usual.

After appel I collected some books from my locker — my locker was in a corner and there was always a pile of block rubbish in front of it so that it was a business to open and shut the door — and went out towards the library. A British orderly and a Polish civilian were pumping filth from one of the lavatories into a long cylindrical cart. The pump leaked and a jet of yellow liquid splashed onto the path with every stroke. I waited behind the cart for them to stop and let me pass. As I waited, Ryan came out of a near-by block and called to me:

'Can I have a word with you, old boy?'

We went out onto the circuit.

'Look, it so happens that a number of people have dropped out of the scheme for one reason or another, and there's now a place for you at the end of the team. Now, I feel I ought to warn you: you won't have quite such a good chance at the end as you would have at the front.'

He paused. Perhaps I was expected to say something. I made a non-committal cluck at the back of my throat, but it came out higher than I had intended.

'Not that I think there's any danger of anyone getting hurt,' he added. 'Absolutely none at all.'

He looked firmly ahead. I got the impression that he had had to use this look rather a lot lately.

'Still, it's up to you.'

Now, I thought, now. Now's your chance to get out of this. He's made it perfectly easy for you, and nobody will think any the worse of you for getting out. Now.

'I'll risk it,' I said, with an unnatural smile.

Oh God. An alarm bell was ringing in my stomach.

Ryan stopped and clapped me on the shoulder.

'Bloody good show, old boy. It probably won't be long now. We're going to make use of this moonless period, but we'll try and give you a practice run over the ladder before the big night. Get all your gear ready. See you later.'

'Yes,' I began, 'I should just like a practice . . .'

But he had left me and broken into a trot towards his block. A little unsteadily I wandered away to the library, but I found it difficult to concentrate on the uses of the Russian Imperfective.

It was the day of parcel issues and as lunch time approached I tried to forget the future in the pleasure of the present. There was always something extra for lunch on 'parcel' day. When I got back to the block there it was sitting on the table beside the empty bowls waiting for soup: an extra biscuit each, spread with liver paste, and half a quarter pound slab of chocolate.

'Oh, goody goody,' said Malleson coming into the room at the same time. 'This is the life: stuff, stuff, stuff away all bloody day.'

He looked happier than I had seen him for weeks and there was colour in his cheeks.

After I had eaten my biscuit I climbed up onto my bunk with the chocolate and took off my boots.

'For Christ's sake be more careful when you're climbing up,' said the man who slept underneath me. 'I'm always finding mud from your boots on my pillow.'

'I've got to climb up somehow.'

'Yes, but not that how.'

'Sorry.'

I reached for *The Mayor of Casterbridge* which I knew was somewhere in the bed. I was determined to let nothing, not even my pride, interfere with the little pleasure I had left. I put a piece of chocolate into my mouth and opened my book . . .

'Could I have a word with you, old man?'

It was Ryan.

'Of course.'

I untied my boots which were laced together round one of the bed-posts, put them on and jumped down.

'And mind those bloody boots when you get up again,' said the man who had complained before. He was lying down now and his face shone palely out of the gloom of the lower bunk like that of some animal in its hole.

'Oh, shut up,' I said.

Outside, Ryan said:

'Do you mind if we do a circuit?'

'Not at all.'

'Rather an unfortunate thing has happened, I'm afraid. The goons have discovered part of an old dismantled ladder which we'd used for earlier trials and we think it may put them onto something.'

My heart leapt like a lift for joy. Visions of an endless life of eating chocolate and reading Hardy rose before me. I would even take care not to wipe my boots on Roper's pillow.

'Of course we're going through with it,' said Ryan. 'It'll just mean speeding things up a little.'

'I see.'

'The net result for you, I'm afraid, is that you won't be able to get any practice on the ladder. You see, we've decided to go tomorrow night and we daren't risk another trial before then. There'll be no moon, and if this wind holds it should help us a lot. Also, the goons will hardly have had time to make anything out of those bits of wood by then. Now, do you think you can be ready?'

'I should think so.'

Ready?

'I can let you have a copy of the local map and some civilian buttons to sew onto your great-coat. Everything else you'll have to fix up for yourself. You must have your face covered up in some way on the night: I suggest a balaclava worn back to front, with eye-holes cut in it. There'll be a meeting for last minute instructions some time tomorrow afternoon. O.K.?'

'O.K.,' I said feebly.

He went into his block.

These practical details solidified my fears. I knew that I should not be able to forget them again until the business had been resolved one way or the other.

I continued to walk round the camp. I thought, I must get as much walking practice as possible between now and tomorrow night. By tea-time I felt that I conformed more to the recognized pattern of an escaper.

But, back in my room, all sorts of hopeless thoughts again attacked me. I began to feel sentimental about the familiar squalor. I should be quite content, I thought, to live here for ever, smelling the cooking and the lavatory and the dust, looking forward to my two slices of bread at lunch or tea and my Red Cross stew at supper, thinking about all the books I am going to read and how nice it is going to be when I can speak German and Russian fluently; I only want to be allowed to live, and enjoy the sun when it shines, and wait for it when it goes behind a cloud.

'I hear you're going tomorrow,' said Malleson. 'Let me know if there's anything I can do to help.'

It was like one of the sentences that used to come in letters from home: 'Do let me know if there's anything I can do.'

'Thanks very much,' I said. 'There are one or two things.'

Jefferson overheard.

'You leaving us?' he said chirpily. 'Good show.'

He was an Australian and it sounded nasty the way he said it.

Everyone at the table turned towards me.

'Well, well.'

'You kept that pretty quiet.'

'Marge, please.'

Roper said: 'Good luck, old boy,' and I was surprised to see that he meant it. Still, it would mean a clean pillow for him.

The only person who really said anything helpful was Jack Nopps.

'Sheer bloody suicide,' he said slowly in his deep thick Cockney.

I felt that he and I had something in common.

After we had been locked in I spent the evening making preparations with Malleson's help: sewing on buttons, dubbing my boots, making a pillow case into a rucksack and staring at a map with unreal names on it like Danzig and Berlin. One of Jack's 'tame' Germans came round about nine o'clock to exchange wireless parts for his weekly ration of Red Cross coffee. He had a nice face and I had got used to him. I should miss him too.

I woke very early the next morning. The peace of the barrack block was startling. I had never been awake in it as early as that before. One or two people at the other end were snoring and once someone quite close to me shouted in his sleep:

'Oh, for Christ's sake, stop bitching!'

But on the whole the bundles of blanket and piled clothing in the beds did not seem alive at all and I might have been alone in the block. It was like finding oneself alone at Piccadilly Circus. It was too cold to push my face far out of my sleeping bag but I could see the yellow damp stain, like a map, on the wall opposite, and the little nest of cobwebs in a corner of the ceiling. I wondered if I should ever see them again. I lay there for a long time unhappy and hardly noticing the daily noises of the block assembling round me. At least, I thought, by this time tomorrow it will be all over. I was surprised at the deterioration in my nerves since my flying days. Perhaps this was what those few loud-mouthed rabbit-eyed creatures who dropped their bombs at the first flak and then came back and talked about the target area had felt like. I had never been able to understand them then, but I sympathized with them now. I would have given anything to be able to get out of this.

In the end I was nearly late for appel.

'Come along, hurry up there.'

The Wing Commander was lucky. He had an outlet for his temper at the beginning of a new day.

Still, I thought as I waited in thick over-coated ranks for the Germans to come and count us, it'll all be over by this time tomorrow. Tomorrow. Tomorrow.

Actually the day passed more quickly than I had expected.

There was still a good deal to be done: studying the local map, persuading a naval man to lend me his dark blue trousers, and buying a filthy cap for a hundred cigarettes from a Pole working in the washroom. But there was a flat period just after lunch when there seemed nothing to do but wait for the special meeting at half past three.

I walked round the camp for what I thought was half an hour, imagining myself hiding in woods, boarding goods trains, stealing food, doing anything except clamber over the wire. Then I discovered that it was still only ten to two. I decided to go back to the block and rest for a little. But as I was going into it the sun came out, challenging the smell from the night lavatory. I decided to fetch a book and read out of doors in my overcoat. Surely I could forget my surroundings for an hour and a half. After the meeting there would be so much to do that the time would pass quickly.

I looked through the books in my locker: Tristram Shandy, P. G. Wodehouse, Marcus Aurelius, John Stuart Mill and the Spanish grammar. The grammar turned the whole of my stomach over like a huge unwieldy omelette. I had borrowed it about a week before.

Spanish was to have been my next language: my winter's task. For some reason I had put off starting on it and had even begun to convince myself that it would be better to leave it until next winter. Now I felt that I wanted nothing else in the world but to be allowed to read this dismal grammar all winter. I took it down from the shelf in my locker and went out of doors.

Close to the block there was a steep bank looking onto the football ground. Most of the grass had already been worn away by cheering trampling spectators but it was still pleasant to sit there when it caught the sun. I opened my grammar. I would begin Spanish now just to reassure myself that I expected a future in which I could pick up past threads.

'It is suggested that this grammar should provide the basis for a year's study of Spanish. If all the lessons are worked through conscientiously and results compared with a key . . .'

A year. It sounded so comfortable and reassuring, like the drone of a distant mowing machine through the class-room window at school. A year. But tomorrow? I read on quickly.

'The basic principles of the Spanish language . . .'

A game of football had started below and the familiar quarrels of sportsmen were already floating up to me.

'Look here, are we playing an off-side rule or not?'

'Oh, stop bitching: of course we are.'

'Who's refereeing this game anyway?'

'That's just what I'd like to know.'

'Oh shut up and get on with the game.'

Somehow the afternoon arrived at half past three.

I made my way round the football pitch towards the library. There was a queue outside the parcel store and people were coming out with newly opened clothing parcels in their arms. Those still in the queue peered inquisitively at the contents jumbled loosely together in brown paper wrapping.

'The bloody goons confiscated my sponge-bag.'

'Good parcel, Prince?'

'Excellent: nine and a half pounds of chocolate and a pair of socks.'

A man with a pencil and a list saw me and shouted:

'Clothing parcel for you. Collect it after tea.'

'Thanks,' I said.

I thought of the little touches of home there would be inside it: the hand-knitted pullover, the familiar English toothpaste, and the razor blades fastened together with an elastic band.

I walked into the library.

A man was standing in the shadow behind the front door.

'You for the meeting?' he asked.

'Yes.'

'It's in the back room. Tell them it's all clear again, will you?'

The library consisted of two rooms, but the only entry to the inner room was through the outer. The outer room was already full of readers but people were being turned out of the inner room to make way for the meeting. They were streaming through the connecting door, muttering discontentedly and clutching their books and papers as they looked hopelessly around for somewhere to sit. There was a great noise of shuffling boots and dropped books, and the readers already established in the outer room looked up and clicked disapproval with their tongues. A man leaning against the wall with a copy of *The Golden Bough* in his hand, screwed up his eyebrows in disgust.

'These bloody escapers,' he said loudly.

I pushed past him into the inner room.

The door was shut. The sudden contrast was magical.

The room was quiet with tension. Ryan stood on the little platform by the blackboard, cleaning the board with a rag. Some chairs had been arranged on the platform and two senior officers were sitting there with bland smiles like judges at a beauty competition. I sat down at the end of one of the tables and looked around me. There seemed to be a lot of faces I had not noticed in the original team. We all looked anxiously towards the platform.

When Ryan turned round, I said:

'The man downstairs says it's all clear again now.'

'Good show, old man. Well, in that case, sir,' he turned to the most senior of the senior officers, 'I think we might as well start.'

The most senior officer nodded profoundly.

Ryan began to explain exactly how the scheme was to work, drawing little diagrams with chalk on the blackboard.

'All members of the team are to be down in the lower block, with their kit, half an hour before lock-up . . . Zero hour will be half past nine. At that time the first five of the ladder party must be standing ready by the window with the ladder. The rest of the team will be assembled in their right order in the block corridor. They will be ready to follow the ladder party as soon as they see its last man go through the window. The actual signal for the ladder party to open the window and go will of course be when all the lights in the camp go out. The signal for the lights to be fused will be given by Wing Commander Sawyer here.'

He pointed to someone sitting in the front row.

'The Wing Commander won't do that of course until we're all ready inside the block. When we're ready, that is at zero hour, he will climb out of the night lavatory window and first make sure that the immediate area round the block is clear of goons. He will then watch the patrolling goon on the wire. When this goon is at the point of his beat furthest away from our stretch of wire, the Wing Commander will give the signal to Clinker here —' a dark beetle-like man stood up for a moment and sat down again, '— who will fuse the entire lighting system of the camp including the searchlights.'

The beetle-like man nodded quietly.

One of the senior officers looked up and said to Ryan:

'Oh, it will be including the searchlights?'

'Yes, it will be including the searchlights.'

'That was something I was going to raise: whether the fusing of the lights would include the searchlights or not.'

'Yes, it most certainly will.'

The senior officer nodded.

'Good,' he said, 'sound.'

There was a pause while Ryan tried to remember where he had got to. In the silence the beetle-like man spoke very slowly and clearly:

'There wouldn't have been much point in fusing only half the lighting system, would there?'

He said it straight at the senior officer, who looked for a moment as if someone had cracked a whip in his face.

Then Ryan, who had not noticed the embarrassment, went on with his explanation. He described how the ladder was to be set up against the wire, how people were to clamber over and how they were to swing themselves clear through the gap at the end.

'. . . And personally I'm absolutely confident —' he repeated the word — 'confident, that the whole show will be a hundred per cent. success.'

The senior officers both nodded emphatically.

I tried to absorb some of Ryan's confidence. After all, he ought to know. He had done this sort of thing before. He had planned the whole scheme and ought to have a better idea than me of what was going to happen. Yet I found my own conviction that the attempt would result in my death steadfast and stubborn.

'And now I'll hand you over to Vincent, who will brief you from the Intelligence angle. He is very unselfishly standing down from this scheme although the Group Captain did offer him a place on it in recognition of his services to the committee. But as I say, he unselfishly insisted that he should not be given a place on any scheme in which he hadn't taken a personal part. However, he has a lot of valuable information about the surrounding countryside, and the frontier crossings which I will ask him to give to us now.'

Vincent stood up at the back of the room and walked modestly along the wall to the platform. He was a man twenty years older than most of us who, though he held a junior rank and had no real ties with the service, had obtained considerable influence with the senior officers in the camp. He was well-read and clever, and he made it easy for stupid men to respect his intellect if he thought they could be of use to him. No-one knew much about his past. He had been at Cambridge just after the last war, had fought with the International Brigade in Spain and had joined the R.A.F. as an air-gunner in 1940. He had a lean, controlled face and spoke with confidence.

'All the available data goes to show that you will find the local Polish population friendly,' he began.

The Polish population? How had he managed to get us as far as that? In contrast with my wishful thinking of the day before, I now found it impossible to visualize anything after the moment when the lights would go out and the window of the block would be thrown open.

Ryan's last words had been disturbing. If Vincent had rejected a place on the scheme, then it was certain that he thought it would fail. I remembered how once, when a tunnel had been successfully completed contrary to expectation, he had jockeyed himself into a position on the team which finally escaped although he had never done any of the work.

'Or, of course, if you don't like the idea of crossing the Swiss frontier, you could always try something quite different, such as making your way down to Yugoslavia and joining Mihailovitch. . .'

He might have been planning a Cooks' Tour. The senior officer nodded approvingly.

By the time the meeting was over I was in such a state of excitement and fright that I forgot all about the clothing parcel I was supposed to collect.

No-one said much to me at tea, although I caught them looking at me sometimes as they sipped at their mugs. Jack Nopps tried to be kind.

'Thought about your plans for when you get outside at all?' he asked casually.

'Yes,' I lied.

'Where are you going?'

'Danzig.'

It was a safe answer.

He looked out of the window.

'Well,' he said. 'You never know.'

'Rather him than me all the same,' said Jefferson, the Australian.

Afterwards Malleson helped me to get my things together. We cut a mask for my face out of a balaclava and made it black with boot polish. I looked at myself in the mirror. The mask made me look terrifying and rather professional, like a commando. I felt better.

Malleson carried my things down to the other block under his greatcoat and I followed him down the path about twenty yards behind. Inside the block I said good-bye to him.

'But there's another hour before we're locked in.'

'I know, but I'd rather be left alone down here. I want to calm down a bit.'

'O.K. Well, all the very best.'

'Thanks.'

He put his hand into his pocket.

'Here,' he said, 'take this. You've got more use for it than I have.'

It was a half-pound slab of chocolate. He hadn't had a clothing parcel for a long time. He must have been saving it for months.

'No,' I stammered, 'I can't possibly . . .'

But he had pushed it into my hand and walked abruptly out of the door.

I looked through the gap between two lockers into the first 'room' in the block. A man was preparing something for supper at a table. Someone lying in the gloom of a lower bunk was reading a book. Otherwise the room was empty.

'May I come in here: I'm on this scheme for tonight.'

The man at the table straightened up and looked at me. He held a newly-made fish cake in his two hands like a cricket ball he had just caught.

'Can't say, I'm sure, old boy. You'd better wait until the others come back, and ask them.'

'But I understood that it had been arranged that one of us was to go into each room.'

'I dare say it has, old man, but you can't do that sort of thing without asking the others, can you?'

He leant over the table and started to make another fish cake.

'Well, can I stay in here until the others come back?'

He didn't answer at first. I was beginning to think he hadn't heard when he said:

'There's not really much room in here, you know. Why don't you try one of the rooms further down?'

The man on the lower bunk put down his book.

'Oh, for Christ's sake, Birkett,' he said, 'don't be so bloody uncivilized.'

He dropped one leg from his bed onto the floor and turned to me.

'Sure, come in. You'll find an empty bed over there which belongs to a chap in sick quarters. You can use that.'

'Thanks very much.'

I put my things on the straw mattress.

'How about food? Would you like to have supper with us?'

I saw Birkett straighten up sharply.

'No thanks very much,' I said, 'I've brought all my own food.'

'Oh, O.K.' He lifted his leg off the floor with one hand and put it back on the bed. 'Well, if there's anything you want just let us know.'

Birkett shrugged his shoulders and went on with the fish cakes.

I lay back on the empty bed and looked at my watch. There was another three and a half hours to go.

At first it was pleasant to lie back on the straw mattress and relax. Most of the inhabitants of the block were walking their last circuits before being locked in, and there was an absence of noise which merged with the deepening gloom. It seemed that it must take a long time for such peace to be broken. Wrapped in it like a butterfly in its cocoon, I felt secure.

The lights were switched on and the harsh familiar outlines of beds, stools and tables forced me back into reality. The little pin of anxiety in my stomach began to dance. People began to come back into the block. The noise swelled until it had the jarring monotony of

108

traffic. The shutters were banged shut. The outside door was locked. People began to wonder how they were going to get through the evening.

'This chap's on the show tonight. He's spending the evening with us.'

Two of them looked down at me.

'Oh, really. Hallo, old boy.'

'Hallo.'

I didn't feel like conversation.

One of them turned away.

'Poor sod,' I heard him mutter.

'The moment those lights go out,' said Birkett, 'I'm getting behind that stove and I'm staying there until the whole shooting match is over.'

I pulled a paper-covered Anthology of verse out of my pocket. There was an advertisement for tooth-paste on one of the back pages and I thought at once of the clothing parcel I had not collected. I turned to the front of the book.

'Fear no more the heat of the sun,
 Nor the furious winter's rages;
 Thou thy worldly task hast done,
 Home art gone and ta'en thy wages . . .'

'Good show, old boy.' It was Ryan. 'Everything on the top line?'

'Yes thanks, sir.'

It made me feel better to call him sir. It helped me in my desperate attempt to respect his judgement.

'Good man.' He paused. 'I think we've a very good sporting chance,' he added confidentially.

'. . . Golden lads and girls all must
 As chimney-sweepers come to dust.'

After about an hour Birkett began to be very busy about the room collecting a saucepan and a baking dish made of hammered-out tins and chipping little bits of wood for a fire. Four people were playing bridge on a blanket spread over one end of the table. Over the other end a man was reading the *Völkischer Beobachter* with the aid of a dictionary.

'Three spades.'

'I'll be wanting to lay the table in a minute.'

'No bid.'

'Four spades.'

'Did you hear that everyone? I'll be wanting to lay the table for supper.'

'Double four spades.'

'Anything in the paper today, Larry?'

'A lot of bull about some wonderful new weapon they'll be using soon.'

'All right, if you don't want the table laid, don't move. I don't care a damn.'

'Oh, yes you do. It's about the only thing you do care about. You've got the soul of a housemaid. Now shut up and let them get on with their game.'

It was the man who had been lying on his bed when I arrived.

'There's no need to be impertinent, Trench.'

Birkett flounced out of the room with his tins and his little pieces of wood.

It was interesting to watch the life of my own room being reproduced in such detail. It was like recognizing the germs of some disease under a microscope.

By the time Birkett came back with his hot fish cakes and his prunes, the bridge players and the man reading the newspaper had moved.

'Here you are, chaps. Come and get it.'

'Jolly good show.'

'What, prunes as well?'

'Goody, goody.'

'Well done, Birkett.'

They rushed at the table from all sides, scrambling over stools, jumping down from top bunks like pigeons clattering down for crumbs. They ate quickly and in silence.

I took out some of the bread and cold meat roll I had brought as my supper. It was just after eight o'clock.

'You all right there?' said someone from the table to me.

They all turned, still eating, and looked at me.

'Yes, thanks.'

'When does it start?' one asked another.

'Half past nine, I think.'

'Yes,' I said, 'half past nine.'

110

I was glad to be able to say something. They all turned and looked at me again.

After supper I walked up and down in the corridor for a bit. Although there was now little more than an hour to go, the actual moment when the lights would go out remained stubbornly remote. I imagined the whole business of running to the wire, and setting up the ladder a thousand times, but I could never get beyond the point when I set my foot on the bottom rung.

Trench came up to me as I turned to walk down the corridor again.

'Come and have some coffee with us,' he said, 'it's just ready.'

I made a show of looking at my watch.

'Yes, I think I've just got time.'

But it must have been clear to him that I was not a professional escaper.

The bridge four had started again. Birkett was pouring the coffee out into mugs.

'Sugar?' he asked, offering me a mug.

'Oh no, really, thanks.'

'Come on. Of course you want some.'

He poured in a large teaspoonful of sugar. I was astonished.

'Thanks very much.'

He grinned and handed round the rest of the mugs.

I took my coffee and followed Trench over to his bed.

'How are you feeling about all this?' he asked.

It was suddenly a great relief to be able to speak the truth.

'I don't like it much,' I said, 'but I think there's a chance.'

'Yes, I think there's a chance, too. Of course, I must be honest: I think some people will probably get hurt, but I suppose that's a risk which everyone's got to take in war.'

'Yes.'

'The only question is: are we still in a war, or not?'

He sucked slowly at his pipe and blew out a cloud of smoke which disappeared into the haze all around us.

'I can't say I feel much as if I am,' he added.

'I don't either.'

He looked at me and then sucked at his pipe again and shrugged his shoulders.

'Still, I suppose you know what you're doing.'

Ryan came into the room.

'Ah, there you are. All set? I think I should begin to get changed now if I were you. We want everybody to be ready to fall into their places five minutes before zero hour.'

I went over to my clothes on the empty bed.

It was going to happen. There was no way out. However much I might take refuge in the present in which it had not yet happened, there would be a moment when the present was the present in which it was happening. The darkness. The sudden cold night air. Running across the open flower beds to the warning wire. Over the warning wire. Shouts from the guards in the boxes. Across the raked earth to the ladder. The sound of a machine-gun. The scramble round the ladder. And then?

The picture in my imagination dissolved. However often I lived through the moment, and I had just lived through it so vividly that the palms of my hands were sweating and my heart thumping, I could not make it last beyond that point.

I put on a clean pair of socks. Then the airman's tunic with the civilian buttons. Collar and tie.

Trench had settled down to his book again. One of the bridge players saw me dressing and said:

'My God, is it starting now?'

'About another twenty minutes, I think.'

'Christ, let's pack up chaps.'

'Time for one more game.'

'All right. Whose deal?'

He turned to me again.

'But you'll let us know when it's about to start, won't you?'

'Yes.'

I was ready now. I tried to sit down on the bed and wait.

I looked through the contents of my pack again. Yes, it was all there: bread, biscuits, local map, cheese, plaster for the feet, a spare pair of socks, chocolate. I fingered the mask I had made. The boot blacking came off on my hands and I wiped it off on the side of the bed. I stood up and went out into the corridor.

It was full of people strangely dressed in plus fours and navy blue suits, with packs strapped to their backs. They were bustling anxiously from room to room, forgetting things, making last minute plans, asking each other how they looked.

I had a moment of panic. Everybody seemed ready except me. I ran back to my room and collected my pack and my mask. I could not speak to anyone, but when the bridge players saw me they threw down their cards and jumped up from the table.

I ran out into the corridor. I saw the Wing Commander who was to do the reconnoitre and give the signal for the fusing of the lights talking anxiously to Ryan. Ryan had his mask on, only pushed up above his eyes like flying goggles before take-off.

Ryan and the Wing Commander separated.

'Come on now,' said Ryan to those of us huddled together in the corridor, 'sort yourselves out into the proper order.'

We pushed each other around for a few minutes.

I found that so many new people had come into the scheme at the last moment that I was now four from the end.

'Come on, you're in front of me.'

'Who comes after Gus?'

'Come on, hurry up for Christ's sake.'

Now that so much was happening I felt better. Perhaps it really would work after all. Anyway, we should know soon enough.

From my place in the queue I watched through a chink between two lockers the ladder party assembling by the window.

'Everyone in their right places now?' Ryan was jumping to and fro between the room from which the ladder was to be launched and the corridor.

'O.K., Wing Commander!' he yelled up the passage.

I watched Sawyer disappear into the night lavatory.

The rest of the barrack was absolutely quiet, waiting to see what would happen.

Ryan had just said: 'O.K., you can bring the ladder out now,' when all the lights went out.

'What the bloody hell?'

'Quick, out with that ladder,' said Ryan, 'there must have been a balls-up.'

In the sudden darkness it was impossible to see anything. There was a clatter as the ladder was dragged across the floor. Everyone was talking at once.

'For Christ's sake, hurry up.'

'What the hell's happening?'

The man behind me kept pulling at my coat.

'Stop pulling, damn you.'

'Get the window open.'

'What the hell are they waiting for?'

113

'I'll say there's been a balls-up.'

With a loud report the shutters of the launching window were thrown open.

The boundary lights were out. There was no moon and a high wind. The night was a sea of darkness and the unknown. The wind carried the shouts of the guards away from us so that they sounded like the shouts of men drowning.

'Go on, for Christ's sake; what are we waiting for?'

I could hear them fumbling with the ladder at the window.

Like a jet of blue fire one of the searchlights from the boxes played straight up into the sky. Then it splashed furiously into the camp. Everyone threw themselves onto the floor. There was a pop as if someone had exploded a huge paper bag, a disappearing electric sizzle, and the searchlight went out.

'Good old Clinker.'

'Get that window shut.'

'No, now's our chance.'

'Come on, chaps, every man for himself.' It was Ryan's voice.

But something had gone wrong with Clinker's fusing. A great blue flash lit the darkness. It was followed by flash after flash, sheets of blue light which stabbed flat at the camp. With each sound went the silky sound of electricity. It was like being at the source of the lightning.

We lay on our stomachs watching each other. Every time the blue light filled the block we saw ourselves silhouetted against the floor. Nobody knew what to do.

There was another loud report as someone slammed the shutters closed again.

'O.K., chaps,' — it was Ryan's voice — 'pack it up. We'll abandon the scheme.'

When the lights went on five minutes later, we were still all lying on the floor.

The exact cause of the fiasco was the main topic of argument for weeks. Some said that Ryan had made a mistake in failing to get everything ready in the block before he sent Sawyer off. Others said that Sawyer had panicked and gone straight out and given the signal without first doing the reconnoitring for which Ryan had allowed time. Others said that Clinker had gone mad at the fusing point and couldn't restrain himself. I don't know why the people who argued so much about it didn't go and ask these three what had happened. Between them they could probably have established the reason for the failure quite easily. Personally I had nothing but an overwhelming feeling of gratitude for whoever had made the attempt impossible. I went about the camp like a man reprieved while on his way to the chaplain and the hangman. I collected my clothing parcel the next morning and there were the razor blades and the tooth paste just as I had expected. I took my friendly Spanish grammar to the library every day and tried to be polite to Jefferson when he maddened me at meals. For a week or so I was even careful not to wipe my boots on Roper's pillow.

As clearly as any incident of those years I remember the books which I read.

We could not have lived without books. They were the only sure support, the one true comfort. When food was short, clothing scarce, blocks overcrowded and underheated, and war news bad, there were always books. In reading one had a pleasure of which, like sleep, one could never be deprived. I remember the books which I read in that time with a great love.

I think chiefly of novels: all Hardy, Adam Bede, Tristram Shandy, The Newcomes, Henry Esmond, The Old Wives' Tale, Sentimental Education and many others, but every sort of reading was happiness. As supply was limited, and controlled by censorship, reading was conventional, but one soon discovered that it would be possible to spend a life-time reading books which were not obscure and still not exhaust everything that was worthwhile.

I even remember books I disliked with affection. During the worst period for external conditions of the whole three years the only book I could get hold of (and then only after putting my name down on a waiting list) was Somerset Maugham's enormous Of Human Bondage. I read it, literally hungrily, for four days, stopping only for the daily half pint of soup and four slices of bread, and sleep. I did not think it a good book, but I shall always be grateful to it. Now I can only remember one thing about it: a passage which refers to the death by starvation of a girl in Paris because she only had a pint of milk and a loaf of bread a day. At that time I should have considered a pint of milk and a loaf of bread a day paradise.

From a book, The Modern Short Story, by H.E. Bates, I remember a criticism of Hardy which made the blood rush to my head with anger:

'. . . So what one remembers out of Hardy is not the philosophic vapourings or the spiritual anguish, all impossibly unreal today . . .'

Silly literary prig, I thought, and how typical of a man who thinks that good writing can only be learnt from good reading to find spiritual anguish unreal. But I was grateful even to Mr. Bates for giving me something to read.

There were many copies of plays in the camps. Among those which gave me the greatest pleasure I remember the whole of Shakespeare, Shaw's *Androcles and the Lion*, and Thornton Wilder's *Our Town*. For the first time in my life I found the real Shakespeare. At last I understood the fanaticism which during my schooldays had always struck me as so forced. The stuff of the plays (Jaques on life, Falstaff on honour, Claudio on death, Hamlet on everything, and so on) became essential to me. I used to go to his characters for help as a Catholic might go to a priest or a sick man to his doctor. How ridiculous to think that these plays had been thrust at me when I was ten! As this was long before I had any real experience of life myself it was hardly surprising that Shakespeare's comments should not have meant much to me then. What can *As You Like It* possibly mean to someone who had never been in love, or *Hamlet* to someone who has never felt 'how weary, stale, flat and unprofitable seem to me all the uses of this world'. I made a vow that I should not allow my children to look at Shakespeare until adolescence. For myself I knew that I should go on finding greater and greater depths in Shakespeare as I grew older, and that I should die and still not have found the bottom.

This personal quality of books was their greatest worth. Every prisoner suffered from cycles of depression, more frequent but almost as regular as the changing seasons. With some people the effect was just numbing: the man would lie on his bed all day like a piece of dead wood. With others it brought a violent distress of spirit often visible on faces for days on end. In one such mood I turned for the first time to Marcus Aurelius. The strong simplicity of his ideas about life and the universe made it easy to link him with other men of understanding, so that for me the book seemed to be ringing with echoes of Hamlet and Richard Jefferies and the New Testament. 'Of course, it is not important philosophy,' all the commentators were careful to point out. To me in that mood it seemed more important than philosophy, like the poetry of Keats or the music of Sibelius.

But undoubtedly the most satisfactory reading of all was poetry. Always the most directly relevant to a charged state of mind, even though it wasn't always modern, it was thus the most comforting and the most healing. If anthologies ever needed any justification they received it for me at least during those years. Under such conditions one could not afford to despise what was well known. One needed it too much for its own sake.

Every year, about eight weeks before Christmas, we began to talk about laying down a 'brew'.

'Oh, for God's sake let's ignore Christmas this year.'

'There's nothing more depressing than pretending to be jolly in a prison camp.'

'But everyone else is having a brew. It won't make Christmas any less awful if we don't have one.'

'I agree. It's the line of least resistance.'

'It's not worth the fruit and the sugar.'

But in the end someone usually found a barrel, and scrubbed it, and poured in the raisins and the sugar and the water. As Christmas approached we would become affectionate about the brew and go and raise the lid and listen to it working quietly away in its corner.

'I think I've got a way of making it taste a little less foul this year,' said Jack Nopps one Christmas. 'There won't be quite so much for everybody as usual, but it will be stronger and it won't make us all sick quite so easily.'

In the evenings he would sit on his bed beating old tins into strange shapes with a hammer. One evening he clambered down with an armful of tin pipes and funnels, scooped a cupful of fermenting liquid out of the barrel, and disappeared into the lavatory. Half an hour later he came back, his yellow teeth flashing in a confident cockney smile.

'Trust your Uncle Jack,' he shouted, 'you'll be drinking apricot brandy for Christmas. It's a first-class still.'

About the second week in December he began taking his still into the night lavatory every evening. He would sit by the little fire he had built underneath it, watching the drops of spirit trickle out of the tubes into bottles partially filled with apricot jam.

By Christmas Day he had twenty-four little medicine bottles filled with a pale opaque liquid.

'Three bottles per man,' he said triumphantly. 'But one will be quite enough for most of you.'

There was the usual extra food for Christmas and we allowed ourselves three slices of bread each for breakfast instead of two. The snow sparkled in the sunshine outside the window and nobody really minded much when people came into the room and said 'Happy Christmas'. But about lunch-time the drunks began to look in.

'Merry Christmas, old boy. Got any brew?'

'Hullo, Ken, come in.'

'I said have you got any bloody brew?'

'Yes, but we're not starting it till this evening.'

'Unsociable bastards.'

He slammed the door, kicking a locker as he went.

There was the roaring and stamping of a herd of drunks at the other end of the corridor.

Tessel, the Canadian, opened the door.

'Sex rears its ugly head,' he said, and shut it again.

We decided that it was time to start on Jack Nopps' apricot brandy.

It tasted of petrol, mixed with creosote and hair oil. Jack took one gulp, said 'Lovely stuff', and went off to tune in to the King's Speech on the secret wireless, which only he could operate. Soon it was dark and the Christmas evening was in full swing.

The drink made me excited and confused so that time seemed to be moving in a series of huge uneasy jerks, sometimes accelerating wildly and sometimes standing absolutely still.

First I was in a room where people stood crowded together in the atmosphere of a cocktail party.

'Of course I was on the same squadron as him for a time.'

'If I can get drunk enough on this stuff I might be able to get away with it at the next repatriation board.'

'It was one of the finest knocking-shops in Cairo.'

'If only we can get a foothold round Calais.'

Every now and again people would step neatly aside while the person they were talking to was sick on the floor.

'Awfully sorry, old boy . . .'

The floor was slimy with sick like the deck of a channel steamer after a bad crossing.

Then I was in the corridor, having an intimate talk with an old friend who could no longer stand.

'Of course, you know, I'm not really tight. It's just this bloody hooch. It goes straight to the stomach.'

All down the corridor people were propping themselves up

118

against the walls, or lying on the floor singly or in couples.

The Germans had allowed us to walk between the huts until midnight. I passed from one block to another.

In the soft snow-lit darkness people were systematically sicking up the food which they had saved for so long. I debated whether to be sick or not myself, and decided that I could hold out for another half hour.

In the next block a man I had never seen before rushed up to me with a jug.

'Have some of my hock: it tastes of furniture polish.'

He splashed some down the front of my tunic and was gone.

I walked in at the first door I saw. The smell of crude spirit was overpowering, like an anaesthetic. Sitting astride one of the beams that spanned the ceiling was Tessel. There was a little crowd underneath him, beseeching him with the heavy solemn common-sense of drunks to 'come down and not be a fool'. Tessel said nothing but looked down at them with contempt. His face was green. He had a bad squint anyway, but now his two eyes seemed completely dissociated from each other and wandered restlessly round different corners of his head, apparently quite out of control and enjoying their surprising liberty.

From the room next door came a heavy tuneless chorus:

'Fuck 'em all, fuck 'em all,
The long and the short and the tall . . .'

I found myself face to face with Jack Nopps.

'What did the King say, Jack?'

He was so drunk that his words came thickly and with great difficulty as if he had been wounded.

'He said . . .'

'. . . So cheer up my lads, fuck 'em all.'

'He said . . . the prisoners of war . . . were conducting themselves . . . with great dignity.'

Tessel slipped heavily from the beam and slumped onto the floor.

Finally I remember many small things which no longer have the coherence of an incident: stray wisps of thought, ends of conversation, odd corners of moods and impressions.

A bad weather front feeling its way over from the west like a nasty white octopus in the blue summer sky.

Hate for a man. Smashing his face against the floor in a horrible day–dream fight.

The long gaps that sometimes occurred between letters. It was as if you were swimming out at sea with a piece of string tied round your middle attached to someone on the shore. When there were no letters the person on the shore disappeared below your horizon and you thought you were alone. Then came the pull on the string and you had to think about something else besides the water and the sky and the sun.

A story about a R.A.F. Flight-Sergeant who noticed that a recruit was still wearing his hat in church. 'Take your hat off, you silly bugger,' he yelled across the pews, 'don't you know you're in the 'ouse of God?'

The interminable searches − 'We are only doing our duty, gentlemen' − and returning to find books and food and clothes scattered in chaos on the floor.

The day when the search guards were given orders to act roughly, and the little R.A.S.C. captain who came running out of the block with his mouth still bleeding from a blow with a rifle butt.

Running in a half-mile race with little pains tearing at my chest and my knees sinking lower and lower as if I were running across quick-sands. The thought that came into my head as I rounded a corner into the straight: 'Why add this to it all?'

The vividness with which stray insignificant pictures from childhood would suddenly appear before me. It was as if an antiquated lecturer, standing somewhere behind me, had slipped a slide into a magic lantern and brought it sharply into focus. Going to sleep or opening a book: an old garden, a childish fear, a face seen casually and quickly forgotten, would take possession of my mind as if there had been no time between.

'. . . But I think your attitude is completely unreasonable . . .'
    Slowly the argument began to change colour. His face shrank into lines of hostility and I felt my right knee twitching with anger inside my trouser-leg.

The grey clouds, the strong dry wind and the leaping dust of a summer evening.

Rain, driving perpendicularly into the ground in long sharp needles, and the sweet smell afterwards and the feeling that life was worth loving after all.

Days when the colours were cold and bleak, the hardening arteries of summer.

Days when my mind was like those days, grey and comfortless for no particular reason.

Days when the summer was like a beauty in her early forties, full-blown and creasing, but warm and dear.

Snow lying in the sun and making the place we had lived in for years suddenly fresh and rare.

A moment at a gramophone concert when the badly-tuned loud-speaker suddenly blared Beethoven's Ninth Symphony into the theatre like a roundabout organ on Hampstead Heath.

The screams of a man who had tried to cut his throat.

A present from a Russian prisoner: a very fat pink pumpkin.

Part Three

1

One incident stands out like an oasis in this desert, fresh and clear and, by contrast with the surrounding time, magic and unnatural.

Lying on my stomach in the dark tunnel, smelling the earth and keeping touch with the heels of the man in front, I still could not believe that I was going to escape.

It was nearly four months before that we had begun this underground life, wriggling down through a lavatory seat and a hole cut in the brick foundations to hollow out a chamber and start a tunnel. Late autumn, midwinter, and now premature spring – in all weathers we had made the furtive journey to the large lavatory block and crawled in through the hole, or received the cans of earth for dispersal, pouring it down through the seats and ramming it into the filth with long poles, or stood about in the gloom, watching for the inside patrols and conversing with those prisoners who came and sat long on legitimate business. The routine had become part of us, and though we often hated it and grudged the time, we felt affectionate and possessive about it. There was something stimulating about the hours spent digging at the tiny face, tugging on the rope for the earth to be dragged away and receiving the faint answering tug from the other end, or squeezing backwards cursing to join the rope where it had snapped under the strain. When we came up to the familiar tea and the squalor and the faces it was as if we had spent the afternoon in another planet.

And very slowly, almost unnoticed, something had grown out of it all. The rope on the trolley became longer and the pull became harder. Soon it was necessary to station someone half way down the tunnel to help the man pulling from the chamber, then two men at intervals. Unintentional deviations in the level became noticeable: the lamp carried by the workers at the face was no longer in sight from the chamber. People began to measure the amount of tunnel already dug, and as the weeks went by the imperceptible progress of each day consolidated in astonishing 'footage': thirty feet, fifty feet, seventy feet. People began to measure it the other way round: the amount of footage still to be dug. But it seemed impossible that it would ever lead to an escape. No-one really thought about that very much; it was all just a daily routine to be worked through. And then a mathematician went down with a set-square and a lead weight tied to a piece of string and found that the tunnel was fifteen feet deeper than it was meant to be. Nobody believed him so he did it all over again and got the same result. So the tunnel started to go upwards, while people stuck probing sticks up through the roof for safety. And one day one of these sticks came up above the ground and it was exactly where the mathematician had calculated it would be, many feet outside the wire.

And so on, until one night I found myself listening in the darkness to my heart beating against the packed earth of the floor, clutching an attaché case filled with escape food and fingering a pocketful of false papers, but still not really believing that I should escape. The inside patrols would discover the trap. There would be a snap roll-call in the blocks. Somehow, I was sure, the alarm would be given before anyone had got away and we should all be hauled ignominiously out again. Or if that didn't happen someone would be seen scuttling across the open field to the cover of the wood before my turn came to emerge. There would be a shot, a thumping of heavy boots down the path over our heads and then, provided that the guards did not start more shooting, fourteen days solitary in the 'cooler'.

Sammy and I had drawn places No. 16 and 17. We were lucky in so far as there were thirty-five people after us, but as we were both certain that something would go wrong before our turn came, wherever we were, it made little difference to us whether we were Nos. 16 and 17 or 51 and 52.

The first two needed complete darkness to dig the final break-through. There was half an hour of light left. Even when they had started digging it might take them another half hour if their calcula-tions of the amount still to be dug were wrong.

Sammy, lying behind me, pulled at my ankle.

'I wish they'd hurry up,' he said, 'this is bad for my claustrophobia.'

Occasionally messages were passed down the tunnel from the chamber to the head or vice versa. As we were lying about half way down it and it was necessary to speak in whispers we knew that the messages we received bore little relation to what had originally been said or to what would arrive at the other end. But we passed them on.

The man in front of me, whose name was Warburton, turned his head as much as it is possible to turn a head without moving one's shoulders and hissed:

'The Emperor says, there's simply got to be more air.'

I passed it on to Sammy, who said:

'I don't know who the Emperor is, but I couldn't agree with him more.'

I heard him emend it into:

'People are fainting; there's got to be more air.'

Certainly the air was bad. There were about thirty people lying in a hundred and fifty feet of tunnel, and another twenty waiting in the chamber. Somewhere in the chamber there was a man working himself into a state of exhaustion on an air pump made out of a kit-bag, but in the middle of the tunnel it was difficult to believe in him while, at the head, people were obviously convinced that they were being suffocated.

'Are you passing these messages on?' hissed Warburton furiously, 'more air for Christ's sake.'

Once there was the dreaded sound of boots running overhead. My heart beat so loudly that I couldn't tell which was boots and which was heart. Sammy took my ankle.

'We've had it,' he said.

But ten minutes passed and nothing happened. Then Warburton said:

'It must have been the patrolling goon trying to keep warm. You don't need to pass that on, by the way.'

For a long time we lay there in silence. I hardly thought at all about the weight of fifteen feet of earth above us or the impossibility of going backwards or forwards if the tunnel collapsed. There had been moments of suppressed terror when we first started the work, but the cumulative effect of nothing going wrong day after day for four months was to build confidence. Now I thought as little about the possibility of the tunnel collapsing as I used to think about the

125

possibility of the wings falling off an aeroplane when flying. I lay there wondering whether there wasn't perhaps a chance that we might get away after all.

Sammy passed up another message:

' "How much longer before they break?", and there's to be less smoking. The latter probably a free translation of talking.'

I changed it to 'talking' and passed it on.

About ten minutes later the answer came back.

'It's in the chamber.'

'What is?' I asked.

'I don't know,' said Warburton peevishly. 'I'm just passing it on.'

'Yes, but what are you passing on?'

'How the hell should I know? It's the answer to the last message, I suppose.'

'But the last message asked when they were going to break.'

'Oh, shut up.'

Five minutes later the proper answer came. It was a draught of cold night air.

'Thank God for that,' said Sammy.

Very slowly we began to crawl forward.

It was not a continuous progress but a series of rare tiny jerks. Sometimes we remained stationary for five minutes at a time and often I decided that at last something had gone wrong. But always we moved on again, and each time we moved on the possibility of escape became more real and exciting.

A message came down from the head of the tunnel:

'Seven men out.'

Sammy said: 'Good God, only seven! This seems to have been going on all night.'

I was sweating. My elbows, sore from weeks of work in the tunnel, were becoming more and more painful. I badly wanted to stretch my neck.

After a long time I noticed that we were jerking uphill. That meant that we were on the last stretch. I told Sammy.

'Quiet, for Christ's sake,' said Warburton, much louder than I had spoken, 'I can see the sky.'

It seemed to me that it was getting very much more difficult to move. There was no longer room for my attaché case by my side and I had to wait until there was sufficient space between me and Warburton before I could push it ahead. The walls of the tunnel were

126

becoming narrower and narrower. My shoulders were pressing hard against them on each side and every time I moved my back brushed the ceiling, bringing down a fine shower of earth.

Now I understood the reason for the long pauses in our progress. The earth which had been dug away to break the tunnel had not been sufficiently dispersed in the excitement of success and as a result the tunnel, like a bottle of hock lying on its side, grew elegantly narrower towards the exit. Each man had to stop and fight his way out. I could hear Warburton panting and wrestling with the walls and realized that it would be my turn next. Occasionally he kicked earth into my face as he fought for the pressure to be free. I lay wondering if I could maintain the tension inside me long enough to get myself out. Every second it was necessary to screw it a little tighter and success now seemed to depend solely on time. If I did not get out before the tension snapped I should never get out at all. At this rate I gave myself about ten minutes.

It was some time since Warburton had kicked earth into my face. I looked ahead to see if he was through. There was only blackness. I thought he must have got stuck in the exit. Then I looked up and saw, light by contrast with the inside of the tunnel, the blue of the night sky. I had expected the exit to be as gently sloped as the whole of the last ascent. I now saw that it went vertically upwards into the night. Warburton had probably left some minutes ago. Guiltily, I heaved myself up.

To my surprise I got my head and shoulders out quite easily. There was a strong wind blowing and the night was overcast. The mathematician and the two who had broken the tunnel had worked accurately. I was looking out of a ditch that ran close to a potato-clamp. It was perfect cover. I was about thirty yards outside the wire.

I saw the patrolling sentry coming down the wire towards me. He stood out clearly in the light of the arc lamps and I thought I must stand out just as clearly to him. But he passed by the place where he could have seen a head and shoulders planted in the stubble and, humming and stamping his feet, ambled down to the other end of the wire. This was my chance.

I tried to pull my arms through and found that I was stuck.

For a long time I knelt there, pinioned by the noose of earth. Then I succeeded in getting down and starting again. This time I put my arms through first but stuck at the waist. I was wearing a thick cut-down R.A.F. greatcoat and the pockets were stuffed with food.

Anyway I had forgotten my attaché case so I went down again. I pushed the attaché case through first, then my arms, and again stuck at the waist. I could hear the sentry coming back up the wire. I struggled wildly, thrashing with my feet in the earth below me. I wondered what Sammy was thinking. The sentry was only about twenty yards away down the wire and coming up it fast. He would be bound to see me this time if he looked my way because so much of my body was above the ground. I made a final effort. I thought that I should break in the sides and spoil the chances of the people coming after me. I got through just before the sentry came level with me. I lay flat on my stomach in the ditch and waited for the shot.

The sentry ambled by, whistling this time, to the other end of his beat. I had about a minute's worth of tension left inside me.

I scrambled along the ditch on my hands and knees to the end of the potato-clamp. There was some open ground to be covered before reaching another ditch and another potato-clamp. I turned to look at the camp. From this distance I could see both ends of the stretch of wire under which the tunnel had passed. In the tall towers at each end the sentries occasionally switched on their searchlights, passed them slowly up and down the wire, swept them, like some one sweeping crumbs off a table, across the camp itself and then switched them out again. They never seemed to think of turning them onto the field outside the wire.

There was no sign of the patrolling sentry so I crawled out of the ditch and across the open stubble to the next clamp. We had been told to crawl with our stomachs flat to the ground for safety, but I wanted to get to the next ditch as soon as possible. As a sop to my conscience I went on two legs and one hand (the other carrying the attaché case) with my bottom high in the air. Just inside the next ditch someone lay on his stomach panting with exhaustion. It was Warburton. I crawled over him, hurried to the end of the ditch and again looked back. This time the camp had shrunk considerably. It seemed to hang in the darkness on the chain of lights which shone at regular intervals all round it. I crawled out of the ditch, under a flimsy wire fence and into the next field. There was still about two hundred yards to go to the wood, but the field sloped downwards about a quarter of the way across and once in the dip there was no danger of being seen from the camp. I moved forward as quickly as possible, this time not even bothering to touch the ground with one hand but running with my knees bent and my body crouched forward. I was suddenly aware of several other figures running across the field in similar positions. We went over the rise into the dip like soldiers of the '14–'18 war going over the top.

Inside the dip I threw myself down and rested. In the open space that still separated me from the wood I could see other dark smudges against the light earth of the field. We lay there for a while panting, like fish that had jumped out of a net onto the deck of a fishing boat.

I had arranged to meet Sammy on the edge of the wood. It was typical of our lack of belief in such a meeting that we had arranged nothing more definite. When I got there the wood was alive with English voices.

'Hist — Percy?'

'No.'

'Hist — George?'

'Hisst!'

'Hist!'

'That you, Taft?'

'No.'

'Hist!'

'Percy! Percy!'

I was leaning against a tree and thinking that I should never find Sammy when he came straight up to me out of the field.

'Wait till I get my breath back,' he said and collapsed beside me.

I looked at the square chain of lights and relaxed. It was safe to relax now. This was the beginning of something else.

'How did you get on?' Sammy asked.

'I wouldn't have believed that the same five minutes could be both so bloody and so wonderful.'

Sammy had less breath.

'I got stuck,' he said.

I realized how small the opening must have been for he was a little man and very agile.

A figure tip-toed past a few feet away from us.

'Percy! Percy!' it whispered and disappeared into the trees.

'Let's go,' I said to Sammy.

'When I've got my breath back.'

'The sooner we put some distance between us and the camp the better.'

'I quite agree, but I can't do that without any breath, can I?'

I realized the strain that was going to be placed on our partnership.

Our fate and actions were now linked together as closely as those of Siamese twins and every decision contained a potential quarrel.

'All right,' I said.

I pulled off the old black-dyed pyjamas I had worn over my clothes to keep them clean in the tunnel, and threw them away into the wood. Then I pulled out the cap which a man who normally spent his time reading Lucretius had made for me out of a German blanket, and tidied myself up.

'How do I look?'

'O.K. Let's go.'

Sammy pulled out a naval officer's cap with the badges removed. I could only see his outline against the cloudy sky, but I knew what he looked like from the dress rehearsal we had carried out the day before. In daylight he intended to wear a pair of dark glasses because his face had been burnt when he was shot down and he was afraid that this would attract attention. He was better dressed than I was. His threadbare naval uniform with civilian buttons, the green half-length overcoat which he had bought from the Pole who drove the sewage cart, and his cap, were at least consistent and plausible. He did not look well-dressed but he did look like the sort of person you would expect to meet in trains and railway stations and take no notice of. He was described in his false identity card as a 'machinist' and he had something of the seedy confident look of people who spend much time with oil-cans and machines. His dark glasses even gave a hint of his having once had some quite advanced specialist knowledge and for a time we considered describing him as an 'engineer'. But my own appearance would have been inconsistent with anything so ambitious.

'I'm afraid it'll have to be machinist after all,' he said resentfully when he first saw me in my clothes.

He seemed to take it as quite a blow to his pride. Certainly I did not look convincing. In addition to my blanket cap and my cut-down R.A.F. greatcoat, I wore a pair of naval trousers, a tie which I had often worn as an undergraduate and which had somehow not been confiscated from one of my clothing parcels, and a dyed R.A.F. airman's tunic which we hoped I should never have to reveal because it was so obvious that I had altered the cut. Altogether I had a mad artificial appearance. I looked like someone who had dressed up.

But it was my boots that worried me most of all.

'Be sure to see that your boots are all right,' Sammy had said to me about a week before.

I had been in a hurry to book my place in the library for the morning and, looking down at the boots I was wearing, had decided that they would do.

'Yes, of course,' I had said crossly.

And then, on the afternoon of the break, my toe had appeared through the top of the leather. For half an hour I had scurried round the blocks trying to borrow another pair. Eventually I found a pair which fitted me and which the owner was prepared to lend.

'The only snag,' he said, 'is that I stuck the sole of the right boot on with glue and I shouldn't like to guarantee it.'

'That'll be all right,' I said confidently.

But what if it wasn't? Could anything be more bogus or more paralysing than a boot without a sole?

I tried to forget about it.

As we set off I said to Sammy:

'You know, I think we look quite good really.'

'Yes,' he said, 'in the dark.'

2

Sammy had a luminous compass and we started to walk north-east in the direction of the Bromberg railway. It had looked quite simple on the map: some open country first, then up a secondary road until it turned in the wrong direction, more open country, across a main road and then the railway line. The field we started to walk across was very muddy and we moved slowly. It was necessary to skirt the camp, and the boundary lights were visible all the time a quarter of a mile away. There was something nightmarish about our heavy mud-clogged steps and the continual presence of the camp from which we were trying to escape. After we had crossed the field we came to a sort of heath. Sometimes the grass was long, sometimes short, sometimes there was gorse and sometimes there were little winding paths which led nowhere. All the time the boundary lights pricked out the shape of the camp just over our right shoulders.

'The balloon doesn't seem to have gone up yet,' said Sammy.

'I'll feel happier when we can't see the camp any more.'

'I think we'd better walk separate — one about fifteen yards ahead of the other, so that if we run into someone one of us will have a chance of getting away. I'll go first.'

'All right,' I said, 'but don't go too far or I won't be able to see you.'

It was very dark and the wind made the night darker. Neither of us yet fully understood the fact that we were free and we expected to be caught at any moment. The darkness seemed to be full of clever Germans with excellent night vision who knew all about us and were biding their time. The ambitious plans that we had made for our journey now seemed more hopelessly unreal than ever. '. . . make our way to Bromberg before it gets light . . . catch the early morning train to Berlin . . .' And here we were after half an hour, still floundering about in the darkness scarcely out of reach of the searchlights.

Sammy stopped. I wondered if there was something wrong and stopped too. After about half a minute he came cautiously back towards me.

'Is that you?' he said.

'Yes.'

'What are you doing?'

'I stopped because you stopped.'

'Well, for Christ's sake — I stopped because I wanted you to catch up with me.'

'How was I to know that? I thought that something had gone wrong.'

'Well anyway,' he said, looking at his compass, 'what I wanted to say was that we've got to keep further over to the right.'

'But that's the direction of the camp.'

'I don't care. That's where we've got to go. If we don't hit the railway line we'll get hopelessly stuck — wandering about like this until morning. Once we get to the railway line we don't need to worry about direction any more. We just walk straight up it to Bromberg.'

'All right.'

He set off in front again, leaving the path. The camp lights grew larger. I could even pick out the silhouette of one of the guard towers.

We had found another path and had been walking along it without difficulty for about ten minutes when I heard a noise. I saw Sammy stop and crawl quickly away into the long grass. I did the same and listened for the sound of footsteps. My heart beat loudly and irregu-

132

larly so that I was afraid the sound might give me away. But no-one came. Very carefully I crawled forward to find Sammy. I almost crawled on top of him before I saw him.

'Didn't you hear someone?' he whispered.

'Yes.'

'Sh.'

We listened together.

'There doesn't seem to be anyone there now.'

'Perhaps they're waiting for us to show ourselves.'

'We'll have to go on. We've wasted nearly an hour already.'

'All right.'

This time I went ahead. The compass was reassuring in the darkness like a pilot's instruments in bumpy cloud. I noticed with surprise that the camp was now behind us although at no time did we seem to have passed it. Once, when we went down into a hollow it disappeared from sight altogether. But it was there again the next moment, though the lights were smaller. They looked almost small enough for the wind to blow them away altogether. I stopped and waited for Sammy.

'Anything wrong?' he asked.

'No. We should be getting to the road soon which will be a relief.'

'Good. Look out where you're going though. I seem to remember from the map that there's some marshy ground close to the road.'

'What about having something to eat?' I said.

'Already?'

I was troubled by a secret fear that we should be caught before we had had time to eat any of our specially prepared escaping food. If we were caught after eating, at least we should feel that we had got something out of the escape. Otherwise the thought of all our confiscated uneaten food would torment us for months when we were back in the camp.

'Just to keep our morale up?' I said. I could not help smiling. Sammy smiled back.

'I think we might allow our morale a few raisins,' he said, 'but we ought to keep moving.'

We munched raisins as we walked.

I was still leading when I saw the dusty white secondary road just ahead of us and a little to the left. I was so relieved that I left the path we were on and made straight for the road. There was a slight slope for a few yards. I ran down it. Falling suddenly, like a drunkard, I was up to my waist in thick muddy water. I trod furiously, splashed with my arms to save myself from overbalancing. I got out again onto the path. My boots and trousers were heavy with muddy slime. Sammy ran up.

'Oh Christ,' he said, and stared at me appalled.

The water was soaking through to my skin and I felt the beginning of a clammy despair. The only consolation was that I had not lost my attaché case.

'We'll have to hope the mud dries before morning,' said Sammy, 'and we'll try to brush it off.'

We both sat down while I emptied the water out of my boots. Then I took off my trousers and we wrung them out. After I had put them on again I dried my feet with a towel and put on a clean pair of socks out of my attaché case. The touch of the dry wool was comforting. I laced up my boots and felt better. I hoped that the dampness round my stomach and at the small of my back would go as I walked. The stimulus of recovery from mishap was flowing through me and although, logically speaking, we were now worse off than before, because the whole bluff of our appearance was prejudiced, I felt more confident than at any time since we had started. I picked up my attaché case and we followed the path onto the road.

'Good,' said Sammy, 'now up here for about a mile, then cross-country again for a bit, over the main road, and we should hit the railway.'

I had gone a dozen yards when I heard a queer flapping noise as I walked. I looked down. The front part of the sole of my right boot had come unstuck with the water. I did not dare to tell Sammy.

We walked close to the side of the road so that we could leave it quickly if we heard someone coming. But the whiteness of the road made it easier than before to see that no-one was coming and our progress was less neurotic. It was no longer possible to pick out the lights of the camp individually. There was just a big distant glow and this too was comforting. I even began to think that we might reach Bromberg, but the idea of buying tickets and catching trains still seemed ridiculous.

When we came to the bend in the road where we had to strike across country again, Sammy said:

'What about a rest and some food?'

We sat down on open ground a few yards away from the road and unpacked raisins and chocolate. The camp had become a faint white glare in the sky from somewhere just below the horizon. As we lay on the grass, eating unrestrainedly for the first time for years, watching the black clouds chase each other across the starlit sky and hearing nothing but the wind in the darkness, something began to thaw inside me. I was aware that I was free. No voices — arguing, shouting, whining, asking, telling. No cramped little room. No cramped little brain. No demands. No obligations. No covering up. Just myself and the sky and the dark empty countryside and the wind blowing over it to eternity.

After about half an hour Sammy said:

'I suppose we'd better get on.'

'I suppose so.'

We started walking again.

The glare from the camp disappeared altogether below the horizon.

The going was easier than I had expected. We found a path that ran beside some ploughed land and followed it until we came to a different type of country. There were fields with hedges, mostly pasture, and there were woods dotting the rising ground. It was like parts of England. For me our journey became like a dream. The dark fields and the blurred trees against the skyline seemed to contain a great mystery. I felt that I could never be happier. I wanted to be allowed to wander through the night and this precious cold landscape for ever.

We walked down a sloping triangular meadow, enclosed on two sides by deep black woods. This place, I thought, is the heart of the earth.

I looked at my watch. It was half past one.

'We'll have to hurry up if we're going to catch the eight o'clock from Bromberg,' I said.

'My feet hurt,' said Sammy, 'I want a rest.'

'Let's rest when we get to the railway line. We'll know how much time we've got to waste then.'

'Oh, all right. But my poor dogs!'

We were walking together now. There did not seem much chance of meeting anyone in open country and we both felt more confident. I was almost dry and had even stopped worrying about the sole of my boot. I could not hear it flapping so often on the grass as on the road.

We discussed our plans.

'We've got to get to Bromberg before it's light. We mustn't be seen wandering about here in daylight.'

'No, especially with you covered in mud.'

'It depends on when the alarm is given. I suppose they might not discover the escape until morning appel. But even then it wouldn't be safe in Bromberg after about ten. Anyway I think we would look suspicious wandering about like this whether the alarm was up or not.'

'The next train after the eight o'clock is not until half past one.'

'We'll just have to make the eight o'clock then.'

'What worries me is: how are we going to get through the cordon which they'll obviously throw round Bromberg as soon as the balloon goes up?'

'We'll just have to hope it doesn't go up. Anyway, that's the point of walking up the railway line instead of the road.'

We had talked about all these things a hundred times before, but it eased our minds to talk about them again now when the unknown was so soon to become known.

Once we stopped by a ditch full of water and Sammy bathed his feet. I was thirsty and had already drunk all the water from the little medicine bottle I had brought with me, so I drank from the ditch. It was stagnant but not unpleasant.

We went on again.

After a long time we walked over a rise and saw a light below us in the distance.

'What the hell's that?' said Sammy.

We sat down under a hedge and he struck a match and looked at the map.

'Christ, I suppose it's that railway crossing,' he said, pointing at the crumpled piece of paper. The wind crackled the edges. 'It's much further south than we ought to be. Almost due east of the camp. Still, it means that we're nearly at the railway line.'

A few minutes later we found a path which led us to the main road we had expected. We stopped and listened before crossing it, and then ran over it quickly as if we were under fire. The light we had seen was brighter now and a dog was barking. We made a small arc to the north.

'I don't see any railway line,' said Sammy.

'It must be here somewhere. The ground rises in a minute.'

I stared at a single tree on the skyline just in front of us. Then I realized that it wasn't a tree but a railway signal. For some reason we had expected to find the railway line running flat across the countryside as it did on the map.

We ran up the embankment. It was high and very steep. Sammy stopped half way up for a rest and I was glad to sit down at the top. We could still see the light, only fainter again, down the line to the south.

'We must have a look at the map,' said Sammy. He took it out of his pocket and tried to strike a match.

I knocked it out of his hand.

'For God's sake be careful.'

'What the hell are you panicking about?'

'I'm not panicking, but it's mad to strike a light up here.'

'Well, we've got to see where we are, haven't we?'

'But there may be people about, especially close to that crossing.'

'Oh, balls.'

'Well, I'm not going to stay here while you do it.'

I walked away up the line. After I had gone a hundred yards I looked back. There was no sign of Sammy or the match. I felt mean and a fool. I went back. Sammy was folding up the map.

'Sorry,' I said, 'where are we?'

'That's the level crossing all right.' He pointed towards the light. 'It means we've about eighteen kilometres to do up the railway. What's the time?'

'Just after three. That leaves us about four and a half hours. We should just do it.'

'Oh Christ,' he said, 'my poor dogs!'

We set off. It was a single track and we again decided to take it in turns to walk ahead.

I soon discovered the disadvantage of walking along a railway line. The sleepers were too close together for it to be possible to walk a normal regular pace. The same thing applied to the spaces in between them, and it was impossible to put one foot on a space and another on a sleeper because the spaces were irregular in depth and always lower than the sleepers. I tried walking along the narrow path between the rail and the embankment but this was continually disappearing or leading off down the embankment. In the end I became resigned to a short mincing step over the sleepers. This was ridiculous and tiring.

I found Sammy sitting by the side of the line.

'God, this is hell, isn't it?' he said.

'Hell.'

'I'm just going to take off my boots for a minute.'

'All right.'

I looked at my watch.

'We might as well have a few raisins while we're about it,' he said.

He knew how to win me over.

We stopped like this two or three times during the night. Once we even left the line altogether for twenty minutes and sat in a little copse eating biscuits and cheese. We knew it was unpractical but at the same time it seemed madness not to enjoy food and freedom while we had them.

'We don't want to let ourselves get run down,' said Sammy.

Once we stopped to wash in a pond by the side of the line, and Sammy tried to brush the mud off my trousers and the bottom of my coat. My feet were sore too by that time and they felt better for being washed.

Once we passed through a deserted village station. The concrete platforms rose up to our shoulders on either side and there was a blurred building on one of them which presumably held the ticket office. It pleased me to think of the respectable citizens who would stand on these platforms next day, waiting for their train with tickets in their pockets and knowing nothing of the two figures that had passed through during the night.

We knew that about seven kilometres from Bromberg there was a bridge where the railway went over the canal. We expected it and dreaded it. It was generally supposed that all railway bridges in Germany were guarded. On the other hand people who had escaped often came back and talked of finding them unguarded. For weeks we had tried to find out about this bridge over the canal. We had gone to Vincent, the 'Intelligence' man.

'I think you can assume it's guarded,' he had said.

'Why assume it if it's not though?' said Sammy.

'Why not assume everything you can?'

'But we don't want to assume it,' I said.

'Oh, I see. Well, in that case I'll try and find out for you.'

'Don't strain yourself,' said Sammy.

Then we had tried asking Jack Nopps' tame German.

'English or American?' I had said, offering him a cigarette.

'Thanks.' He took a fistful of both.

'Supposing one ever succeeded in escaping from here, would it be safe to go over bridges — say, railway bridges — or would they be guarded?'

'Fatal. Guarded night and day,' he said, putting the cigarettes away into an inner pocket and lighting the stubbed out end of an old cigar.

When I told Sammy he said that he too had asked him the same question.

'What did he say?'

'He said they weren't guarded.'

'What did you give him?'

'Some chocolate.'

'I gave him cigarettes.'

'That brings us down to: "Which does Jack Nopps' goon like best, cigarettes or chocolate?" '

Then, just before the tunnel was due to break, Vincent had come to see us.

'I've got some information for you two,' he said. 'About that bridge you asked me about — I've collected a good deal of evidence and it seems impossible to say categorically one thing or the other. On the other hand I should say there is a tendency for it to be guarded and should avoid it at all costs.'

I could see that Sammy was going to say something rude.

'Thanks,' I said, 'thanks very much.'

And now it was only a kilometre away. Sammy caught up with me.

'I wonder which way it's tending at the moment,' he said. 'We'd better go slow and approach it very carefully. If we see it's guarded, we'll have to leave the line and try and get across the canal some other way. We'll toss up to see who goes first. Whoever goes last can stay well behind. If he hears a fuss he can run off into the darkness.'

He picked up a stone from between the sleepers and held out his hands.

'Left or right?'

'Left.'

'Sorry.'

He let the stone drop from his right hand.

'O.K.,' I said, 'keep well behind.'

I set off.

I expected to come to the bridge so often in the next ten minutes that when it did loom out of the darkness ahead of me, like a prehistoric monster lumbering out of primaeval slime, I was surprised to find it so close on top of me. I began to crawl along the side of the line towards it. I kept stopping to listen for the sound of a sentry but could hear nothing. The steel structure looked enormous from so close to the ground. When I was about ten yards away I saw the faint glitter of the water in the canal. Then I heard a solitary definite 'plop'. I stayed quite still on my hands and knees. A fish? Or a bored sentry throwing in a stone? I lay flat on my stomach and listened. There was no other sound. A minute passed and I was afraid that Sammy would be catching me up. Suddenly I could stand it no longer. If there was anyone there I should know in fifteen seconds. If there wasn't, there would be no harm done. I stood up quite noisily and walked quickly towards the bridge.

No-one at this end. The girders rang with the sound of my boots. The sound echoed up from the water beneath. But that was all.

There was no-one on the other side.

I ran back to tell Sammy. We crossed together.

'Good old bridge,' said Sammy, slapping the iron-work affectionately as if it were a horse. 'Of course you might give the man his due, he did only say it had a tendency that way.'

When we got to the other side we sheltered in the dark hollow under the bridge. Sammy lit a cigarette. He brought out the map and read it by pulling hard on the cigarette and then putting the glowing end close to the paper.

'Well, there we are,' he said, pointing to a place on the map where the caterpillar railway line crossed the worm canal.

It was comforting to know our position as definitely as that. It made me feel that in spite of confusion and Sammy's feet and my muddy trousers and flapping sole we had been competent.

It was a quarter past six. We had seven kilometres to go and about another hour of darkness.

'I don't think we're going to make it,' said Sammy, stretching himself flat on the bank.

'We've bloody well got to.'

'I don't think we will all the same.'

'We'll have to walk the last bit in daylight if necessary.'

'Risky,' he said.

'Well, don't be so bloody objective about it. It's you it's going to be risky for as well as me.'

140

'Oh, I know, I know.'

'Well then do something about it.'

'Oh, shut up.'

Our voices rose and boomed fatuously under the bridge.

Sammy lit another cigarette.

We sat in silence until we both began to get cold.

'Come on,' he said.

It was half past six. We might just catch the train but we had no chance of getting to Bromberg in darkness. Sammy realized this too, but we said nothing as we walked on together.

Even so the dawn surprised us. Somehow I had expected to see it coming and to be able to put on a spurt to beat it. But before it was possible to say definitely that night was going it was suddenly not night at all but day. We walked on without speaking, Sammy a few yards ahead. I could see him clearly now. His small hunched figure with its little legs prancing nimbly over the sleepers had a queer mad quality. He looked like an Edward Lear illustration to a Limerick. He turned round and looked at me.

'Oh, my God,' he said, stopping and doubling up with laughter. 'Oh, my God! I wish you could see yourself.'

'What's the matter?'

'You look absolutely mad. And bogus as hell.'

He went on chuckling to himself under his dark glasses for some minutes.

All this time it was getting lighter. We knew that we looked suspicious, especially walking down a railway line, but we were both too tired to bother much and just walked on. Sandy pinewoods stretched away on either side of the line. They had the dirty worn-out look of parts of Surrey.

'These woods are on the map. They're about two and a half kilometres from the town.'

We were walking on carelessly so that we forgot all about the line crossing the main road until we were there. The shock woke us up.

'What the hell are we going to do?' said Sammy. 'We can't go on like this, we look too awful.'

'I think we'd better hide up in the woods for a bit and get ourselves tidy. We'll have to give up the eight o'clock to Berlin. Perhaps there'll be a local one going in the right direction later in the morning. We can get some sleep that way.'

'It'll be risky in these woods. They don't look very thick.'

141

'The whole thing's pretty risky by now. Anyway we haven't done badly to get this far.'

Sammy thought for a moment.

'Let's go up the railway line rather than along the road anyway,' he said.

'All right.'

As we crossed over the road we saw a man coming down it towards us. Neither of us looked at him. We walked on and across the line. The road ran away from the line at a slight angle and after a minute I could see the man staring after us. He obviously thought it odd that we should choose the railway line in preference to the road. When we were enclosed by trees again, Sammy said:

'I can't stand much more of that. Let's hide up.'

We turned off into the wood. It was now quite light though the sun was not yet up. There were bushes in parts of the wood, also patches where small trees grew close together. Even so it looked much thicker from a standing position than when we were actually lying down in it. The woods were covered with intersecting paths as if people walked there often.

'It doesn't matter,' said Sammy lying down under a bramble bush, 'we haven't done badly to get this far.'

I lay down too. I couldn't remember whether it was he or I who had said that before. I was very tired. I expected to be woken up by a policeman or a forester. But I didn't care. I went to sleep.

3

The first thing I noticed when I woke up was the green purplish colour of Sammy's burnt face in the early morning light. A minute later long dancing fingernails of sunshine probed into the wood from the horizon. It was very cold.

Sammy moved a long curling bramble away from his eyes.

'What's the time?' he asked.

'A quarter past eight.'

He let the bramble fall again.

I went to look for some water. We seemed to be in the thickest part of the wood and there was no sound of anyone else. I found a stream and came back to tell Sammy and to fetch my washing things.

After we had washed and cleaned our teeth, and eaten great

quantities of bread and butter and corned beef, we felt better. Sammy brushed my trousers again.

'Is it coming off?' I asked.

'I don't think so, but it's going in which has much the same effect. It doesn't look too bad.'

We allowed ourselves some chocolate and sat down and talked about what we were going to do next. We both felt a pleasant recklessness about the future. Our original plan had collapsed and theoretically we were now due to be caught. But we had not been caught yet and every additional minute was a triumph in itself.

We decided that the woods would be one of the first places to be searched when the escape was discovered and that we ought to leave as soon as possible. We agreed to try and bluff our way into Bromberg by walking openly down the main road.

'Somehow I don't think they'll expect to find escaped prisoners walking down a main road in daylight.'

'We'll try and look like two ordinary chaps going to work.'

'When we get to the station we can find out the time of the first train going west, and then hide in the lavatory until it goes.'

Such a plan would have sounded hopeless and lunatic the day before. Now we both accepted it as reasonable and set off with confidence.

We had to cross the railway line to get to the main road and as we came out into the clearing a little train rattled up towards Bromberg. We stopped to let it pass, trying to look as if we always came out of a wood at that time of the morning. One man in a corner seat looked at us and then turned away, taking us for granted. This increased our confidence and we walked happily over the line to the main road.

We had gone about a hundred yards when Sammy noticed the flapping noise.

'What the hell's that noise?' he asked.

'I think it's the sole of my boot. It's come unstuck.'

'Oh, my God!' he giggled. 'Oh, my God!'

It did not seem to matter at all now. It was just one more contribution to the illogicality of our still being free.

It was pleasant to walk along a flat road after the railway line. We passed through a small village. A woman was hanging up some washing. A boy was sitting on a doorstep. A man, dressed rather like Sammy, was bending over a car in a garage. The sun shone. The air was clear. There was a quiet background of country sounds.

'Remember the name of that village,' said Sammy after we had passed through. 'We can say we've come from there if anyone asks us.'

A horse and cart was coming down the road towards us. We mumbled incoherently at each other to give the impression of conversation. As it passed the man who was driving said: ''Morgen.'

''Morgen,' shouted Sammy heartily. This frightened me because his accent was arrogantly English. But the man on the cart didn't look back.

'For God's sake, don't do that again,' I said.

'Sorry, I really meant it in a way.'

The cart had had a little notice printed on the side: 'Heinz Renner, Friedrichstrasse, Bromberg.'

'We'll say we're going to work for Heinz Renner,' I said.

The pine woods came down to the road on each side. Soon we would be seeing the outskirts of Bromberg.

'The aerodrome's somewhere near here,' said Sammy, 'if there's a barrier across the road anywhere it'll probably be here.'

I again became conscious of the flapping sole of my boot.

A short burst of tommy-gun fire ripped the quiet of the woods and Sammy jumped high into the air. There were shouts in the wood and I could see grey Luftwaffe figures in steel helmets running through the trees. There were more shots.

'Keep on walking,' said Sammy under his breath, 'but I think we've had it.'

I was far too frightened to do anything but walk.

An N.C.O. with a tommy-gun ran out of the wood onto the road about twenty yards ahead of us. His face was red and sweating and his helmet had slipped onto the back of his head. He ran up the road towards us. Other soldiers ran after him. There were more shots in the wood.

'Jesus Christ,' said Sammy, 'I don't like this. Quick, look as if we're having a conversation.'

I opened my mouth but could make no sound at all.

The N.C.O. and the soldiers ran straight past us into the wood. There were more shots and a whistle blew. Then there were no more shots. There was no more shouting. Bored and panting, the soldiers fell in by the side of the road. A few hundred yards lower down we passed the aerodrome.

My heart was beating so heavily that I thought I should have to sit down.

I don't know which was the greater shock: the first sound of the shots or the final realization that it was all only part of a military exercise and had absolutely nothing to do with us at all.

We walked down the hill into Bromberg.

I felt so confident that I stopped a Pole and asked him the way to the station.

'First on the left over the bridge. Second on the right.'

'Thanks very much.'

'Bitte schön.'

'Too easy,' said Sammy.

We arrived as the station clock struck a quarter to ten.

4

The more people we saw the more confident we became, for no-one paid any attention to us. There was a large bustling crowd in the hall of the station and we wandered through it trying to find out the times of the trains going towards Berlin. Our chief difficulty was communication between ourselves. I was described on my identity card as a French worker and Sammy on his as an Italian, these being the languages each of us knew best. Sammy's Italian was excellent, but I knew none at all. Sammy's French was elementary and mine was very little better. At first we tried talking together in a heavy schoolboy French, but we misunderstood each other so often that we were reduced to mumbling in English. This must have given us a furtive appearance as we had to withdraw from the crowds to discuss what we read on the notice boards.

Finally we decided to catch a local train to Schneidemühl, about fifty kilometres away to the west. It was due to leave at twelve o'clock.

I had left Sammy and was moving across to the booking office when a little man in S.S. uniform came up to me.

He rattled a money-box.

'Eine kleine Spende.' The Party made regular collections for winter relief.

I had no coins. The money which we had got in the camp was all in notes. I stuffed a one mark note into the little slot. The man looked surprised. I stuffed in another. He looked more surprised still.

'Danke schön, danke schön.'

I shuffled quickly away.

I was nervous buying the tickets and gave a whole five mark note too much. But the man, his eyes glazed with the bored superiority of the petty official merely thought that I was stupid and slapped the note back to me.

When I told Sammy about the man with the money-box he giggled.

'Of course he was surprised. An interpreter in the camp once told me that no goon ever gives more than ten pfennigs.'

We went up to the barrier.

'Your train doesn't go for another two hours,' said the ticket inspector.

'We'll wait.'

He punched the tickets and we passed through.

There was a long concrete subway underneath the station and steps led up from it at intervals to the separate platforms: one, three and five down one side; two, four and six down the other. We followed the sign for the lavatory.

A man was adjusting his bow tie in front of a mirror. This made it impossible for us to talk to each other. We took off our coats and washed. We took towels from our attaché cases (furtively, to avoid disclosing unnatural quantities of chocolate) and dried our hands and faces. The man was still there fiddling with the ends of his tie. I noticed that Sammy had 'Gift of the British Red Cross' stamped across his braces, and I put on my own coat quickly, hoping that he would do the same. But he was being purposely slow and played maddeningly with the taps.

Then the man at the mirror undid his bow tie altogether, pulled it off his neck and stuffed it away into his pocket. He pulled an ordinary tie out of another pocket, tied it quickly, turned down his collar and left.

We began to whisper.

'For God's sake put on your coat.'

'Quick, get in there.'

'We mustn't talk unless we're certain no-one's about.'

'All right, but get in.'

'And we'll stay until the train goes.'

'O.K.'

When I went to the door of the first cubicle and saw the little semi-circular 'Besetzt' on the outside it was as if someone had dropped a stone into the bottom of my stomach. A man must have been sitting inside listening to us. A feeble hope made me push the door and it swung open with a creak: the lock was broken; there was no-one there. I hurried to the other doors. 'Frei.' 'Frei.' 'Frei.' Sammy and I locked ourselves in next to each other.

Soon I saw a piece of paper being pushed under the partition between us.

'If you've anything to say, write it down.'

A few minutes later a large biscuit followed with some cheese and a note on the top: 'For the morale.'

I tore off a sheet of lavatory paper, wrote 'Thanks' on it and pushed it under the partition. Then I ate the biscuit and stared at the pornographic drawings on the wall.

Tiredness emphasized the strangeness of our position. A phrase which my grandmother always used when discussing the unorthodoxy of other people's behaviour went echoing through my head: 'Where will it all end, my dear? Where will it all end?'

I began to be frightened in a new way, in a way that was no longer either amusing or exciting as well. Perhaps it was because we were now quite trapped if anything should go wrong, or merely because I was tired, but I now began to understand the full strength of our enemy. It was no longer just a matter of a few guards to be outwitted. A whole society was against us and for practical purposes that meant all society, the whole world.

The main door into the lavatory opened. There was the clatter of a pail and the slobbering of some sort of rubber mop on the floor. The station char was on her rounds. In a few minutes I heard her in the next cubicle to mine, slamming up the seat and pulling the plug. The dirty water from her mop edged its way under the partition into my cubicle. She tried my door. I rustled the lavatory paper. She tried Sammy's door. He was more realistic. She moved away, singing to herself and slobbering around with the mop somewhere else in the room. Then she came back and rattled our doors impatiently. I realized that if she was determined to come in we should have to leave, but I could think of nothing to do but wait to see what she would do. I could hear her waiting and breathing on the other side of the door. She waited for about two minutes and then kicked the door and shouted in a German which I did not understand. I pulled the plug and left with a show of dignity.

147

She was fat and short and her thick black hair was done up in a bun at the back of her head. She muttered at me as I passed. I heard Sammy pull his plug and went outside to wait for him in the subway. The same S.S. man as before came up to me.

'Eine kleine Spende.'

I gave him some of the change I had got with the tickets.

Sammy came out and we went towards our platform. I slammed my feet as we walked so that the echoes rang in the hollow place. Somehow it released some of the tiredness in my head.

I bought a newspaper and we went and sat in the waiting-room. It was almost empty. There were two or three genuine foreign workers, whose dishevelled appearance gave me confidence. There was a tired looking young mother, a pale father and a screaming baby. A middle-aged woman in black was pushing plates along a marble-topped counter and flicking crumbs off it with a duster.

'We'll be able to have soup later,' said Sammy.

With the exception of fish it was the only unrationed food in Germany.

We sat down at a table which had fresh coffee stains on it.

'I'm going to sleep,' said Sammy, 'I think it's safer.'

I began to read the German High Command's communiqué in the newspaper.

'Between Tripoli and Mareth our rearguards . . .'

Tripoli. Somewhere between Tripoli and Mareth the world changed. Somewhere in that desert there was a point beyond which it was no longer necessary to disguise personality, hide in lavatories, fear everyone who passed. Tripoli didn't seem to have anything to do with this stuffy Polish railway station. The two worlds existed but there was no link between them. We were sitting on the Polish railway station and our world was one of humiliation and deceit.

Tiredness was like a bog into which I was sinking. The use of my muscles was becoming difficult. It was a great effort to put down the newspaper, to shift my bottom and to move my head. I saw the dark green glasses on Sammy's false looking nose and the pale father slapping the baby and the mother watching in despair. Then I was sucked into the sour sticky blackness of the bog.

5

Though I was awake for most of the next two days I never completely shook off sleep. The few short intervals of sleep which I did get, such as this one of an hour with my head slumped over my arm on the coffee-stained table of a station waiting-room, were never sufficient to absorb more than a small quantity of tiredness. Tiredness grew continually. Each sleep made me feel better than before I went into it, but always worse than after the previous sleep. For two days my limbs grew heavier and heavier. Material things became more and more remote as if held at a longer and longer arm's length. My mind had to work harder and harder for less and less result. I walked and thought in a cocoon of frustrated sleep, and people and incidents often took on the fantasy of a morning dream.

The waiting-room was suddenly full. There were people sitting on their luggage in the spaces between the tables and chairs. A big woman with a rucksack was looking down at me as if she expected me to offer her my seat. There was a waiting-room hum, occasionally broken by the yell of a child or someone trying to order coffee from a hot waiter.

Sammy leant across the table. His eyes flickered furtively under the green lenses.

'Une demi-heure encore,' he said slowly. 'Too much of a crowd for soup, I think,' he added.

It seemed the next minute that he leant across again and muttered: 'Ten minutes to go.'

Just after that we began to step over people and luggage on our way to the front door. The big woman sat down on my chair.

On the platform were two British soldiers in clean battle-dress, side hats and well polished boots. They were walking up and down in step, like officers waiting for a parade to begin. Their escort must have been close by but I could not see him. I wanted to talk to them, to say: 'Pst — you think I'm a German civilian, but I'm really an R.A.F. officer', but somehow they looked forbidding in their correctness as we slunk past, content to be despised by them too.

At the other end of the platform, standing discreetly at the back of the crowd in a check cap and a smart blue mackintosh, was Willy Myers.

It was such a surprise to see him that at first it did not seem a surprise at all. Then I looked quickly, guiltily away. I knew Sammy had seen him too because he said 'Good God!' quite loudly beside me. I allowed myself another look at Willy. He gave me the sort of smile one gives people one meets every day but wants to keep at a distance. Sammy and I turned towards the line and waited for our train.

'It's Willy Myers, did you see?'

'Er–oui, je l'ai vu.'

I think the dark glasses must have made it easier for Sammy to keep control of himself.

An official wearing a blue peaked cap came up to us.

'Where are you going to?'

'We're going to Schneidemühl. We're . . .' I reached into my pocket for our papers.

'That's right,' said the official, 'this is your train coming in now.'

We pushed our way into a third class carriage through elbowing widows and old men with baskets.

It was a long carriage without compartments and the brawl for seats continued inside. We sat down together among four soldiers. I wondered if Willy Myers had got a seat. The soldiers were combining their contempt for civilians with the joy of going on leave by talking very loudly and bouncing about on their seats as if there was no–one in the carriage. Occasionally the eyes of one of them would stray to see what sort of impression he was making.

The train started.

The jolting of the carriage and the hardness of the wooden seat worked into my disjointed dozing. I thought that I ought to keep awake and was continually forcing my head up and my eyes open. Every time I awoke the world seemed freshly raw. I was hot and sticky under my thick coat. The stuffiness of the carriage had a foreign smell. All round me German voices talking of market and rationing and bombing reminded me that I had no place among these people. One of the soldiers started to whistle an old dance tune called 'Goody-goody'. Sammy had taken his cap off. A woman was eating some bread and a pink juicy sausage.

We stopped at a station. Nakel. I remembered staring at the name on the local map.

I started thinking about the tunnel and our journey of the night before. I wanted to digest the experience. But it changed into a game I was playing at school. Someone was 'He' and we all had to go and hide. I went down into the fives courts, through the swimming bath, past the rifle range and out onto the main road. Where was I going? I wanted to stop. I was afraid.

We were at another station.

No-one seemed to get out, but a lot more people got in. A soldier took out a mouth organ and began to play 'Lilli Marlene'. Several women held string bags full of vegetables. The train started again.

To market, to market to buy a fat pig, to market, to market jiggedy jig. My own Lilli Marlene. There was a shout down the compartment behind me. I was wide awake.

People were fumbling in their pockets. I knew I looked calm but I tried to feel it too. After all, our papers were perfectly forged and Sammy swore that they were copies of an original.

It was only the ticket inspector. He clipped our tickets and passed on. Sammy never even woke up.

The next time I woke up I realized at once that I had been asleep for a long time. The carriage was almost empty. It was as if most of the people had been made to vanish by the wave of some magic wand. Even the soldiers had quietened down. I was refreshed. I looked at my watch and saw that we were almost due at Schneidemühl.

This, I thought, is quite an achievement. We are more than fifty miles from the camp.

Sammy was sitting upright, looking pleased with himself too.

On the platform we met Willy Myers again almost at once. He was greatly agitated because although he had bought himself a second class ticket he had got into a third class carriage by mistake. This had offended the ticket inspector who had insisted that he moved. When he had moved into a second class carriage he had found himself sitting within a few feet of one of the camp interpreters going on leave.

'Phew,' he said, 'it was a nasty couple of hours.'

'It serves you right for travelling second class,' said Sammy.

Walking slowly with Willy towards the station time-table Sammy and I discussed our plans. Our long term plans had always been extremely hazy, mainly because we had not believed that we should ever be in a position to use them. Sammy had talked mysteriously about some contact he knew of on the Belgian frontier. 'We'll make our way by train to Aachen,' he had said, authoritatively one evening in the camp, 'and then go on to this address I know.' And he had gone off to play roulette until bed time. (He won £500 that night, but the money was just about as unreal as the train to Aachen. You could not buy food or clothes or books with the £500 and you did not need a train when the furthest you could go in any direction was two hundred yards.) A day before the tunnel broke he had sewn a map of the Belgian frontier into the lining of his coat, but after that we were too busy with immediate practical problems to think anything more about it.

Now magically we were on a railway station fifty miles away from the camp. Though the Belgian frontier was not yet by any means real it was clear that reality was changing and that we should have to adapt our ideas to meet it.

'If there's a train going to Berlin tonight,' said Sammy, 'we'll go through with the old plan. We could always spend the night in the waiting-room of a big station without being noticed. If there's not, we'll think again.'

We nosed round one of the time-table boards.

There were no more trains to Berlin that day.

There was a train to Stettin with a change at Küstrin, in three hours time.

Sammy and I withdrew to discuss it.

'Why not?'

'O.K.'

'We'll try and get a boat. At least we'll have made a shot at it that way.'

'O.K.'

Willy Myers had disappeared. We looked for him for a few minutes and then decided to spend part of our three hours wait in walking round the town. We gave up our tickets and went out of the station. Half way up the hill we saw Willy.

We caught him up. He seemed rather annoyed to see us.

'Couldn't you wait for us?' asked Sammy.

'You looked so bloody furtive whispering together. Besides,' he pointed at my trousers, 'look at that mud. Socially, it's not giving me a chance.'

He stalked on offended. For a moment it was difficult not to believe in this prim bourgeois Dane (he had been the only one out of fifty to pose as a Dane) in his neat clothes and well polished shoes.

'What are your plans?' I asked.

I thought it was up to me to make amends in some way. He was flattered.

'Well, as a matter of fact,' he said, 'I haven't told anyone in the

152

camp my plans, but I don't mind telling you two now, in the circumstances.'

We had passed over the railway bridge and were walking down a row of seedy but pretentious villas.

'I know a German family somewhere up on the coast north of here. I shall go and see them and get them to give me a rowing boat to go to Denmark in. Once in Denmark, of course, I'm all right. I've got plenty of connections there.'

'Where does this family live?' asked Sammy.

'Well as a matter of fact I don't exactly know the name of the village. You see I never actually stayed with them. I was staying with a family somewhere inland and we just went up to this other family once for the day.'

'Oh,' said Sammy.

We walked down another row of villas. We told him our plan. Although to me it seemed no more impractical than his own, he was sceptical. He made the most of our having completely changed our plan en route.

'I've had this plan of mine worked out for nearly six months,' he said.

We walked about for an hour and then came back to the railway bridge.

'The dogs are getting tired again,' said Sammy. 'Let's go into the station and sit down.'

'There's another two hours to wait.'

'We can have some soup or something.'

'Oh, all right.'

'I think I'd better get out of town and find somewhere in the woods to sleep,' said Willy.

'So long, then. All the best.'

'Good-bye,' said Willy, raising his cap politely. 'Good luck.'

Sammy and I went back into the station.

6

When I asked for two tickets to Stettin the man at the booking office said:

'Are you a Pole?'

'No, a Frenchman.'

I took out my identity card.

He waved it away.

'All right,' he said, and gave me two tickets. 'Poles aren't allowed into Stettin without a special permit, that's all.'

I told Sammy.

'Oh, God,' he said, 'I hope they aren't going to be particular about Stettin.'

Two hours later we were on the train to Küstrin. We found a compartment to ourselves. It was a faster type of train and more comfortable than the first one. It soon grew dark and the darkness was friendly. The speed of the train too was on our side, for it gave greater value to every minute that we continued to survive. The train stopped once and a man and a woman got into our compartment, but they did not even look at us. I began to feel quite confident and enjoyed my sleep.

We were due at Küstrin in about half an hour and I was congratulating myself on our good luck in having had no identity check when the cry I had dreaded rang through the corridor.

'Ausweise, bitte. Papers, please.'

A neat middle-aged civilian came into the compartment.

'Ausweise, bitte, meine Herren,' he said in the polite inhuman voice of the German official.

I showed him mine. He looked at it and held it.

He asked for Sammy's. He looked at it for a moment and handed it back to him. Then he handed mine back to me. A policeman in uniform came into the carriage.

'Two Frenchmen,' the civilian said to him.

I was afraid this might lead to a muddle. Sammy's card said that he was an Italian.

'Where are you going to?' the policeman asked me.

'Stettin.'

'You've got your workers' cards, I hope?'

Something in his tone made me think that he wouldn't ask for them.

'Yes.'

'Because you'll need them to get into Stettin.'

They left the compartment.

A quarter of an hour later we came into Küstrin where we had to change.

'I don't like the sound of Stettin at all,' said Sammy on the platform.

'Neither do I.'

'Let's change back to the original plan.'

'O.K.'

I wondered what Willy Myers would have said.

'We'll spend the night in the woods outside this town and get a train to Berlin in the morning,' said Sammy.

We found the notice boards and saw that there was a train to Berlin at half past six the next morning.

'That'll do,' said Sammy.

I was just about to give up the tickets at the barrier when I remembered that they were for Stettin.

'We're coming back later,' I said, showing them to the collector.

He let us through.

I realized how much confidence we had gained in a day. Earlier this problem of the wrong ticket would have required long planning and argument.

'Now we'll get out of the town,' said Sammy.

This was easier said than done. It was quite dark and the black-out in Küstrin was merciless. It was all very well to pull out the luminous compass and say: 'We'll steer due north, we're bound to get out in the end,' but you can't steer a course through a brick wall or somebody's front door. We had to follow the streets and, though we tried to compensate for enforced deviations in one direction by voluntary deviations in the other, it was clear after an hour that we were making no progress.

'We should have got out of it by now,' I said.

'Perhaps it's just a very big town.'

'But there's no sign of it ending yet. We must have gone wrong.'

Sammy closed the compass with a snap and put it away in his pocket.

'Stop nagging, can't you? You're like a bloody old woman.'

'Well, it's all your fault for playing with that compass like a boy scout. We could have found our way out by common sense hours ago.'

'Funny sort of common sense that can see in the dark.'

'Oh, shut up.'

'Oh, for Christ's sake.'

We were standing on the corner of a pavement. A door close by with a little blue light just inside it kept opening and shutting. It was either a pub. or a lavatory. There was the high maniac shriek of a drunken girl. A soldier bumped into us, swore at the darkness and staggered on. We moved further up the road.

'O.K.,' I said to Sammy, 'let's try again.'

'Common sense or compass?'

'Compass.'

He pulled it out of his pocket.

The little yellow needle swung delicately through the darkness.

I had been suspecting for a long time that we had been going round in circles, but I was only certain when we crossed the same bridge twice from the same end. I did not want to annoy Sammy again so I said nothing.

When we got to the other side he shut the compass up again and put it away.

'You noticed, I suppose?' he said mournfully.

'Yes.'

'What the hell are we going to do?'

It was past eleven o'clock. The number of pedestrians was already growing smaller and we would soon look suspicious wandering round the town. A night wind blew over the bridge, and the sound of the river underneath was impersonal and cold.

There was an area of what looked in the darkness like waste ground stretching down to the river from our end of the bridge.

'What about down there?'

It looked the sort of place where rubbish is tipped in spite of notices. There wasn't likely to be much cover.

'You mean down there?'

'Yes.'

'I suppose we could go down and look.'

It was not a rubbish dump. We were walking down a cart track. The ground was uneven on either side and there were stray clumps of bushes. It seemed an odd place to find in the middle of a town. Probably it was a very ordinary place; we never knew. The wind and the darkness and our sense of the enmity all round us made it mysterious. Below, the river catching a drop of light from a momentary gap in the clouds flashed a cold star at us and rushed on invisible.

We left the track and found a gentle hollow sheltered by bushes. We lay down for sleep. I was very cold and I curled up and pressed my head and body into the ground to try and get below the wind. But though I had longed for sleep I could think of nothing but the cold. Tiredness merged with the ache of cold in my thighs and shoulders and with the shivering round my sides.

Sammy knelt up from the little dark ball he had been on the grass beside me.

'This is impossible,' he said, 'let's go and look for some cover.'

'Yes.'

I was so cold that I was beginning to hope that we would be caught and given the warmth of a cell.

About twenty yards away we found two houses set together in isolation in the middle of the strange heath. There were no lights and no sounds. In the front garden of one of them there was something that looked like a low wooden hut. We climbed over the garden wall and looked at it.

It was tilted onto one side and when Sammy crawled into it it tilted over onto the other side with a crash and a rattle of stones. I waited for a minute to see if anyone had heard us. The houses still stood cold and dim in the darkness. I crawled into the little hut.

'For Christ's sake be careful,' said Sammy, 'it's not safe to move.'

I crawled out gently again to see if I could discover the cause of the tilt.

I saw that the hut was the top of a disused dove-cot, which had been broken or cut off its pole. The stump of the pole remained and acted as a pivot. It was obviously dangerous to move any weight from one side of the dove-cot to the other. I crawled in again and told Sammy.

We lay together on the downward slope. There was no straw or covering of any sort inside but the wooden walls were shelter from the wind and I slept a little.

When I woke up I was as cold as if I had been lying in the open. It was the ache of the cold which made sleep impossible.

Sammy was awake too.

'Christ, it's bloody cold.'

'Have you been asleep?'

'I think so.'

We clung together like lovers for warmth. Sometimes one or the other of us slept for about ten minutes, but what I remember of the night besides the cold was the sound of a distant clock striking every quarter. I longed for the time when we could consider it morning and move and get warm.

'How early do you think we can leave?'

'The train goes at 6.30.'

'We could leave at five. Lots of people must go to work about that time.'

'Yes. We'll try to look as if we're going to work.'

Sammy snored once or twice and I copied him to pretend to myself that I was going to sleep.

Sometimes the wind suppressed the sound of the clock striking, and when I heard it again I would find with joy that we were a whole quarter of an hour nearer morning than I had expected. Sometimes the gap between quarters would seem so long that I would be sure that I had missed a chime. Then it would strike the quarter that I hoped I had missed.

'Listen, I think there's a sentry on the bridge.'

The wind rubbed against the wooden sides of the dove-cot.

'I can't hear anything.'

'It's gone now.'

'We must be careful when we move anyway.'

'How long before we move?'

'Only another two hours.'

'Christ.'

At four o'clock I disentangled myself from Sammy and crawled out. I walked quickly and softly round and round the dove-cot trying to get warm. I practised a silent version of the hugging exercise which taxi-drivers use. The clouds had broken and run before the wind. They straggled in flight across the black sky and the stars.

I crawled in beside Sammy feeling warmer. But the ache was in my bones again within five minutes and spoilt all sleep. I went out again and walked about the garden. This time I thought I heard the nailed boot of a sentry on the bridge. But the wind and the river made it difficult to be sure.

At a quarter to five Sammy crawled out.

'I can't stand it any longer,' he said, 'let's go.'

'What if there's a sentry on the bridge?'

'Too bad. We must walk normally along the pavement as if we always went to work at this time.'

We picked up our attaché cases and climbed over the garden wall.

As we crossed the bridge we saw the sentry leaning against the parapet on the other side of the road. His steel helmet gave him the familiar impersonal look. We walked along the pavement with a determined everyday step. I tried to think myself into the part of a man going to work on the railway. Without moving from the parapet the sentry turned and looked at us. Then he turned back and looked at the water again. We passed over the bridge towards the railway station.

We found it easily without having to ask the way. There was still an hour before our train left, but we decided to go straight to the platform and find a lavatory. All the lights were on in the station, but it seemed deserted. It had a queer clinical look as if we were walking about an enormous dirty hospital.

Though it was pleasant to be warm and out of the wind I was already feeling the effects of the night. My limbs and brain were moving slowly, automatically, and there was a stiffness round my eyes.

We passed through a ticket barrier with no-one standing at it, walked along a subway and up onto the first platform.

'We'll feel better when we've had a wash,' said Sammy.

We were just going into the lavatory when I remembered the tickets.

'We haven't got the right tickets. We've only got the ones for Stettin.'

'My God, I'd forgotten all about the tickets.'

'So had I. I'd better go back and fetch them.'

Sammy sat down on a platform seat and I went back the way we had come.

This time there were two policemen and a railway official standing at the barrier. They were talking loudly and laughing. Their voices rang in the subway.

I tried to walk past them.

'Hi! Where are you going?'

'I just want to go outside for a minute.'

'Have you got a ticket?'

I remembered the ticket to Stettin.

'Yes.'

I pulled it out of my pocket.

'Who are you? A Frenchman?'

'Yes.'

They all laughed.

159

'All right. Go on.'

There was a girl in the booking office. I had been frightened by the policemen and stumbled in my German asking for the two tickets.

'Who are you?'

'A Frenchman.'

'Let's see your identity card.'

It looked less impressive now than when I had first seen it. Some of the forged printing had smudged a little through being rubbed in my wallet.

'I've never seen an identity card like this before.'

'Well, it's the one I was issued with.'

I wondered if Sammy was getting worried waiting for me on the platform and whether he would be able to get away if I was caught.

The girl turned the identity card over and over as if this would give her some clue to the queer document. I thought of the mild little Yorkshireman who had made it with mapping pen and Indian ink in the afternoon stuffiness of the barrack block.

People were forming a queue behind me.

'I suppose it's all right,' said the girl.

She handed it back to me and gave me my ticket.

The policemen and the ticket collector laughed again when they saw me and waved me through.

Sammy was walking up and down the platform. He looked the sort of person who is impatient to get at his day's work.

'What the hell have you been doing?' he asked, agitated.

'Come into the lavatory and I'll tell you.'

'I was getting quite worried.'

'You needed to be.'

It was a smart modern type of lavatory. There were separate compartments with wash basins and water closets together in each. We both locked ourselves into the same one. While Sammy took off his coat and shaved I sat on the top of the seat and told him what had happened.

'Oh, my God!' he kept saying, chuckling to himself in the mirror as I talked, 'Oh, my God!'

'I'm sure she knew it was phoney, but she just couldn't be bothered to do anything about it.'

'Oh, my God!'

He looked fresh and respectable when he had shaved. While I took off my coat and tied the towel round my neck he took my place on

160

the seat. The water in the basin was pleasantly hot.

'Did I ever tell you about the time I nearly drowned an Air Marshal in the North Sea?' he said.

'No.'

'We were supposed to be doing a black-out test over Norwich . . .'

The cold and anxiety of the night in the dove-cot were forgotten. This was suddenly a game we were playing and we were enjoying it very much. We packed up our washing and shaving things and unlocked the door.

A man was standing just outside it staring at us like a fascinated child. It was the spectacle of two men coming out of the same lavatory which seemed chiefly to astonish him. We had heard no-one come in. He was just there as someone in a dream is there.

We tried to keep up a show of confidence by walking slowly over to the large communal mirror and adjusting our ties. I was wondering how long he could have been there. We had only talked in whispers, but if he knew English he would probably have recognized the language. Anyhow the fact of the two men whispering together in the same lavatory, whatever the language, was suspicious.

The man made a show of combing his hair and left.

'That's torn it,' said Sammy.

'Let's get out of here.'

I was dismayed at the thought of being deprived of our game just as we were beginning to enjoy it.

It was too late. We saw him about thirty yards down the platform talking to two civilians in hats and pointing towards the lavatory door as we came out of it. We tried to look calm. Sammy strolled to the edge of the platform and looked enquiringly up and down it for a train. It was not our platform but he looked quite innocent, almost pathetic. The two civilians were walking quickly towards us.

'Good morning, gentlemen. Your papers, please.'

'Kriminalpolizei,' added the other apologetically.

It was all very polite.

Each took an identity card. They exchanged them. One detective seemed more satisfied than the other.

'What are you doing here?' the unsatisfied one asked.

'We're travelling for Krupps — specialist armament workers. We've just been doing a job here. Now we're going on to Berlin.'

I had practised the phrases a hundred times.

161

The satisfied detective nodded and looked at his watch.

The unsatisfied one said:

'Have you got anything to prove this? Any letters or anything?'

We had a letter. We had decided to use it only in an extreme emergency, because it could not stand close examination. It was written in long-hand by a prisoner who knew German perfectly and it purported to come from 'the works manager of Krupps'. The heavily embossed heading 'KRUPP' at the top of the paper designed by the man who had forged the identity cards, was the only substantiation of this. The letter was addressed to 'all whom it might concern'. It informed them that the Frenchman, Pierre Durand, and the Italian, Giuseppe Mantini were travelling through various armament factories on work in connection with new weapons and it asked them to give these two foreign workers every assistance.

'Yes,' I said, 'we've got a letter.'

A train was drawing in at a platform on the other side of the station. The satisfied detective grew impatient and pointed out the train to the other who said:

'Moment.'

'Let's see your letter,' he added.

The train stopped. I gave him the letter and he read it through under his breath.

'For God's sake, man, come on — the train!' said the satisfied one, and started to move away.

The other read the letter through again to himself and then handed it back reluctantly. He said nothing but ran off down the platform after the other to catch the train.

We watched it anxiously. It began to move while they were still on the footbridge. They shouted, but it paid no attention. They ran down the platform, jumped onto the moving train and buttoned themselves in.

'If this goes on much longer,' said Sammy, 'I shall have a nervous breakdown.'

We walked quickly to our platform where we had only a quarter of an hour to wait for the express to Berlin.

After what had happened to us at Küstrin the check of identity papers which took place on this train seemed a mild affair and we were not in the least surprised when we survived it. We were now confident that we would survive anything.

In Berlin the sun was shining from a blue spring sky. I understood

162

from the conversation of a man and a woman in our carriage that there had been an air raid two nights before. There were isolated signs of damage: some houses down by the railway, a burnt-out church — less on the whole than could have been seen from a train passing through London at that time. But the effect of morning sunshine on the roofs of a terrorized city was much the same and even to us sitting in the train it seemed very good to be alive.

7

Just outside the Charlottenburg station we sat on a public seat in the middle of a square. A straight broad street led off it into the city. The sun still shone and the trees on the pavements were sticky with buds. I wanted to wander round Berlin but Sammy said that this would be silly.

We discussed our plans. By now some general principles had been accepted by both of us and this saved much time and bad temper. We agreed that we were travelling to Aachen; that, where possible, we would travel by short stages and slow trains (there was a theory, which seemed to be confirmed by our experience, that identity checks occurred only on the fast trains); and that we would spend time between trains in lavatories or in waiting rooms.

We had to stop talking when an army officer and a tall smart woman came and sat on the other end of the seat. They looked resentful at finding such a class of person there and soon moved away.

Sammy furtively brought out a corner of his silk handkerchief-map.

'Where shall we take the next train to?' he asked.

It was just a matter of going in as straight a line as possible towards Aachen. It was worth making the line a little crooked however if it saved us from having to wait about on stations for long periods.

When we got back to the Charlottenburg station we found that the most convenient immediate destination would be Stendhal. We bought our tickets, drank coffee and soup in the second class refreshment room, munched raisins and chocolate in the lavatory and caught the train.

It rattled out through the suburbs into the still sunny afternoon which lay over the Central German Plain. The flat open countryside was heavily cultivated, and from the carriage window it had the monotony of a calm sea. The carriage was comfortably empty. There was an atmosphere of siesta. I felt warm and secure as the little train went steadily about its business, dropping some people at country stations and picking others up, but always after a few minutes taking us further and further on our way. I tried to think about Aachen and Sammy's Belgian contact, but it still seemed unreal and I was content to look out of the window and think that in an hour or two we would be in Stendhal.

There was no check of identity papers, and I got out at Stendhal confident and happy.

'That definitely proves the theory that there are no identity checks on the slow trains,' I said.

'Not necessarily.'

It maddened me to have my confidence questioned.

'What do you mean?'

I tried to think that I had mistaken his tone, but I could see from the way his eyes were concentrated down either side of his nose that there was trouble coming.

'Just what I say. I don't think it necessarily proves anything of the sort.'

My confidence was transformed into wild irritation and unreason.

'Oh, Christ, what's the matter with you?' I said.

He looked at me with offended dignity.

'Absolutely nothing at all, thank you very much.'

We walked a little way down the platform in silence.

'You feeling all right yourself?' he asked suddenly.

'Oh, shut up.'

The fact that we had to talk out of the sides of our mouths made this sort of quarrelling very tiring.

When we came to the time-table boards I read them as if nothing was wrong. The fast trains were printed in red and the slow ones in black. There was a red train to Hanover in half an hour's time. There was a black train, also to Hanover but stopping at every station on the way, ten minutes later.

I drew away from the board so that I could talk it over with Sammy. He went on looking at the board for a little while and then came up to me.

'There's a slow train in forty minutes,' I said before he could have a chance of speaking.

'There's a fast one in half an hour.'

'Yes, but I thought we'd agreed that we don't want to use fast trains because of the identity checks.'

'I think the slow trains are a waste of time. I want to get on.'

We drifted down the platform again.

'Well, we can't hang about here much longer like this. We'll begin to look suspicious.'

We walked down the steps to the subway. It was cool and empty. For the first time we were able to face each other with our arguments.

'I think you're being most unreasonable,' I said. 'You know we've agreed on this. We're much safer on the slow trains. They just don't bother about checks on them. That last train proved it.'

'What if it did? We know our papers are good enough to survive checks. And the longer we expose ourselves on these train journeys the greater the general risk. We'd get to Aachen in half the time if we went by express from now on.'

'Well, I think it's absolute madness.'

Sammy shrugged his shoulders. There was no way out of this nightmare quarrel.

'If you feel as strongly about it as all that,' said Sammy, 'you'd better go on by yourself.'

The flesh on my cheeks began to twitch as if pulled by tiny invisible reins. God, I thought, what a miserable humiliating end to our escape. I could not understand how it had happened so suddenly. Half an hour before I had been almost completely happy.

'All right,' I said, 'I bloody well will.'

I had only gone a few yards when I stopped and turned round. Sammy had started to follow me.

'All right,' he said, 'we'll go by the slow train.'

'No, no . . . Well, wait a minute . . .'

I felt thankful and ashamed.

'Yes,' said Sammy, 'this time we'll go by the slow train. We'll start up the argument again when we get to Hanover.'

I knew quite well that I would never risk that sort of argument again.

'All right. But I daresay you're right, you know. I mean . . .'

My apology tailed away in embarrassment. Sammy was embarrassed too. We both needed a silence.

The train from Stendhal to Hanover was very like the train from

Berlin to Stendhal. We settled ourselves into corner seats of the long 'bus type carriage and as soon as the train moved I began to feel better. The journey would take five hours. That meant that we were safe for another five hours.

I dozed between stations. As before, few people got on or off. The sun was a little lower in the sky, but it still shone brightly over the growing corn. Inside the carriage silky threads of cigarette smoke weaved lazy patterns over our heads before being sucked into the gaps at the top of the windows and rushing out with the speed of the train. I stared at Sammy's sleeping face. He was a good companion: the sort of person you could quarrel with without it mattering.

After some time my bottom got very sore on the hard wooden seat and my back ached. I went to the lavatory for a change of scene, and stood there for a time eating chocolate. It was a very dirty lavatory and something had gone wrong with the flushing arrangements so that I soon found I had not got much of an appetite for chocolate.

I came back and stared out of the window again. There were still several hours to go.

I had ceased to pay much attention to the stations we stopped at, although I was always happier once the train had restarted. But I had long ago dismissed the idea of any trouble before Hanover. So I was astonished when the policeman in light blue-green uniform came into the carriage and asked for papers. It was at least ten minutes since the last stop. He must have been working his way up the train. I kicked Sammy's foot and he woke up, quickly replacing a look of panic by one of elaborate calm.

The policeman stopped in front of me.

'Ausweis, bitte.'

I had already got out my identity card. I handed it to him and looked out of the window. I looked out of the window for a long time. Then I thought that this would be unnatural for anyone under the circumstances and looked back at the policeman. He seemed puzzled by my identity card and was turning it over and over as the girl at Küstrin had done. He looked down at me.

'You're a Frenchman,' he said.

'Yes.'

He read the identity card all over again.

'Are you alone?' he asked.

'No, there's a fellow worker with me, an Italian.'

166

I pointed at Sammy. The policeman looked across at him and nodded, but did not ask for his identity card.

I began to feel alarmed.

'Have you any other papers?'

'I've a letter here from our firm, Krupps.'

He read it through slowly. It seemed to impress him. He even handed my identity card back, but he did not stop asking questions.

'Where are you going to now?'

'To Hanover.'

'Why?'

'We're engaged on the installation of new plant into armament factories. I can't say more than that. In fact I shouldn't really be talking about this at all. But that is our job.'

'Where have you come from?'

'Stendhal.'

'What were you doing there?'

'We had to visit a factory there.'

'What was the name of the factory?'

'Karl Brückner A–G.'

'In what street?'

'Friedrichstrasse.'

He took Sammy's identity card.

I could not decide whether he was really suspicious or just stupid and covering his perplexity with this calculated thoroughness.

He handed Sammy back his card. With the same look on his face as when he had asked us all the questions, he saluted.

'Danke, meine Herren.'

He moved over to the man sitting on the other side of the compartment.

Sammy put his identity card slowly away into his pocket, but as he turned to look out of the window I noticed that his face was a purplish green.

A few minutes later I heard the policeman putting the same sort of questions to someone else further down the carriage. I strained my neck to see what was happening. A foreigner was in trouble. He was a dark, olive-skinned man and his face was hot and flummoxed as he stared helplessly at the policeman, answering his questions. All the time his hands were searching his pockets for something. But all they found was torn bits of paper and string.

'I have lost it,' he said slowly in a queer accent.

A harsher note crept into the policeman's voice.

The train stopped soon afterwards and through the window I saw the olive-skinned man being led away down the platform. The policeman had the look of a man who thinks he has done a really good job of work. When Sammy saw what had happened he nudged me with his foot and put his hand over his mouth like a naughty little boy.

8

When the train drew into Hanover it was almost dark. The station was full of the noise of steam and wheels and the platforms were like congested pavements. This activity caught us unawares after the stuffy peace of the train. We were pushed along the platform by a current of anxious men and women, and I lost Sammy and found him again several times before we were sifted by the barrier. The main hall of the station had been damaged in air-raids and wooden scaffolding and blocked exits increased the confusion. The only advantage was that against the background of noise we could talk to each other in English without being overheard.

When we found the arrival and departure board I took care to forestall trouble.

'There's a fast train at one o'clock.'

Sammy was a good tactician. He knew when he had won.

'Can't we get a slow one before that?'

'I don't think we want a slow train even if there is one. I quite agree with you: we don't want to hang about more than we can help.'

'Just as you like. I don't want to persuade you.'

'No, I want to get on too. We'll get the one a.m. express to Cologne.'

'O.K.'

We went to the waiting-room. There were nearly seven hours to wait.

It was a very large waiting-room, like a Lyons Corner House. We found two seats at a table near the door. I went and bought some black coffee from a bar at the other end of the room, then some beer and then some more black coffee. Sammy looked at my watch.

'Good God!' he said, 'is that all? I feel as if we've been here for days already.'

Various people came and sat down on the other seats at our table, looked round the room for a few minutes or read their newspapers and then went away to catch trains. We watched the population of the waiting-room change two or three times over. After about two hours we agreed to take turns going for a walk round the station. I went first.

People were still bustling about with as much determination as before. A porter riding on an automatically propelled trolley drove ruthlessly through the crowd, dispersing worried looking women carrying suitcases and pale well-dressed men in pince-nez. There was a short queue outside the lavatory, but it was moving quickly and I went in and had a wash. My clothes were sticky and rough on my skin, but after washing my face and neck I didn't notice this so much. I wandered round the station again. The dim blue lighting added urgency to everybody's business and I felt out of place with nothing to do. In one part of the station there was an exhibition of captured allied equipment in aid of the German Red Cross. I wanted to go in, but so few other people were visiting it that I thought I should be conspicuous. I went back to Sammy.

'There's just been an identity check,' he said.

My heart jumped.

'What happened?'

'They arrested two scruffy looking chaps on the other side of the room. They never asked me for mine.'

He was obviously proud of his social success.

When he went out for his walk I dozed with my head slumped on the table, and when I woke up he must have been back some time for he was leaning back in his chair with his eyes shut.

'Did you have a nice walk?'

'Got into conversation with a tart.'

'What did she say?'

'She said she always found foreigners the most interesting.'

There were still three hours to wait.

Sammy had bought an evening newspaper. I read the High Command communiqué and then went to sleep again.

A young Luftwaffe Gefreiter with long black hair came and sat down opposite us with his girl. They were confidentially amorous and paid no attention to us.

In the end they sat us out. Sammy tapped my watch and raised a bored eyebrow. It was half past twelve. As our chairs scraped backwards over the floor the Luftwaffe man slipped his hand into the girl's blouse.

There was the same bustle as existed all over the station in the queue at the booking office. I was drowsy and could not make myself part of it. I gave the man more money than was necessary for the tickets.

'Come on, wake up.'

He pushed the notes back at me.

The woman behind me clicked her tongue impatiently.

We found our platform and waited for the express to Cologne. There were constant announcements about trains on the station loudspeakers and we soon heard the first mention of our express. It would be arriving in ten minutes time. It would be arriving in five minutes time. A mistake had been made. The express for Cologne was late: it would be arriving in eight minutes time. Second and third class carriages would be at the rear and middle of the train, first class carriages at the front. This announcement about the position of the carriages was repeated three or four times.

A young man in a wide brimmed hat walked past, looking at us. He turned and walked past us again. From the corner of my eye I saw him walking round behind us, like an officer inspecting troops. He came and stood in front of us.

'Excuse me,' he said, 'the front part of the train will come in here. The third class carriages will be further down the platform.'

The strange thing was that he did not say it unpleasantly, but rather as if he was trying to save us trouble.

'Oh, thank you very much.'

'Not at all.'

'What bloody cheek,' said Sammy as we moved down through the crowd.

9

The express came in slowly but powerfully. A huge stallion of a train it snorted and made the platform tremble.

The rush for seats approached a panic and it was very difficult to keep with Sammy. When I had fought through the pressure at the door I saw that there was no chance of a seat. It was already almost impossible to walk down the corridor. There was a sudden violent surge of people. I stuck out my elbows, holding the standing room I had won for myself in the corridor, but Sammy was swept past me. I watched him come to rest some yards further down.

The train was scheduled to stop three times on the seven hour journey to Cologne, but it looked as if the crowded conditions would make any identity check impossible. I was surprised when soon after the first stop I heard the familiar 'Ausweise, bitte,' in the corridor. The man, an elderly civilian in a soft grey hat, came fighting towards us. He was finding it impossible to carry out a thorough check and was asking individuals for their papers at random. I wondered if he would ask me. I suddenly began to hope very much that he wouldn't. A few minutes before I had thought that I was confident about our papers. But now I realized that the fact that they had been so successful so often was in itself no guarantee that they would always be. Each policeman or detective saw them for the first time and each had a completely fresh chance to suspect them. It was only because I had got used to this chance being missed that I was confident, but the papers were still just as false as they had always been.

The detective was forcing his way towards me. It was some time since he had asked anyone for their papers. The train rocked furiously over some points in the darkness.

'You,' he said, stopping and tapping the man next to me on the chest, 'your papers, please.'

The man had a lot of difficulty in getting them out of his pocket in the crush. The detective shone a little blue lamp onto the Ausweis and handed it back.

'And you?' he asked, turning to me, 'who are you?'

'An armament worker.'

He nodded and elbowed his way to other parts of the train.

The train rushed fiercely through the night, rocking us as we stood in the dimly lit corridor and sometimes knocking us helplessly on top of each other as it rattled over complicated points. The corridor emptied itself a little at one of the stops and when we started again I saw that Sammy was now only one place away from me. There was a little woman in black between us and she turned to Sammy and started talking to him. She said something about opening the window, but Sammy didn't understand it at all.

'I'm afraid my friend doesn't speak German,' I said.

'Oh, I see. Thank you.'

She looked at Sammy as if she thought he ought to go to a doctor.

'Well, would you mind opening the window for me? I feel rather faint. Thank you. Thank you so much.'

The next time we stopped I looked out to see if I could read the name of the station.

'Hamm,' said the little woman.

I remembered how the name had become something like a music-hall joke in England during the early part of the war because of its regular appearance in Air Ministry communiqués. And I remembered myself flying over it in the nose of a Hampden, staring down through the darkness at the little red fires.

There was another identity check soon after that. There was more room now and the uniformed policeman was able to look at everyone's papers in turn. He shone a torch from my identity card to my face and back again. He stared at the card and brought his torch close up to it. He rubbed the lettering with his thumb. I got the impression that he suspected the document but didn't want to admit that he had never seen one like it before just in case it might be a real one. He continued to look at it for about five minutes and then handed it back without saying a word. On the whole I was glad that it was dark and that he had a lot of other papers to examine.

The night went on and on, like the train.

When we made our third stop my watch told me that it was just before dawn, but it was as dark as ever. We knew that this was the last stop before Cologne. Sammy and I were able to get seats in one of the carriages. It was very good to sit down.

Soon it would be light and soon after that we would be at Cologne, thirty miles from our destination at Aachen. For the first time I began to think seriously about Aachen. What sort of man would the 'contact' be? Would we find him easily? Would he hide us, or put us in touch with the Belgian Underground straight away? What would the Belgian Underground be like? Would they try to get us out through Switzerland or Spain? I looked through the window and saw that once again the moment of dawn had escaped me. I watched the new day as it lay dully over fields and roads and farms. Then the sun broke over the horizon, leaping across the frosty grass, stirring the day to life and warming my cheek through the window.

Sammy looked comfortable and happy in his corner. I think he felt much as I did: the night had been like another long tunnel. Now we were through it and out on our own. All the first part of our escape seemed far away, an old story. We had crossed Germany and were beginning a new adventure. When I heard yet another cry of 'Ausweise, bitte', in the corridor, I regarded it merely as a bore.

The fat young man in civilian clothes to whom I handed my well-worn identity card disliked it at once.

'Have you any other papers?'

He kept the identity card.

I handed him the letter. He folded it up and put it into his pocket.

I realized that something was going wrong. I began to tell him our story. He listened politely, but somehow I could not bring the same enthusiasm into the details as before. It disconcerted me that he had not asked any questions, and I felt that I was telling the story to someone who knew it already.

'I see,' he said when I had finished. 'Well, you'll just have to come along with me for questioning at Cologne.'

He had collected Sammy's identity card and put it into his pocket with mine and the letter. The other people in the carriage were eyeing us queerly.

'We're in rather a hurry,' I said, 'we've got a business appointment in Cologne and we can't miss it. It's important armament work.'

'All right,' said the fat young man, 'I don't expect we'll keep you long.'

A uniformed policeman, who was his partner on the patrol, came into the carriage and had the situation explained to him. They whispered together like parents discussing something important in front of the children. The policeman stood just outside the door of the carriage while the fat young man continued the patrol. Every time I looked at the policeman I caught his eye and he looked quickly away. Sammy was looking unconcernedly out of the window, but I think he too knew that there was now no hope.

The three of us got out onto the station at Cologne and the fat young man joined us. He had bright red cheeks and was very energetic, bouncing about the platform taking decisions and changing them and shepherding us in and out of the crowds. There was little sign of air-raid damage and this added to the accumulating humiliation.

He led us down some passages and past a barrier marked 'No Admittance'.

'It won't take long, will it?' I asked feebly, 'we've got this appointment and . . .'

'All right, all right,' he said.

He pushed open a door and we were in an underground room full of blue-green policemen. They did not pay much attention to us as we came in because they were examining a dirty looking fair-haired man who had apparently been taken off another train.

He was speaking German with great difficulty.

'I was . . . factory somewhere else . . . Now I come here . . . Dutchman . . . I look for work . . .'

One of the policemen snapped a pair of handcuffs onto him while he was still talking and bundled him away. The fat young man pushed us forward.

'Who are you?' he shouted harshly, conscious of his audience.

The other policemen crowded round, interested, like medical students at an operation.

I began the old story. I knew he didn't believe it, but I couldn't bring myself to give it up. Besides I didn't know if Sammy was ready to give it up. I looked across at him for some sign of what he was thinking, but I saw only the Italian machinist staring placidly at me from under his dark glasses.

'. . . installation of factory plant in connection with new weapons . . .'

The fat young man grew bored. Again I was not telling the story well and when he moved over to a desk with our identity papers in his hand and put a watchmaker's magnifying glass into his eye I tailed away. He studied the papers calmly for about a quarter of a minute while the other policemen held their breath. Then he threw the magnifying glass and the papers onto the desk and pulled a revolver out of his pocket.

'Forged,' he screamed, and rushed at me, 'these papers are forged!'

He stopped when the revolver stuck into my stomach. His working red face blotted out the rest of the room. I put up my hands.

'British officers — escaped prisoners of war,' I panted.

His face relaxed. He stepped back and put the revolver on the desk. As he wiped the sweat from his forehead there was an approving murmur from the circle of policemen. Sammy took off his dark glasses.

'Of course,' said the fat young man, 'I knew that you were prisoners immediately. You have come from the Oflag in Poland.'

'You'd heard about the escape then?'

'It's known all over Germany,' said a goggling simple looking policeman close to my ear.

'They have all been caught again, of course,' said another.

'I would have known you were prisoners anywhere,' said the fat young man, 'and do you know how?'

I thought it was necessary to make him feel as pleased with himself as possible.

'No. How?'

'By your leather boot-laces.'

'Elementary, my dear Watson,' said Sammy.

'That and the khaki clothing,' said the fat young man. 'They told us you would all be wearing leather boot-laces and khaki clothing.'

'But we aren't wearing any khaki clothing.'

'No, but I would have recognized it if you had been. Besides, it wasn't necessary: you were wearing leather boot-laces.'

'It is not so easy to fool the German police,' said the man close to my ear.

The policemen were all smiles now, offering us cigarettes, betting us that the Invasion would never be a success and reassuring themselves that we were officers.

'Were you here for the big air-raid last year?' Sammy asked one of them.

I had remembered the first thousand aircraft raid as soon as we had arrived in Cologne and had hoped that the subject would not be mentioned.

'Yes,' said the policeman conversationally. 'I remember it.'

'There were a thousand aircraft in that raid,' said Sammy, 'and that was nearly a year ago. Think what it's going to be like this summer.'

'All British propaganda,' said the policeman.

10

We got to know the fat young man quite well during the next twenty-four hours. He took us to his own police station where he was supposed to look after us until we were handed over to the Luftwaffe authorities. He put us together in the same cell, but he was always visiting us or having us out into his office on some pretext or another, further questioning or further searching.

His name was Ernst. He had just got married. His wife was in the

Luftwaffe equivalent of the W.A.A.F. He could say 'Good morning', 'Son of a bitch' and 'Winston Churchill' in English and thought that the Germans and the English ought to be fighting the rest of the world. He attributed the British bombing of women and children to Jewish influences.

During the afternoon while Sammy and I were enjoying our first real sleep for days he came and woke us up.

'Only you,' he said, pointing to me, 'the Chef wants you for questioning.'

I put on my boots which still had traces of mud on them from the bog outside the camp. The sole flapped nostalgically as I put it to the floor.

'If you can't think of anything to tell them,' said Sammy as I went out of the door, 'make it up.'

Ernst took me to his office first.

'Just before we go,' he said, 'I want to show you something.'

He went to a drawer in his desk and pulled out a photograph.

'This is me in uniform,' he said, handing it to me, 'I don't want you to think that I am not a front-line soldier like you two. I thought perhaps you might have been wondering about it. You see, in Germany the police are a military organization and we carry rifles and fight just like any other soldier. That photograph of me was taken last year when I was mopping up behind the lines in Russia.'

He took it back and put it away carefully in the drawer.

'Now we will go to the Chef.'

The Police Chief was sitting behind a large desk in an otherwise almost empty room. He was wearing a double-breasted brown suit and a bow tie, and he looked rather like the editor of a newspaper. He rose magnanimously as I came in and told me to sit down on a chair that was already placed opposite his desk. As I did so I noticed a man with a notebook sitting on a chair in the corner behind me.

'You speak German?'

'Yes.'

'You have not been very clever. Not clever.'

He smiled, showing gold in his teeth.

I shrugged my shoulders.

'No, in fact you have not been clever at all. Why did you come this way? Did you expect to reach the Channel and go to England by boat? That, you must know, is impossible. Every year many are shot or drowned trying to escape that way, but none succeed. No, you

176

were not clever if that was your plan.'

He stopped to shift his position on the chair. His tone was authoritative but friendly, like a sensible schoolmaster rebuking a boy for cheating. He recrossed his legs and folded his hands. None of the windows in the room were open and there was a dry smell of furniture.

'On the other hand you may have been trying to do something quite different.'

He fingered some papers that were lying on the desk.

'I have here a report from the Gestapo chief of Cologne.'

He paused on the word 'Gestapo'. I heard the man who was sitting in the corner behind me move very slightly.

'The Gestapo' — again he enjoyed the word — 'have recently detected and rounded up a British sabotage group which was dropped by aircraft in the Aachen area. Now, is it possible that you really had no intention of escape at all, but had been informed by code from England of the presence of this group and were on your way to join them?'

The words made me jump. If this was their line of thinking there would be a charge of espionage, a firing squad perhaps.

'That is absurd,' I said quickly, 'our only idea was to escape back to England. That is within our rights as prisoners of war.'

The smile increased. He began to select something from among the documents.

'And yet, do you not think it strange that these maps, found in the lining of your friend's coat,' — he drew them out from the pile — 'were made by the Air Ministry and do not take you beyond the Aachen area?'

His manner had changed and he was now like a prosecuting counsel who knows that he has a good case.

'But we only wanted to escape,' I stammered, 'we just hadn't got any other maps, that's all. We weren't really sure where we were going to as a matter of fact.'

I was very conscious of my red face and the man I couldn't see behind me.

'Oh, come, come. Now it is you who are being absurd. Do you mean to tell me that two British officers would take all the trouble and risk of escaping from the camp and yet not be sure of where they were going to?'

That was just what I did mean to say, but I realized that it sounded

177

ridiculous. There seemed nothing I could do.

'Well, that is all, thank you very much. I shall have to give the Gestapo your explanation and then it is up to them to take action if they wish. The matter is out of my hands. But I should like to repeat: you have not been clever, not clever at all.'

A policeman in uniform took me back to the cell.

I told Sammy what happened. His eyes sharpened.

'Bluff,' he said.

But he looked serious.

'That's what I tried to think. But they made me feel very uncomfortable all the same.'

'Did they try to get any information out of you about the actual escape?'

'None at all. That's what was so queer.'

Sammy lay back on his bed and squinted down at his feet.

'My God,' he said, 'if they mean all this we've had it.'

For a long time neither of us spoke. I thought of all I had heard about the two Germanies: the Wehrmacht Germany which saluted when it passed you in the camp and allowed you to write home three times a month, and the S.S. Germany which beat you in the stomach with lengths of hose pipe and shot you in the early morning. No-one would ever know how or when we had disappeared.

Nailed boots rang in the passage and stopped outside our door. The shutter over the peep-hole flicked open and, a few seconds later, back again. Then there was a drawing back of bolts and a policeman came in. He beckoned to Sammy.

'Komm,' he said.

Sammy put on his coat. I could think of nothing to say.

'Good luck,' I said as he went through the door.

Sammy did not look back but went straight out into the passage, and the policeman shut the door and slammed back the bolts behind him.

I lay on my bed staring at the wall close to my face.

After half an hour I began to wonder if I would ever see Sammy again. After an hour I decided that it was unlikely. After that I must have gone to sleep.

The next thing I knew was that the bolts were being drawn back outside. The door opened and Sammy came in looking very tired. The policeman stood for a moment in the doorway behind him. I sat up while Sammy went over to his bed and sat down on the edge of it.

Then he looked up at the policeman. The policeman stepped back and shut the door and rebarred it. Sammy looked over at me and winked. We waited while the policeman played about with the peep-hole. Then we heard him walking away down the passage.

Sammy jumped up onto his bed.

'It's O.K.,' he said, 'they are bluffing.'

'But what's been happening to you all this time?'

'They've been asking me all about the tunnel. How long were we building it and did any of the Poles help? He said they knew that we had got our orderlies to do most of the actual digging for us. But they wanted to know how we had smuggled the civilian clothes into the camp. And where had we got the printing press from to make the false papers with? Oh, it was very rich.'

'But didn't they say anything about the Gestapo?'

'That was the best part of the lot. He started on that line. He said you had probably already told me the serious charges involved, and that he would now ring up the Gestapo to see if there were any fresh instruction. Then he went through an elaborate pantomime of trying to ring up the Gestapo with one finger holding down the telephone. As he couldn't get through, he said, he'd just ask me one or two questions. He said that if we would reveal everything about the escape organization in the camp he was pretty sure that the Gestapo would not press the sabotage charges. Of course from that moment I knew that we were all right. Towards the end of the questioning another high-up came in. The Chef explained that he was "looking into this affair of the escaped prisoners and the Gestapo", but the new chap looked astonished and said: "The Gestapo? Oh, yes, of course, the Gestapo." I felt quite sorry for the poor Chef.'

'Well, thank God for that. I was beginning to get rather worried.'

I felt a fool for having taken it all so seriously.

Later in the day two Luftwaffe men came and collected us from our cell and took us to the local military gaol. They were friendly. After the fright I had had I felt that we were among our own people again.

All the other prisoners in the gaol were Germans serving military sentences. One of them came in to clean out our cell the next morning and told us that he had got twenty years for desertion. He wanted to know when the Invasion was coming.

'This year,' said Sammy reassuringly.

'I wish to hell they'd hurry up then,' he said.

We gave him some milk chocolate as a sort of tip.

We stayed in the gaol for two days. It was a pleasant rest for us as we only wanted to sleep, and we could do this far more easily in our large peaceful cell than we would ever have been able to in the camp.

'What are you going to do after the war?' asked Sammy one afternoon as we lay on our beds listening to the prisoners doubling round and round the courtyard below our window.

'I haven't the faintest idea.'

'Neither have I.'

'What were you doing before?'

'I was a clerk in an insurance office.'

'And you're not going back to it?'

'What, after all this? What do you think?'

Another time he said:

'I once knew a chap who'd been in a glasshouse in England. He managed to get himself classed as one of the people who were a bit queer in the head. He wasn't allowed to do rifle drill, but was given a hatchet and told to go away and chop wood.'

On the evening of the second day we were told to pack up our things and get ready to leave. In spite of all the searches we had been through since we had been caught, the Germans had taken none of our food or clothes.

'Where are we going to?' I asked the soldier who had unlocked the door.

He shrugged his shoulders and said:

'Not home.'

'What do you think he meant by that?' I asked Sammy as we walked down the corridor in front of him.

'A German joke, I expect.'

But when we were pushed into the little office and saw the four quiet men in overcoats and hats, standing round the walls each with a hand in his coat pocket, I began to wonder again if the Police Chief had been bluffing after all.

They looked us over. One of them who wore thick horn-rimmed glasses seemed more important than the others. He took some papers out of a large leather despatch case and checked our names.

'What the hell's all this?' said Sammy.

'No talking!' shouted the man in thick glasses.

Then he looked at his watch and said something to the soldier, who left the room. The six of us stood there in silence for a few minutes. None of the four took his hand out of his coat pocket. They behaved just as I had always expected the Gestapo to behave.

I tried to make conversation.

'Do you speak English?' I asked the leader.

'Perhaps,' he said in German.

There was another silence.

'Where are we going to?' I asked.

I heard the urgency in my own voice.

He shrugged his shoulders, but through the thick lenses of his glasses I thought I saw the possibility of a smile.

'Are we going to the camp?' asked Sammy.

This time there was definitely a smile.

'Perhaps,' he said.

'Who are you?' I asked.

He proudly pulled a little metal disk out of his pocket. On it was cut the word 'KRIMINALPOLIZEI' (Criminal Police).

'Thank God,' muttered Sammy.

'Who did you think we were?' asked one of the others, 'Gestapo?'

They all smiled.

Very gradually they began to thaw out.

The man in thick glasses said:

'You can talk to each other if you like, but it must be in German.'

'But my friend doesn't know much German.'

He considered this drawback for a moment.

'Then you can talk to him in English, but you must translate everything you say into German for me.'

All my fears about these men were now at rest.

While we waited until it was time to go for our train they grew more and more friendly.

'After all,' said one of them to the other three, 'we have got to be with them for the next two days.'

They all nodded approvingly.

They began to show us photographs from their breast pockets of their wives and children. We argued a little about the war.

'But wait until the Invasion comes.'

'It never will.'

'Just you wait.'

181

'It will be driven into the sea. The Führer has said so.'

I asked the man in glasses what he usually did in his job.

'Fraud cases,' he answered, '— fascinating. But I shall enjoy this little holiday.'

On our way back across Germany one of them sang love songs in a terrible high tenor, and the man in glasses told us his theories about the British Secret Service. He said he believed that T.E. Lawrence had not been killed in a motor-cycle accident, but was now our chief spy.

They ate our chocolate with us instead of confiscating it as they might have done, and at the station restaurants they shared their food coupons with us in return.

'Ah,' said one of them, handing me an enormous plate of steak and vegetables, 'it's not worth escaping. Really, it's not.'

When, at the end of the journey, we had been delivered to the camp 'cooler', we found Willy Myers in the next cell.

'What happened to you?' we asked.

'It was maddening,' he said, 'I got caught just short of the coast while looking for that village. Another couple of hours and I should have been all right. If I could only have found that village . . .'

And ten days later we were back in the camp. Sammy went back to his bed at the end of the block, which was near the stove but never got any sun, and I went back to mine near the door, which faced south but smelt of the night lavatory. Sammy began winning hundreds of pounds a night at roulette again, and I revised my Russian verbs.

Except at the twice daily roll-calls or on the way to the lavatory we seldom saw each other, and when we did meet we talked about the things we had always talked about: Red Cross parcels and the Invasion and whether the Senior British Officer was any good or not. Our strange journey had no part in this life and we took it away from the front of our minds.

The corn in the fields outside the wire thickened and grew tall. The heavy chestnut trees along the road grew grey with the dust of midsummer. One day Polish girls with their hair tied up in handkerchiefs came and started to cut the corn. It was time to think about writing home for shorts and gym shoes for the following spring.

182

Part Four

1

With the landing in Normandy in June, 1944, the war took on a new personal meaning.

The war had always been the most consistently popular topic of conversation and there was probably no time from 1940 onwards when someone in the camp did not think it would end successfully 'this year'. But it was always being fought at such a distance, and its end — except to those who practised optimism as others practised spiritualism or football or languages — seemed always so dim and remote that it remained impersonal. It was like a big prize fight about which you argued, took sides, even heard over the radio, but of which the different phases in no way affected your life.

Since the attack on Sicily the emphasis of the war had been growing gradually more personal, but the repeated setbacks and stalemates made it difficult to realize this. As we shuffled out of the huts to roll-call on the morning of the Italian surrender someone said to me:

'Just imagine what the chaps in Italian camps are feeling like now. Lucky buggers.'

A few weeks later they told us exactly what they had been feeling like as they had watched the Germans arrive and take over their camps which in some cases had been free of Italian guards for hours.

Heavy air attacks were made on Berlin. We lay happily in our bunks at night listening to the thunder of death a hundred miles away and feeling the earth tremble. But every morning the war continued as before, and the German radio and the guards were as confident of victory as ever.

The first formations of allied aircraft appeared over the camp in daylight. We ran excitedly to the windows, fighting for space as the siren wailed outside and the single note of bombers filled the afternoon. They passed over to lay their condensation trails elsewhere, and the fighters left behind a scribble in the sky like the marks left by a child who has been playing with chalk on a slate.

On 4th June I won some chocolate with the expiry of a bet about the invasion. The bet had originally set the 4th May as a limit, but when that date came and there had been no Invasion I made it 'double or quits' by the 4th June. As Michael handed over the four precious squares of chocolate he said, to console himself:

'If the Invasion doesn't come this year, Churchill is going to look a bloody fool.'

I had heard the same thing said in 1942. I wondered about 1946.

It rained cleanly all the morning making the stale sand fresh and hard. The Germans counted us just after dawn as we lay in bed and there was no morning parade for roll-call. This was unusual but not unprecedented. Someone in the room sat up and wondered why the routine was different, but the rest of us just turned over and accepted it as a good opportunity for staying long in bed.

It was pleasant to lie back and think that there was absolutely nothing I had to do, that there was no reason why I should not spend the rest of that day and the greater part of all following days in bed if I wanted to.

There were raisins in barley for lunch.

I was lying fascinated by the kaleidoscopic nostalgia which comes before sleep when I heard shouting and the sound of people running down the wooden corridor.

Hammond rushed in, red with excitement, yelling:

'Invasion! Invasion!'

It was all so exactly as I had always imagined it would be that for a time it seemed unreal. But it was true. The news had just been announced on the German radio.

I went out to the loudspeaker in my pyjamas. There was a big crowd round it and a noise like the inside of the monkey house at the Zoo. After the rain the light was bright and brittle. People's movements seemed quicker and more sudden than usual. No-one seemed to have heard the original announcement. A black-bearded Lieutenant-commander said:

'I've just drunk the pongoes' health in hooch.'

It was difficult to tell whether drink or excitement had distorted what was to be seen of his face.

The voice in the loudspeaker barked on, but it was concerned with minor incidents of news or routine propaganda. There was a change in the programme and I moved away, thinking for the first time for years of a future outside barbed wire. The smug, scornful tone of the daily political commentator followed me to the block. He had adapted himself quickly to the news. His arguments and the jargon which padded them were so much the same as ever that it was difficult to tell that he had a different setting for them.

In the afternoon I went for a solitary walk round the 'circuit'. I tried to grasp the fact that life 'after the war' was now a real possibility, but I found myself numb and unresponsive.

2

One evening a few weeks later I was walking round the camp in the late sun, pushing my bare feet through the dusty sand and wondering whether there was enough pressure in the water taps for a wash, when there was an interruption in the programme of the distant loudspeaker.

'Here is an important announcement of the Wireless News Service. Attempted assassination of the Führer.'

I ran across the compound and listened, astonished, to some controlled facts about the plot of the twentieth of July.

The next morning more details were given. It was clear that this had not been the attempt of a semi-lunatic as had at first been suggested but was part of a conspiracy. Some of the camp Germans were standing by the loudspeaker with us, listening with an earnest, incredulous expression on their faces that I had not seen since the day they had heard of the fall of Mussolini.

For a day or two the news which came from the B.B.C. was sensational. There was talk of anti-Nazi tanks racing towards Berlin and of riots in Munich. This was the end, I began to think. Germany was breaking up from within. One evening from my window I heard the music of 'Deutschland über Alles' being played over the loudspeaker and grew sentimental over the changes of history.

The sense of political tension continued for some time. The Germans with whom I discussed the attempt were bewildered. If nothing else had happened, the facade of internal unity had been cracked and with it the popular confidence which was its reflection.

But gradually it became obvious that the plot had failed. Pictures of the tiny German General who had planned to assassinate Hitler at a demonstration of new equipment for the services, by putting a bomb into one of the knapsacks, appeared in the illustrated papers with suitable vilifications underneath. There was a picture of the *Völkischer Beobachter* of Witzleben, in civilian suit and collarless, being tried by the People's Court. The Party salute replaced the military salute in all branches of the armed forces. The officer who took our roll-calls kept on forgetting and giving the old salute by mistake. But soon he was able to take his mistake as a joke and he became as accustomed to the new salute as we did.

There came an August morning which recurred every year. Photographed or seen through a glass window it would have seemed identical with the many other hot, clear mornings which had been seen in the camp during the summer. Yet the mornings of black winds and dust which had come with spells of broken weather had had far more in common with summer than this one of sun and blue sky. For though the leaves of the trees in the road outside glistened as usual like watersilk, and brown bodies lay in the sun, there was the knowledge of coming winter in the air.

There was usually a counterpart to this day in January: a winter's day which talked of spring. It is impossible to say just what it was about such days which suggested the linking of the seasons. Perhaps it was just imagination prompted by a change in the temperature, but their freakishness was none the less real for that. The effect of such days was not so much to make one think of a new spring or winter but of the return of the old one.

I lay on the sand and watched four Focke-Wolf 190's playing follow-my-leader in the sun at about four thousand feet and giving off temporary condensation trails. I liked to think that these clouds conjured mysteriously from the blue air were the invisible winter being forced out of its hiding.

British and American troops were racing across Europe. There had been a landing in the south of France. We will be free, I thought, before that winter comes to stay.

But winter came and with it the dark indoor afternoons and the snow, and we were still there.

3

It was from the east that the real change came.

It was not unexpected. After the news of the Ardennes offensive we had begun to look for comfort to the other side of our maps. Nothing was happening there but at least nothing had gone wrong. 'Just wait for the Russian offensive, old boy,' said Hammond, who was the room strategist, 'that'll do the trick.'

And for the first time in four and a half years he was right.

I heard of the opening of the offensive with quiet satisfaction. There was the usual excitement in rooms and corridors all round the camp. People stood in groups round the loudspeaker twittering, black against the snow, like birds in a tree-top at evening. All this had gone on every time the Red Army opened an offensive. One usually took part in it in a Bank Holiday mood, knowing that when the excitement was over everything would return to normal until next time. But this time, in spite of the familiar reaction in the camp, I could not help feeling that something was different. I went to the library to look at the map of Europe with the Russian front pinned out on it in blue cotton. I measured the distance they had advanced last time and then the same distance from their present position forward. It easily took in the area of the camp. I went to the room to collect the tea can, threw in some tea, and then went and stood in the queue for hot water outside the kitchen. Punctually at half past three the window flew up and Sergeant Wall started slopping out hot water as he had done almost every afternoon for the past two years. It was difficult to believe that this could ever change.

As I walked back to the block I spilled a little tea onto the snow to see if it was strong enough. I always did this when it was my turn to collect the tea, although I don't know why because there was nothing I could do about it if it was too weak.

There was only Mark in the room when I got back to it. We had a full Red Cross parcel every week now and people were not so punctual for meals as they had been when we had had only half a parcel. Mark usually took more interest in his garden than in the war.

187

Even in winter when the ground was hard or under snow he would spend much of his time looking at the onions he had stored in boxes under his bed or planning where to put his tomato plants next year.

'Hullo,' he said quietly, 'I've just been looking at the map in the library.'

'So have I.'

'Of course I know it sounds ridiculous, but did you notice that if they advance the same amount as they advanced last year they will overrun the camp.'

'Yes.'

Hammond came in and took his two slices of bread.

'Home for Easter, chaps,' he said. 'The goons have absolutely had it.' I watched him as he dug his knife into the tin of jam. Then I remembered that we weren't on half parcels any more so that it didn't really matter if he took too much, but it was difficult to get out of the habit of minding.

After tea Simon Green came in. He wanted to produce himself as Othello in the summer and asked if I would do Cassio. He had taken the opportunity of playing most of the great Shakespearian parts while he had been a prisoner. I couldn't help wondering if he would really be glad to get back to his local rep.

The tension mounted steadily. It grew to something unprecedented as the names of places within a hundred kilometres of the camp were mentioned in the German communiqué. As at the time of D Day the library was almost empty all day long, and this time it stayed empty, except after the German communiqué or the reading of the B.B.C. news when people would fight for a place round the map. It was the news from German sources that I found the most satisfying. We had all suffered before at the hands of the B.B.C.'s over-optimism and I had come to regard good news as definite only if the Germans admitted it. The B.B.C. was valuable for filling in details.

As the Russians came nearer and nearer a special Liberation group was formed inside the camp. As a potential speaker of Russian I took part in the discussion of exciting plans for contacting the advancing forces. We studied local maps in secret, and practised unarmed combat and how to roll over railway lines on the floor of one of the huts. The best part of all this was the fact that our group received extra food to strengthen us for the physical exertions which lay ahead. Every day I walked fifteen or twenty times round the camp imagining thrilling scenes of contact in the middle of the battle.

Rumours started, wild contradictory rumours.

'Of course, it's only a rumour, old boy, but . . .'

'Heard the latest?'

Such was the uncertainty and excitement of the time that one had to stop and listen to each, and however improbable each might seem one always wondered if there might not be something in it.

Then came the first rumours of a possible evacuation of the camp. It was like a sudden sour taste in the mouth.

'The S.B.O.'s seeing the Commandant now . . .'

'We'll move on foot, only taking as much luggage as we can carry . . .'

'Johnny Walters says . . .'

For the first time I realized how definitely I had made up my mind that we were going to be liberated.

'The goons would never be able to do it . . .'

'I hope to God the Russians know about our being here . . .'

'The goons will want all their roads for military traffic . . .'

'What's the Russian for prisoner-of-war?'

'I bet you anything you like we don't move.'

'Johnny Walters says . . .'

'How will the Russian aircraft know it's us?'

A few people began to make rucksacks, to decide what they would take if there was a move. One thing was certain: life in that camp would never be the same again.

One afternoon there was a distant sound of gunfire behind the dark green tops of the fir-trees.

'My God, you know I think this is it,' said Mark.

But the sound died away in the night and the next day the German communiqué said that the Russians had formed a temporary bridge-head over the Oder but had been driven back.

'Do you realize that's only fifty kilometres away?' shouted Hammond.

'Yes,' said Michael, 'sugar please.'

'They can't possibly move us now.'

'They've been doing things they can't do for six years. I'm going to make myself a rucksack just in case.'

I felt guilty coming back into the room every evening after my extra meal and sitting down to the ordinary one.

'This sounds a bloody good racket you're on,' said Hammond on the last evening but one.

'Yes, I suppose it is a bit of a racket really.'

The extra food had warmed my spirit as well as my body. I was prepared to tolerate Hammond.

'It isn't a racket at all,' said Michael, 'you have to work bloody hard for it. I haven't walked fifteen times round the camp since I've been here.'

'How much soup do you actually get?' said Hammond. 'I suppose if it's only a spoonful or two it's not really so unfair.'

Sykes, who was the block commander, held a meeting that evening. He substituted seriousness for intelligence. It had made him into one of the finest bomber pilots in the R.A.F.

'I'll try and give you the overall picture, chaps,' he began. He summarized the news of the last few days. '. . . so I think you will agree with me that there is a very good chance of the whole outfit blowing up.' It seemed an unfortunate choice of phrase.

He told us how to take cover if there was any fighting round the camp.

'And one last word of encouragement, chaps,' he added. 'We have reason to believe that with every Russian Division there is a British or American liaison officer. So you've nothing to fear on that score.'

'What are the chances of a move, sir?' someone asked.

'I don't see how the goons can possibly carry it out. No, chaps, I think this is what we've all been waiting for.'

I went to bed confident, and glad that I had not wasted time making a rucksack.

But the next day the rumours of a move were as strong as ever. All over the camp people were to be seen stitching braces onto kit-bags, making haversacks out of old shirts. After lunch I decided that the strain of ignoring this activity was too great, so I started to make myself a rucksack out of a kitbag. I had just completed it when someone came into the room and said:

'The goons are confiscating all the rucksacks they can find in the Sergeants' Compound. That proves it. We're not moving.'

The news was so good that I did not even resent the time I had spent on my kitbag.

I tried to calm myself by spending the rest of the afternoon reading Othello, but it was difficult not to wonder what would be happening by this time tomorrow. It was the uncertainty of the immediate future which was so strange after years in which it had always been as carefully prescribed as medicine.

There was more gunfire during the afternoon. I purposely did not go and listen to the German communiqué, but I was glad when Hammond came in to tea and told us what it had said.

'They'll be here any hour now, chaps. The goons have admitted a break-through.'

After tea I went for my walk.

The roll-call that evening was just like any other roll-call I had ever attended, but we all talked a great deal more than usual amongst ourselves after the officer had counted us.

P.T. for the 'Special Group'.

'This may be the last one we'll have,' said Bunn, who took the class.

The extra meal for the 'Special Group'.

'Stoke up, chaps, we don't want to have to waste time eating when we get back.'

Back to my room for the ordinary meal. It was not ready yet. Mark was looking over the onion box as I came in.

'Hullo,' he said. 'Pity about these in a way. I suppose we could have taken them with us if we'd moved.'

His eyes sparkled. 'My God, though, it's wonderful, isn't it?'

'Wonderful. I can hardly believe it.'

Hammond was lying on his back on his bed, surprisingly quiet. He had a placid expression on his face. I felt ashamed for having disliked him for so long. I took the chance of giving him back a book of his I had borrowed.

'Thanks very much.'

'Not at all, old boy. Enjoy it?'

'Very much, thanks.'

'Well, it won't be long now.'

'No, thank God.'

He lay back again.

'Quite apart from everything else,' he said, 'it'll be good for us to get out of here, won't it? I mean, really, this has been the hell of a life for a man, hasn't it? It'll be good to be able to get things in their right perspective again.'

It was time for me to go back to the 'Special Group' for map reading.

191

Bunn opened the meeting.

'I don't want to waste any time. I expect you've all heard by now that the move is off and that it's as certain as anything can be that this organization will come into force. I'll hand you straight over to Hatter who will summarize as much as we know of the local terrain.'

The faces round the table were grim and excited. We all looked earnestly at Hatter, the South African, who began to talk quickly and competently.

'You're probably all well acquainted with the immediate locality – that is, the Vorlager and the road round it. Don't forget the excellent little slit trench about twenty yards outside the main gate by the way – there's good cover there. With regard to the wood beyond, it's fairly straightforward as far as the river . . .'

It was remarkable how serious we had all become. I had never heard Hatter talk quite like this before. He was usually contemptuous of people who took anything seriously and he was in a position to be for he had done brave things while a prisoner. But he was thinking of a new life now and perhaps he was already slipping off his prison philosophy.

When Hatter had finished, Alec got up and gave a talk about compass reading. His bright red cheeks and glistening eyes flashed excitement. I remembered his lean drawn face at a time in 1942 when the food had run out. He had written some good poetry then. But this sort of thing obviously suited him much better. He wound up his talk.

'And one last thing: don't get so taken up with your compass that you forget to keep your eyes open. Remember there may be an enemy behind every tree.'

An outsider might have thought us overgrown schoolboys planning an adventure. It was true in a way, too. Yet people like Alec and Hatter had already proved many times that they were prepared to go through with their adventure long after schoolboys would have returned home helpless and in tears. Alec had once been out for fifty days. He had walked alone to the Swiss frontier living off what he could steal.

The door opened. Limpet, the camp adjutant, stood just outside in the corridor. He said nothing but stared at us with a supercilious expression as we sat huddled round the table. Bunn who was 'summing up' stopped in mid-sentence.

'I'm afraid we're having a private meeting, Limpet. Anything we can do for you?'

Limpet was probably the most despised man in the camp. All the common man's resentment of the bureaucrat was concentrated against him. Certainly he often deserved it for he was the completely humourless bureaucrat, painful enough in ordinary life but intolerable in a prison camp. Yet he too was something of a contradiction, for without him the camp would never have been run properly and no-one else would ever have done the work.

Alec particularly hated Limpet.

'Go on, bugger off, Limpet. We're busy.'

'There's no need to be rude, Drummond.'

We were all getting impatient.

Bunn said:

'Is there anything you want, Limpet? Because if not I'm afraid we must get on with the meeting.'

Limpet smoothed the little black beard he had grown so carefully.

'Oh, I wouldn't disturb you for the world. I just thought you might be interested to know that the camp is being evacuated in half an hour's time.'

4

Back in the room the chaos was terrifying. Food, clothes, books and cigarettes were scattered thickly over the floor, the table and the beds. One of the beds had collapsed. Carefully built shelves bookcases and lockers, the pride of their owners for years and guarded with strict jealousy, had been torn off the walls or trampled into confusion. The other eleven inhabitants of the room were searching through the chaos trying to decide what to take with them and what to leave behind. Hammond was almost in tears trying to make himself a rucksack at the last moment. Michael was building a sledge out of a bookcase and part of the table, hammering nails in with a flat piece of iron. Only Mark seemed at all calm.

'Of course they say half an hour, but I shouldn't think anything will happen for hours yet,' he said.

'Where are we going to?' I asked him. 'Are we going on foot? How long will it take?'

'Nobody knows anything at all. We're going, that's all.'

I climbed over books and broken cardboard boxes to my locker, pulled out the rucksack I had made that afternoon and began to stuff it with clothes. Then I decided that the only thing worth taking was food. I pulled all the clothes out again.

'What are we going to do about food?' I asked.

Everyone was too busy to take any notice.

I went over to Mark.

'What about the food? It seems to me it's the only thing worth worrying about. I mean, it'll be touch and go whether or not we get through this march. I mean . . .'

'All right,' said Mark, 'calm down. We'll divide up the food in a minute.'

I felt a fool and went back to my bed. I wondered if I should have room for any books. There were all the notes I had made in the last three years too, and the novel I had started.

'Got any more of this strong thread?'

'Anyone seen my blankets?'

'If only we could make one big sledge we could all put our things onto it and take it in turns to pull.'

'What happens if it thaws?'

'Who's taken my boots?'

There was a continual grunting and cursing.

The door opened.

'Anyone want any tobacco? I've got more than I can take.'

No-one paid any attention. The man went away shouting:

'Anyone want any tobacco?'

That morning tobacco had stood at quite a high price on the camp market. Now it was difficult to give it away.

Mark was dividing up the food. He threw the tins which were my share up onto my bed.

'And remember,' he shouted, 'the goons are going to make an issue of one parcel per man as we go out of the gate so leave room in your rucksack for that.'

The tins he had given me half filled my rucksack. I had sewn the kitbag up stupidly so that there was less room than there ought to have been. I should have to leave most of my clothes behind. I looked inside my locker at the new shirts from my last clothing parcel. I had been saving them for the spring. There were some gym shoes too and a little store of fresh clean note-books which I had built up very slowly over a period of years. I should have to leave them all behind.

On the bunk below me Hammond had finished his sewing and was staring at a great hoard of cigarettes which he always kept in a box at the bottom of his bed.

'There are over three thousand there,' he said sadly. 'I'll be able to get in two or three hundred at the most.'

I stared into my rucksack. Perhaps there would be more room if I repacked it. I emptied everything out onto the bed and started again. But this time it was even worse. I had to leave out a pair of shorts which I had got in quite easily before. And I rejected the novel. It seemed suddenly absurd to bother about it. If I could get myself through whatever lay ahead I would have lost nothing. Besides, it was not a very good novel. I got all the food in and tied up the cord at the top. The tins made hard uneven bumps on the skin of the bag.

The door opened and Sykes shouted in at us:

'It's no use any of you making sledges. The goons aren't going to allow them.'

No-one paid any attention except Michael who stopped hammering, stupefied. I remembered that I had not put in any books. We might be at the next camp for years. I unpacked the top of the bag again. Sykes had left the door open and I could hear him shouting into all the other rooms down the corridor.

Other people came in at intervals.

'Anyone want any razor blades?'

'Anyone want any soap?'

Everyone seemed to be taking a masochistic pleasure in ridiculing their own particular hoard. They were bleeding with generosity.

'Anyone want any note-books?'

But slowly the confusion simmered down. Disorder remained, but people had been exhausted by it. They lay on their bunks and blew smoke rings at the ceiling or at the boards of the top bunk.

'I don't care what the goons say. I don't see how they can stop us.'

Michael jumped down from his bunk and started hammering again.

This time it was quite noticeable as a separate noise.

'They'll just take it away from you if they see it,' said Hammond. 'And you won't have time to collect your food and belongings off it when we're on the march.'

Michael went on hammering.

'I bet they'll just shoot anyone who looks like falling out,' said Hammond.

'Oh, shut up,' I said. 'It's bad enough without your trying to panic us.'

'All right, you're not so bloody calm yourself.'

'Anyone want any bread?'

'No thanks.'

'It's mad, isn't it?' added Mark, when the man had left the room. 'People will be fighting for bread in a few days' time.'

In the end I decided to take *Tristram Shandy* and a paper backed *Book of Verse*. I chose *Tristram Shandy* partly because I thought it would bear reading over and over again and partly because the little Oxford edition was the smallest book I had.

There was a shout at the end of the block:

'We're not moving for another three hours at least. The S.B.O.'s just come back from a meeting with the Commandant.'

'There you are,' said Hammond, starting up from his bunk, 'what did I tell you? We're not moving.'

'For another three hours.'

'No, he said we're not moving. Didn't you hear? And that the S.B.O. had had an interview with the Commandant.'

'He said we're not moving for three hours.'

'Wrong again!' jeered someone.

'I'll bloody well find out for myself.'

Hammond ran out of the room.

He left behind a surprised silence. Michael was admiring his completed sledge. I could even hear people breathing on the other side of the room. It was like waking up from a bad dream in the middle of the night.

'Thank God for some peace,' said Mark, breaking it.

All round the block people must have been taking similar rests, shattered by the immediate shock, quietly trying to adjust their minds to the unknown.

Tom Jelliss caught my eye across the room.

'This time tomorrow!' he said, nodding his head slowly. He would have been a good ham actor if he hadn't been a salesman by profession. He believed in himself however big an act he was putting on. Perhaps that was why he was such a good salesman.

'This time tomorrow,' he repeated slowly, 'it seems impossible that it can ever come, doesn't it? What will be happening? Where will we be?'

I looked at my watch.

'It's twenty past ten,' I said. 'I'll remind you of this moment this time tomorrow night.'

'Right,' he said solemnly. 'Twenty past ten tomorrow night.'

Until then a vast dark gulf stretched in front of us. It seemed impossible that we should ever find our bearings in it, recognize time and faces, hopes and problems again. And yet I knew that we would, and that when this time came round again tomorrow night the events of the intervening time would seem solid and almost ordinary compared with the fantasies which our helpless imaginations now suggested but could not even begin to form.

Hammond came back into the room, crestfallen.

'Well?' somebody asked him.

'They don't seem able to make up their minds,' he said. 'Some say he said one thing, some another. I don't know what to make of it.'

Everybody jeered. He slumped onto his bed.

'All the same,' said Mark, 'I don't much like the idea of having to wait for three hours. I'd rather start now and get it over.'

Michael said:

'I bet they go on postponing it all through the night. Just about dawn when we've all settled down to a good fat sleep they'll come round shouting and waving guns and have us all out of bed in a quarter of an hour. But I'm bloody well going to take my sledge if I die in the attempt.'

'Ah,' said Tom Jelliss, 'I shouldn't be at all surprised.'

People were more themselves again now. For a time we had all lost our identities in the terrifying panic of the herd. Now we were recovering. Personalities had adjusted themselves to the upheaval and were beginning to reassert themselves. I felt calmer, almost a little bored.

Soon a sense of anti-climax set in. Somebody at the other end of the room even went to sleep and snored soothingly.

I must have begun to doze myself because when I looked up again, Mark was sitting at the table peeling potatoes.

'It seems a pity to waste them,' he said, 'when we may all be going to starve so bloody soon. I'll fry them and we can use up some of the onions that way too.'

I got down to help him. I was still quite hungry although I had already had two suppers that evening. Besides it was something to do.

When I took the chipped potatoes out to the block stove I found other people cooking too.

'This is my tenth plateful of spuds this evening,' said a huge New Zealander. 'My God I've been waiting for an opportunity like this for years.'

He stuffed in another forkful. Some of the greasy chips tumbled down his tunic onto the floor.

'Besides,' he said, with his mouth full, 'this may be the last decent meal I ever have.'

Looking at his vast frame and fat gross face thick with the grease streaming from the corners of his mouth it was difficult to think of him starving.

We fried the potatoes and the onions and took them back to the room. Everyone climbed down from their beds to eat. As always the food made people mellow.

'Now that I'm all packed up I'm almost beginning to look forward to whatever comes next.'

'Anything will be better than just sitting around like we've been doing for the last three years.'

Even Hammond began to cheer up.

'I've just been talking to a chap at the other end of the block,' he said, 'and he swears that he heard machine-gun fire about half an hour ago. So the goons may be too late after all.'

We went and lay on our beds again. I had rolled up my sleeping bag into a suitable shape for carrying, but now I unrolled it again, took off my boots and crawled inside. I thought of what the New Zealander had said about food. Perhaps this was the last time I should ever lie on a proper bed.

I was quite calm now. I had stared into the unknown sufficiently often during the last few hours for fear to have given place to expectation. From now on I was to live with change, an element that had been missing from my life for years. It would be like recovering the use of an injured limb. It was the first step back to health and freedom.

'Whatever else may happen,' said Michael, 'the old prisoner of war life as we knew it has been completely smashed. That's one compensation.'

'Yes,' said Hammond, 'it's the beginning of the end all right.'

The door opened. It was Jack Nopps. He took a slow, calculating survey of the figures on the beds.

'Of course, I don't know whether you chaps are interested,' he began. I saw that one arm hanging down by his side held an enormous lump of raw meat. 'But I've just broken into the meat store in the cookhouse. It's funny, nobody seemed to have had the idea before. But then people are slow you know, very slow.'

I scrambled out of my sleeping bag and stuck my feet into my unlaced boots. Tom Jelliss was already down and making for the door.

'All right,' he shouted, 'I'll get what I can, but somebody follow me up.'

He pushed past Jack Nopps and ran down the passage.

'Greedy bastards,' growled Jack and stepped aside to let me out.

The news seemed to have spread all over the camp. There was the shuffling, swelling sound of a stampede from several of the other huts as I stepped into the cold night air.

In spite of my hurry and the fact that other people were pushing past me, I stopped for a moment and held my breath in wonder. The silent blackness of the woods beyond the boundary lights and the crisp still snow on the floor of the camp was an apt setting for great events. I had wondered at the beauty of night in a prison camp many times during the last few years. Its peace and dark simplicity were always astonishing after the strain and staleness which had marked the day. It was like seeing the face of a worried man suddenly relaxed into cool refreshing sleep. But this night had a beauty I had never seen before. It was like a great dark bud waiting to burst into history and it suffered its tension with a calmness and serenity which put human fears and ambitions to shame.

'They say there's a whole side of beef there.'

'And two hams according to Sergeant Wall.'

'There won't be anything left pretty soon.'

Dark scrambling figures were streaming out of the huts across the snow. I ran towards the cookhouse.

I got there in time to meet Tom coming out.

'Too late, dear boy. Too late,' he cried mournfully, 'you were so slow. Still I managed to find a little something for all of us.'

He tapped his bulging pockets.

'What did you get?'

'Lamb chops.'

'Good show.'

'I would have got a great deal more if it hadn't been for those racketeers Drummond and Hatter. How is it that they always manage to get onto everything good?'

'We haven't done too badly ourselves.'

'Oh no, we haven't done too badly.'

He chuckled.

We were walking slowly back to our hut, but people who did not yet know that the supply was exhausted were still fighting their way in the other direction.

'Alas!' Tom cried to them as they passed. 'Too late! Too late!'

Somebody stopped.

'What do you mean, "too late"?' he asked.

'I mean,' said Tom, 'that there is no more meat left.'

'Who got it then?'

'Drummond and Hatter seemed to have got hold of most of it. I should ask them.'

'What a bloody swindle! It should have been divided up equally.'

'I quite agree with you, dear boy. But go and tell that to Drummond and Hatter.'

He stalked on into the hut and I followed him.

We were already so full that we were unable to eat it all at one sitting. We decided to save some of it for a final meal just before we left. I climbed up onto my bed and settled down to sleep again.

All this time there had been no sign of the Germans apart from the normal prodding of the searchlights along the wire. The S.B.O. and other officials were continually being rumoured to have got fresh details or instructions from them, but no-one seemed to have had any contact with a German himself.

Sykes came in again and said:

'Apparently there is still some doubt about sledges. The S.B.O. is fighting to have them allowed.'

Michael jumped down from his bed again.

'I think it's just worth making a large communal one for us all on the off chance,' he said. He began to saw up suitable bits of wood.

'But how the hell are fourteen of us going to stick together on the march?' asked Hammond.

'I don't expect we will. But we'll put the parcels that the goons give us at the gate onto the communal sledge and then anyone who wants to separate can take his parcel off later.'

'I don't like the idea of that. I'll take my own parcel, thanks.'

'O.K., I don't mind. Anyone else feel like doing that?'

'Do you think the sledge will really work?' I asked.

'No. That's why I'm hammering it together.'

'Sorry.'

'Not at all. Do you want to secede too?'

'No, no. I was just rather doubtful about whether . . .'

My sentence was drowned by his hammering.

I was far too aware of my own practical incompetence to back up my doubts with action.

'Well,' said Michael, 'I'm going to build the thing and anyone who cares to can use it.'

Mark jumped down from his bed.

'I think you've got something there. I'll give you a hand.'

By now I was growing impatient. I had keyed myself up hours ago for something to happen and nothing at all had happened except that everybody else had got keyed up too. Like a loosely knit bad dream the night kept on repeating itself and getting nowhere at all. The chaotic room, its floor ankle deep in books and food and clothes, just went on and on reflecting the yellow electric light from its wooden planked walls and seemed to have lost all touch with time.

I think everyone else was feeling the same undigested impatience. When Sykes came in about a quarter of an hour later he got the full force of it.

'Cancel my last announcement about sledges, chaps. Apparently the goons have said . . .'

Everyone let him have it at once.

'Oh, bugger off.'

'Why doesn't someone organize this move?'

'Does anyone know what's meant to be happening?'

Sykes stared, appalled. It never seemed to have struck him before that people could admit to feeling helpless.

Tom Jelliss spoke in a deep rich voice.

'Go away and get on with your knitting, you silly old woman.'

It seemed a tactical error. Sykes fastened onto him.

'Who the hell do you think you're talking to, Jelliss?'

Miraculously Tom looked hurt, a broken smile on his lips.

'But, Sykie old man, I was only joking . . .'

It was impossible not to believe him. Sykes went out of the door without another word.

This incident did not make me feel any better. It was the sort of thing that had gone on in the camp in different little forms a dozen times a day for years, and yet here it was popping up as usual as if nothing extraordinary was happening at all. It made me feel that the end was really very far away after all. I turned over on my bed and faced the wall. I thought, if I can sleep the time will go more quickly. I knew that something must come out of all this, if only the day and the turning off of the monotonous electric light, and yet it was as if Time had stuck and would never move again.

When I awoke it was like waking in the night on the last day of term at school. I was immediately conscious of something to be excited about. At the same time I had a headache and an unpleasant awareness in the back of my throat of all the meals I had eaten that evening. The light was still on but everyone was asleep, some people breathing heavily, regularly. Through the wall I could hear someone walking about in the next room. He sounded as if he was looking for something. A lot of time must have passed since I had fallen asleep. That's better, I thought, we are that much nearer to something happening. But when I looked at my watch I saw that it was only twenty past one. I held it to my ear to see if it had stopped but it ticked neatly as it had always done. I was just turning over, disgusted, when I heard a new sort of step in the wooden passage. It was heavily booted and determined.

"Raus, 'raus, meine Herren! Zählappel!'

There were groans from the next room and a thump as someone jumped down from his bed.

"Raus, 'raus!'

A German soldier with a rifle and full marching pack on his back looked in at the door.

'Aufstehen!'

Mark sat up.

'What the hell's happening?'

'Appel. I expect we're going.'

'This is it.'

Everyone in the room was suddenly awake, putting on boots, anxiously collecting blankets and packs. As I waded through the debris out of the room I picked up a mug off the table and tied it to my belt by a piece of string through the handle.

Outside in the snow there was the greatest confusion. The camp Feldwebel was there trying to count us, but he kept on getting the count wrong in the darkness.

'For God's sake, fall in properly.'

'The sooner he counts us and we can get off, the better.'

202

But every time he trudged up the line through the snow, peering at the huddled forms in front of him, he found a different number. And then just when he had succeeded in getting the right number twice, more people came stumbling out of the hut dragging their kit bags on a sledge after them.

We shouted at them, angry and disgusted.

'Oh, my God!'

'For Christ's sake! You're keeping everybody waiting.'

The Feldwebel didn't get the count right again. But I thought he would never give up trying.

We soon lost all interest and, with it, all impatience. The excited conversation which had bubbled through the ranks when we first came out subsided and we stood there dull and dumb like animals, feeling nothing but the cold. We had so long been accustomed to being pushed around like this that we had learnt to develop when necessary the heavy blankness of mind which soaks up all thought and feeling except a numbed resentment.

We had stood there for over an hour when a German officer strode out of the darkness and shouted for the Feldwebel. They spoke together for a minute and then the Feldwebel said:

'Dismiss to the huts, please, gentlemens.'

There was a rush for the warmth of the huts. I knew this Feldwebel quite well so I went up to him.

'What's happening?' I asked.

'God knows!' he answered quickly, 'God knows!'

I went back to my room where they were just beginning to cook another meal.

About an hour later there was another roll-call and again we dragged our packs and sledges out into the snow. The Feldwebel gave it up earlier this time and we were back in the huts again within twenty minutes.

We were exhausted. No-one spoke when we got back into the room, nor even had the energy to climb back onto his bed. Everyone sat down in the first clear space they could find. I sat down on Hammond's bed and he didn't mind.

'I can't stand much more of this,' said Mark quietly.

We were still sitting there hopeless and exhausted when we heard the swelling, shuffling and scraping sound which meant that people in other rooms were moving. I went out into the corridor. The now familiar stream of figures wrapped in overcoats and balaclavas, and

203

carrying rucksacks and dragging sledges was making for the door again.

'What's happening?' I asked someone, 'another appel?'

'No, we're going.'

'Who said so?'

'I don't know, but we're going.'

He ploughed on, his sledge bumping against the walls of the corridor.

And so finally without any further roll-call we streamed out of the camp to the Vorlager. The ragged procession moved so fast that it was difficult to keep up with it in the snow and it was even more difficult for the twelve of us to keep together. But Michael's sledge, with four people pulling on the ropes, ran smoothly.

Hammond said:

'Well, look here, chaps, as I'm not going to make up your party I won't stick with you any more.'

'All right.'

He fell back into the gloom and I never saw him again.

The gates into the Vorlager were thrown wide open and although there were both British and German officials on either side of the gate shouting instructions we surged through without paying much attention to any of them.

I saw Limpet, the adjutant, standing underneath an arc lamp.

'Try to keep in step there,' he shouted in his high pompous voice.

There was a slight check outside the parcel store in the Vorlager where the parcel staff were desperately handing out as many parcels as they could to anyone who could carry them. There was no question of one parcel per man. There were so many in the store that several hundred would have to be left behind anyway. This great quantity of parcels had arrived within the last few weeks after we had spent all the early part of the winter short of food.

People were ripping open the surplus parcels and taking from them the tins that were best food value and at the same time easy to carry. All around in the snow lay boxes and tins of food, trampled and rejected — tins of dried milk, margarine and sardines, boxes of prunes and cheese. The ground was so thick with them that it was quite difficult to walk. For a moment I stared in astonishment. These tins had been the most coveted of all worldly goods for the last three years. The opening of an extra tin of sardines for tea or an extra cheese for lunch had been an occasion for joy, and I had often dreamt

204

of having a whole tin of condensed milk to myself. Now, though all of us knew that they would be more coveted than ever within a few days, we were throwing them away. I found myself standing next to a tall German guard. He carried his full pack, and his rifle was slung across his back. He saw me staring at the ground and shook his head sadly.

'Das ist Krieg,' he said.

We piled the sledge high with parcels and only stopped when Michael said that it could stand no more strain. I picked up some of the tins I saw lying on the ground and stuffed them into my pockets. I ripped open a parcel, pushed the chocolate into my mouth and threw the rest of the parcel away. The S.B.O. was walking up and down beside us with a stick, shouting encouragement.

'Come on now, chaps. Don't waste too much time. Take all the food you can. I don't expect these Huns will feed us.'

Occasionally he would wave his stick in the air as if he were leading a charge. He was a half-ridiculous, half-inspiring figure and I felt better for seeing him. Perhaps because he reminded me of a picture I had once seen of General Gordon, I felt that he was in the great British tradition.

We surged forward again. The sledge needed four people to pull it now, but it was quite easy once we had got it started. Tom Jelliss followed behind, tapping the parcels piled on top of it with a stick.

'O.K., you four,' he cried. 'Keep on pulling. I'll stay at the back and see that none of them fall off.'

He managed to give the impression that he was making a great self-sacrifice.

We swung into the road outside the camp. There was a cry at the head of the column which was repeated like a tardy echo all the way down to us and beyond.

'Halt!'
'Halt!'
'Halt!'

The column stopped clumsily like a goods train. We bumped into the boots and sledge of those in front and then rebounded onto the overcoats of those behind.

'What's happening?'
'They're marshalling the column.'

We stood there for two hours.

The day had broken and I was completely exhausted by the time

205

we finally set off, shambling through the snow and dragging our sledges behind us.

<h1 style="text-align:center">5</h1>

But the effect of starting at last was stimulating. We were a long way from the head of the column and had to march fast to keep up. This was pleasant at first. It released the night's pent-up frustration. Soon the sun was shining through the thick snow-coated woods by the side of the road. The iced branches and frosty twigs sparkled delicately and the tramp of the column found a cardboard echo in the heavy stillness, so that it was as if we were walking through some pantomime set on an enormous stage. The sledge flowed smoothly behind us. The cold air nipped our cheeks and noses, and yet we were snug inside our balaclavas. I was suddenly completely happy.

The Germans had evacuated the camp with us so that they were more like fellow refugees than guards. All had heavy packs and some were pushing bicycles through the snow, with little parcels tied to the handle-bars. They were soon completely absorbed in their own problems, thinking about what they had left behind or wondering if they would have to jettison part of what they were carrying. At any time during this march it would have been quite possible to leave the column and escape. But a primitive instinct forbade it. It was no longer just a question of being on one side or another in a war. In the column there was the solid comfortable protection of the herd. Nobody knew what waited for them on either side of the road.

The success of the sledge was encouraging and when Michael saw a little boy standing with a sledge at some cross-roads, watching the column pass by, he went up to him and offered to buy it.

'I'll give you a whole Red Cross parcel for it,' said Michael.

'Come on,' muttered one of the guards, 'keep moving.'

The little boy followed Michael along the road bartering.

'Zwei Paketen!'

'Nein, eine. Eine grosse Rote Kreuz Pakete.'

'I'll have to go and ask my mother,' said the little boy. 'She lives near here. I'll catch you up and tell you what she says.'

He ran off.

'Damn,' said Michael.

But the little boy came back about a quarter of an hour later, pulling his empty sledge behind him and looking up and down the column for Michael. He was firmly resisting the offers of all other buyers. When he found Michael he said in English:

'O.K.,' and went away happily with his Red Cross parcel.

It was an excellent sledge with iron runners and we shifted some of the load from the first sledge onto it.

'I'll try and keep an eye on that too,' said Tom, tapping at the parcels importantly with his stick, 'but it'd be much easier if I could put my pack onto it.'

'Oh, blow it out!'

'How very rude. And I was only trying to help.'

The effect of these first few hours was exhilarating. We were enjoying something close to freedom and whatever else might happen it seemed certain that, as someone had said during the night, the old life we had hated so long had been smashed for ever. Every hour the Germans halted the column for a short rest. It was pleasant to ease off the weight of a pack and to sit by the crisp dry snow at the side of the road, leaning against a sledge and thinking that we would never see the camp's stale stretch of dust and sand again. Mark came round distributing raw prunes out of a packet.

'Two each,' he said, 'excellent thirst-quenchers.'

He sat down beside me.

'This is rather wonderful, isn't it?'

'I know it sounds quite mad, but I don't think I've ever felt so happy in my life.'

'Where do you think we're going to?'

'God knows! But wherever it is, it won't be for long. This is the end.'

Jack Nopps passed in front of us and overheard. He was so heavily swathed in scarves and balaclavas that I didn't recognize him at first. But I knew the voice at once.

'That's right,' he said. '"It won't be long now." Where have I heard that one before?'

Somehow this rather annoyed me. I didn't want jokes to be made which suggested that we were in for another disappointment.

Jack passed on, but Tom came and sat down beside us.

'I say,' he said, pained, 'that was rather unnecessary, wasn't it?'

And that made it even worse. But we had started again within ten minutes, and as I marched I thought only in terms of a rapid end to the war.

At mid-day we came out of the wooded country and followed a secondary road down to the Autobahn. We halted for a rest just short of it and sat round our sledges eating bread and sardines. Michael produced a large tin with an adjustable ventilator cut in the side, and some chips of wood.

'What the hell's that?'

'It's a home-made stove. It should give us all a cup of brew quite quickly.'

We poured water from our water bottles into another tin which he placed over the top of his stove. Then he lit the chips of wood and quickly heated enough water to give us all a drink of cocoa.

'But when did you make that?' I asked him, astonished.

'Oh, just before we left. I thought it might come in useful.'

He threw away the ashes and packed the stove away onto the sledge again.

Glowing with food and hot drink we sat and waited for the column to start.

The small country roads down which we had passed so far had been empty of any other traffic but ourselves. The front might have been hundreds of miles away. But here on the Autobahn — the main Autobahn running south east from Berlin — we saw the first military convoys. Heavy with snow, the lorries and guns seemed to be going in both directions, but there was no sign of confusion or panic. One of the convoys halted by the side of the Autobahn just ahead of us and I walked down our column to see if I could talk to any of the soldiers. A big man wearing a white fur coat with the collar turned up was sitting at the wheel of one of the lorries eating pink sausage with a pen-knife. I was wondering whether I dared talk to him when he said:

'Who the hell are you?'

'Prisoners. English.'

'What — Army?'

'No, Air Force.'

'Oh.'

'What's happening at the front?'

'How should I know? I'm not there.'

'Well, have the Russians broken through?'

'No. Everything's under control.'

He seemed bored with the conversation and looked away. I went back down the column to Mark, Tom, Michael and the rest.

It was during that afternoon that the rest, one by one, dropped out of our party. It was a good thing really, because eleven was an unwieldy number to keep together and divide the rations among at every meal. They seceded for various reasons, but went on the whole without any trouble.

'If you don't mind, I'd rather be on my own.'

'Frank and I are going to make a Mess of two. We think eleven is too many.'

'I'm going to try fending for myself.'

Apologetically they took their share of parcels off the sledge and left.

Only with Bramwell was there any trouble.

'Oh, and there's one more thing, Mark: what about the sledges?'

'That's easy,' said Michael, 'they're both mine.'

'Yes, I daresay, but I was talking to Mark, not you.'

'That's all right, but you were talking about my sledges.'

'Shut up a minute, Michael,' said Mark. He turned to Bramwell. 'What about the sledges?'

'Well, one of them was bought with one of the room's Red Cross parcels, wasn't it?'

'Yes. I suppose it was.'

'Well, then in that case we've all got a share in it, haven't we?'

Michael's face had grown pale.

'No-one's stopping you having your share in it, are they? You've chosen to go away.'

'That's my affair.'

'Well, it's my sledge.'

'But you've got one of your own already.'

Mark was undoing the top of his own rucksack.

'Here you are,' he said. 'Here are two tins of bully and a box of cheese. At a conservative estimate that's about a quarter of a parcel. Your share in the sledge was equal to one twelfth. Now bugger off.'

'Thanks very much.' He took the tins. 'But there's really no need to be offensive about it.'

'That's what you think.'

There was a sudden movement in the column.

'March!'

I jumped up from the side of the road. There was grunting and swearing and a stamping of boots on the snow. We had almost to run to keep up with the column.

209

'I wish to hell they'd give us warning.'

By the time we had settled down again Bramwell had disappeared.

'Bloody good riddance to that sod,' said Michael, tugging fiercely at one of the ropes of the sledge.

Mark said:

'It always worries me when a Mess breaks up. However polite we may all be about it I always feel it's a bit of a reflection on everyone. I mean we ought to be able to stick together.'

During my time as a prisoner I had seen many Messes break up without bitterness and I had moved two or three times myself from one Mess to another so that Mark's censure seemed to me too severe. For a time one would live together with a set of people so intimately that they would seem as much a part of one's life as the sun or one's own hands. Then the camp would move or the room be broken up in some other way and one would be living on exactly the same terms with a completely different set of people. The camp was peopled with Christian names which one kept at a distance.

'I don't think it's as bad as that,' I said. 'On the whole when people break away from a Mess they do it quite voluntarily and without anyone feeling offended. I mean there's not often any personal antagonism. It's just a sensible admission that human beings aren't meant to live together for years like this. It's not anyone's fault that they can't stand each other after a time. They just need a change of people now and again as they need a change of air.'

Mark sucked at a prune for a bit, then spat the stone from his mouth into the deep snow by the side of the road.

'That's a depressing thought. After all we've got to live with one lot of people or another all our lives, whether we're prisoners or not. If what you say is true, then life's altogether pretty hopeless.'

'Oh, but ordinary life's not the same at all. The conditions in which you have to live with people there are quite different.'

But Mark didn't answer.

The scenery on either side of the road changed like time on the face of a clock. At any given moment it was impossible to detect movement and yet if one paid no attention to it for a little and then looked at it again the change that had taken place would be surprising. Sometimes I would get so sick of a stretch of the road that I would think we had been forgotten by time. The ragged tramp of thousands of boots, the occasional cat-call down the column, the straining of ropes, the creak and jingle of the Germans' military equipment, and the complete silence of the snow-bound woods or the flat snow-blanketed countryside would seem permanent. It was as if I had been put into a picture and hung up on a wall. But always there would be a halt, or a tiny silent village, or a farm first seen as a landmark from afar and then passed as a place with cattle and dogs barking, which would break the picture and show that we were moving.

I asked one of the Germans where we were going to. He seemed pleased to be spoken to.

'Cottbus, they told us this morning. But I don't think anyone really knows.'

'But the Hauptmann must know where he's taking us to.'

'Oh, yes, the Hauptmann does, I dare say.'

'Where do you live?' I asked.

'Aachen.'

'Then . . .'

'Yes, I haven't heard from my wife and children for two months.'

'Oh, I expect they're all right, you know. The Americans don't really murder children.'

'It's not them I'm worrying about. I wouldn't mind being where they are. But what if the Russians get me?'

'They're not really as bad as all that either.'

'Oh, aren't they? Do you know that when they broke into East Prussia they murdered every German who had stayed behind. They threw all the babies into the air and caught them on bayonets and I wouldn't like to say what they did to the women.'

'Who the hell told you that? The *Völkischer Beobachter*?'

'No, but we had a lecture by a man from the Propaganda Ministry about it.'

When I told Michael where we were supposed to be going to he said:

'But I asked a goon just now and he said it was somewhere near Berlin.'

The signposts were no help because, presumably to keep off the more important roads and the Autobahn, we were following a zig-zag course.

'Not that it matters much,' said Michael. 'I don't care if we go round in circles for weeks so long as the Russians catch us in the end.'

The sky was solid with thick low cloud which lay flat above us, a reflection of the countryside. It was a world of no sun. Once there

211

was the sound of an aeroplane muffled by the cloud, but it soon died away leaving the old stillness and the separate rustling, scraping noise of the column. We took it in turns to pull the sledges which were little lighter than before because although the others had taken their parcels off we had now put our packs onto them. They continued to move smoothly over the snow and it was a relief to have no pack, but it was only possible for one of us to take a rest at a time. At first we left it to the good will of whoever was resting to relieve one of those pulling after a reasonable interval and this worked in rotation for an hour or two. But during the afternoon the system broke down noticeably often when Tom Jelliss was resting.

Mark said:

'I think we'll have to do the reliefs regularly. There'll have to be a time limit for resting.'

'Really I don't think you need to look so pointedly at me,' said Tom. 'I'm sure I try to do my share.'

'Well, this'll make it easier for you to succeed.'

Secretly I was rather glad that this change had been made necessary, because I found it an increasing strain to offer to start pulling again before I was ready to. Now that this was compulsory it would be easier.

I suppose we were all getting tired. It was becoming a greater and greater effort to start marching after each halt, like having to get out of bed in the morning before one is properly awake. But this was hardly surprising. We had walked about twenty kilometres by the middle of the afternoon and this was more than most of us had walked for years. Moreover we were not particularly fit for the sudden exertion. It was only during the last two weeks that we had been getting a full Red Cross parcel every week and even that was only sufficient for a relatively gentle existence. To offset this there was the moral stimulus given by the sudden acceleration of our lives, and the excitement of a changing countryside and new conditions. But towards the end of the afternoon the physical strain began to assert itself.

At about four o'clock when night was beginning to show itself as a faint darkening of the horizon, a large prison camp came into sight, its gloomy huts and heavily trodden paths standing out like black sores on the snow. It was a wretched place, quite alone in the countryside, an outcast from the society of civilized dwelling places.

'Perhaps they're going to put us up here for the night.'

'Perhaps this is where we're moving to.'

As we came closer I saw little khaki figures wandering from hut to hut and then stopping and staring down the road towards us.

'My God,' said Mark, 'it looks pretty bad from outside, doesn't it? To think we've been living in a place like that for three years!'

I looked at it again. Of course, it was exactly like the camp we had left. It seemed impossible that anyone could live in there for three months without going mad.

When the head of the column drew level with it, more figures appeared from the huts and ran over towards the wire.

'Look!' said Michael. 'They're wearing red berets.'

By the time we had drawn level there was a large crowd on the inside of the wire and voices were shouting backwards and forwards across the road in English.

'Who are you?'

'Airborne Division most of us.'

'How long have you been here?'

'Four months.'

'Where were you captured?'

'Arnhem.'

'Ah well, it won't be long now.'

'Hope not.'

'Guess who's behind.'

'What?'

'I said "Guess who's behind".'

'Who?'

'Joe.'

'Who?'

'Uncle Joe. The Russkis.'

'Oh.'

There was the embarrassed silence that follows a flat joke. Certainly he couldn't be so close behind as all that if the people in this camp were not being moved.

We tramped past their main gate. The sentries in the towers seemed as interested in us as the prisoners were. More prisoners came out of the huts and the whole of the wire along the road was soon lined with pale eager faces.

'How are you off for Red Cross parcels?' shouted Michael.

'What are they?'

'Never heard of them!'

213

'What, haven't you had any parcels?'

'The sick get them sometimes and there was a week or two at the beginning . . .'

Michael stopped the sledges and pulled a tin of corned beef and some cigarettes out of one of the parcels. He ran across the road and threw them over the wire. There was a scramble on the other side.

'Thanks, chum.'

'Thanks very much.'

Other people in the column began to pull out cigarettes and food and throw them over the wire.

'Coming over.'

'O.K.'

'Got it!'

'O.K.'

There was a sudden wild animal shouting from further up the column. A burst of tommy-gun fire shattered the quiet of the snow. The whole column stiffened and was silent. Then everyone began talking again and marched on, but no-one threw anything more over the wire.

There was a lot more shouting.

'Look out!' said a little German soldier who had been pushing his bicycle along beside us, 'the officer's coming.'

The Hauptmann was running back down the road, yelling and waving his tommy-gun, the skirt of his long coat blowing behind him and showing his high boots and leather breeches.

'March! March, damn you! March!' he shouted in German. 'And you,' he screamed up at one of the sentries in a tower, 'what the hell do you think you're doing? Send your prisoners back into their huts at once.'

The sentry, who so far had been more astonished than annoyed at everything that had happened, immediately started shouting down at the khaki figures along the wire. It sounded like a rude imitation of the Hauptmann. The prisoners in the camp moved slowly and sulkily back to their huts.

The Hauptmann was still shouting at random up and down the road, and it was some time before I realized that his anger was directed almost entirely against the German guards and not against us at all. He shouted at every wretched figure in grey that he could single out from the column. They were all so heavily laden and so encumbered by their extra packages or bicycles that they had diffi-

214

culty in standing to attention while they were being shouted at.

'What the hell do you think you are? A German soldier or a tramp? You're supposed to be guarding these prisoners. You know they're not allowed to communicate with anyone on the march, don't you?'

'Jawohl, Herr Hauptmann.'

'Well then, for God's sake obey your orders, man!'

'Jawohl, Herr Hauptmann.'

'And you –' he said, turning to a man with a bicycle, 'what the hell do you think you're doing with all those parcels tied round your bicycle? You look like an old woman going to market, not a German soldier.'

In his fury he tore at the parcels, but they were well tied on and he merely pulled the bicycle over. He gave it a savage kick as it lay on the ground, its wheels spinning, and strode up to the head of the column again. As he passed me I saw that his face was dark red with anger and sweating.

A prisoner helped the little soldier pick up his bicycle.

'Bloody officers,' mumbled the soldier.

Dusk was already creeping round us. We came to some snug red villas placed at a decent interval from each other by the side of the road. I saw hands grasping the curtains in the rooms inside and faces staring out of the windows.

'Perhaps we're coming to a town.'

'I bloody well hope so. I don't look forward to this sort of thing in the dark.'

A girl in a coat and skirt with a handkerchief tied round her head came out of one of the houses and started walking down the road with us.

'Is there a town near here?' I asked her.

'In about two kilometres.'

Her accent sounded strange.

'She says there's a town in about two kilometres.'

'Thank God for that.'

'Are you a German?'

'No, I'm a Ukrainian.'

I was surprised. She was well-dressed for a deportee. I spoke to her in Russian. She was delighted.

'Ah, but you speak so well.'

'Oh, no, not really.'

'Ah, but you do.'

'How have the Germans treated you?'

'Oh, I can't complain at all. I work as a secretary, you see.'

'Oh. Well, you'll be going home soon, I expect.'

'What do you mean?'

'Well, the Red Army's coming.'

She didn't answer.

'Aren't you glad the Red Army's coming?'

'How far away are they?'

'Pretty close. That's why we're being evacuated. But surely you're glad they're coming?'

'I don't know,' she said after a pause. She smiled.

I couldn't think of anything to say. I was glad when she said, 'Good-bye,' and took a side turning off the road.

There were more civilians walking down the road now in both directions and some stopped and looked at us as we passed. There were signs of a town in the distance. I saw a man standing by the side of the road wearing a Russian fur hat, with the flaps up. It was too big for him and looked like a pie stuck on the top of his head. He had a pale knobbly face and a long nose. I spoke to him in Russian.

'Ah, yes,' he replied, 'the Red Army's coming, I dare say.'

It was extremely difficult to make him say anything else, but for some reason he started walking down the road with us.

'How have the Germans treated you?'

'Badly.'

He looked better off than any other Russian prisoner I had ever seen.

'What does he want?' someone asked me.

'I can't think.'

'Ask him if he could sell us any bread,' said Tom. 'We'll have run out by this evening unless the goons give us an issue. Tell him we'll give him a good price.'

'Have you got any bread?' I asked the Russian.

He smiled, showing black, horrible teeth.

He kept pace with us in silence.

'There's a town just down the road, isn't there?' I asked him, to break the silence. It also pleased me to be able to air my feeble knowledge of Russian.

'Just down the road.'

I never discovered what he wanted though he followed us all the way into the town, and, after we had halted in the market place,

216

stood on the pavement watching us until it was almost dark. Whether he was very cunning or very simple, a loyal Russian or a traitor, and above all what it was that so particularly fascinated him about this ragged marching column of English prisoners I shall never know. But for some reason he has stuck in my memory.

The atmosphere in the market place was encouraging. Packs had been taken off and everyone was sitting or lying on sledges waiting for something to happen. In the shadows civilians of all nationalities hovered furtively round the fringe of the column. There was a general impression that the Hauptmann and the S.B.O. had gone off to look for quarters for the night. And even when I saw the S.B.O. himself sitting disconsolately on his sledge staring at the dirty frozen road I was not particularly alarmed. We were in a town. We would sleep in a dry place with a roof. I turned my attention to the civilians flitting round us in the dusk.

For every German in that town there must have been at least five foreigners. I suppose there was a big factory near-by employing foreign workers, but what was really surprising was the variety of nationalities. One expected the French, the Poles and the Russians, even the Italians — slave workers had become a part of society in Germany — but here were also Rumanians, Spaniards, Lithuanians, Czechs and Dutchmen. The news that there were English prisoners in the market place with tinned food to exchange had spread rapidly through the town. It was like the arrival of a trading team in an Esquimo settlement. The dusk lingered as dusk often does in late January, hinting at longer evenings, and trade was brisk.

All around was to be heard the thick ponderous abuse of languages as bargains were struck in the shadows, sardines exchanged for bread, soap for eggs, pullovers for margarine. One Frenchman on hearing of the arrival of the column had quickly hammered some boards together into rough sledges and was now selling them fast for cigarettes to those who had not brought sledges from the camp. John Waggot was buying eggs from an Italian in Latin. Two boys in the uniform of the Hitler Youth on the other side of the road had loaves under their arms, but were afraid to come across and mingle with the column. They made their bargains by a sort of tick-tack method and then threw the bread across the road in return for cigarettes.

In all this the guards made little attempt to interfere. Occasionally they would gently shoo away an Italian or a Pole, but when he came back the second time they would look first to see if there was an officer coming, and if there wasn't take no more notice. I had just agreed with a Frenchman to exchange thirty cigarettes for a loaf of bread when an officer came down the road. A guard who had been standing near me and paying no attention to what I was doing saw him and quickly shouted at the Frenchman, prodding him with the point of his gun. But when the officer had passed, taking no notice at all, he went after the Frenchman and brought him back, so that he could hand over the loaf.

Tricks were played in the gloom by furtive figures who snatched at cigarettes and ran without handing over anything in return, but on the whole the trading was honourable and temporarily stable prices were evolved. These however were constantly being upset. Complaints were heard up and down the column.

'You know people are spoiling the market.'

'No-one should give more than ten cigarettes for an egg.'

'I got one for eight just now.'

'I had to give forty for a loaf of bread.'

'There you are, you see. That's how the market gets spoilt.'

Soon however it grew dark and the bartering died down. Traders of all nationalities slunk away to their holes. We returned to our sledges and waited. The interest and excitement of the extraordinary scene had kept us warm, but now as we waited we began to feel the cold. There was no sign of anything happening. People still talked about the Hauptmann and the S.B.O. looking for quarters. A little wind blew down the street. Gently at first and then more solidly it began to snow.

As the wind blew more strongly and the night settled in the snow drove harder and harder. It came at us almost horizontally so that one had to bend double and turn one's back to avoid it. Even so it soaked into my balaclava and froze my neck. My woollen gloves were soon wet and freezing and my fingers grew so cold that I could not feel them any more. I banged them repeatedly against my sides. When the blood began to return it was as if my hands were being burnt raw and I jumped up and down in pain. They were cold again within five minutes.

Somebody tugged at my elbow. A civilian wearing a cap but no overcoat, with the collar of his jacket turned up and thick with snow, was standing beside me. He was a German.

'Come with me,' he said, 'I have something for you.'

'I don't want to buy anything.'

'It's being given away.'

He had a torch which gave out a feeble blue light and I followed him a few yards down the pavement to where a woman was standing with a steaming jug.

'Would you like some hot coffee?' she asked.

I pushed my mug greedily in front of her can and she poured out a thin brown liquid. The warmth came through my wet gloves to my fingers. I kneaded the palms of my hands carefully round the mug and raised it to my lips, sipping at the coffee. Immediately the warmth flowed to every inch of my body. I went on sipping it noisily, breathing into the steam so that it spread all over my face.

'This is my wife,' said the man who had fetched me, 'if any more of your comrades would like some . . .'

I called out between sips:

'Anyone want some hot coffee?'

There was a rush for the woman.

It was not until I had finished my mug that I thought of thanking her, but by that time she had run out and gone home to fetch some more. I went back to the sledges and told Tom and Mark and Michael about her. They shook some of the snow off themselves and ran to her, untying mugs from their belts.

I was just beginning to think that we should have to spend the night in the market square, when there was a sudden animation in the column, and a shout from the head of it. People stood up adjusting their packs. There was the distant shuffling sound of marching.

'We're off!'

We heaved at the sledges which had become embedded in the road.

We marched round the market square and down a side street. We came to a halt in front of a church. The wind blew in gusts down the street and snow drove at us from all directions. Rumours were talked up and down the column in the blustering freezing darkness.

'We're going to sleep in the church.'

'The church is full of Americans from some other camp.'

'The S.B.O. and the Hauptmann are trying to get alternative accommodation.'

'It's locked and the S.B.O. and the Hauptmann have gone to look for the key.'

We waited outside this church for nearly two hours. I could think of nothing but the cold which made my feet and hands numb,

219

stiffened and grazed my nose and ears and burnt into every bone in my body like a sharp icy acid. I longed for the soft shelter of the church. I thought of the hundreds of churches I had looked into in the past, admiring an arch here or a tomb there and sniffling the quaint musty smell. I had never imagined that one day my only wish would be to be allowed to sleep on the floor of one. Once there was a cry that the gate was being opened and that we were moving in. We collected all our belongings and waited, but nothing happened.

The four of us were so cold and tired that the whole of the time we waited outside the church we hardly spoke to each other. In spite of exhaustion we had to keep moving to keep warm and we wandered endlessly up and down the column always hoping that when we were at the point furthest away from our sledges something would happen to make us go running back to them. But it never did.

More German women, with blankets over their shoulders and scarves tied round their head, came out with jugs and buckets of hot liquid: tea, coffee, weak soup or even plain hot water. It didn't matter what it was so long as it was hot. I wandered about, searching for these women and pushing my mug at every one I saw. I tried to make up for my greed by thanking one of them profusely for her kindness.

'It's nothing,' she said in a gruff, hoarse voice, 'you're human beings after all.'

Another said:

'I hope some other mother would do the same for my son.'

We never went into the church. I had given up all hope of the snow ever stopping or the column ever moving when I heard the familiar voice of Limpet, the adjutant.

'Fall in again, please chaps!'

'Come off it, Limpet. What's happening?'

'Fall in there, please. The S.B.O.'s got the goons to let us into the school.'

Nobody knew anything about the school, but a great cheer went up at this. I was surprised to find that I had the energy left to take part in such a cheer.

'I'm very disappointed we couldn't go into the church,' said Tom. 'I should have loved to spend a night on the altar.'

The column shambled off down a slope, cheerful and animated. In five minutes we arrived at the school. It was a large building with three storeys. Even so, when a thousand of us had swarmed into it, stamping up the stairs, spreading out fanwise at each landing and filling each room like human lava, there was little floor space left anywhere. We left our sledges outside, but took all our parcels and packs in. The floor of the room in which the four of us came to rest was soon solid with packs and bodies, boxes and cooking pots. Somebody even had a rifle.

'Where the hell did you get that rifle?'

'A goon gave it to me before he buggered off.'

'Who buggered off?'

'The goon. He said he just couldn't stand this any longer.'

Tom who had been first into the room had got into a dispute with Hatter about a strip of space along the wall.

'Hey, get up out of there, Hatter. I was there first.'

'What do you mean, you were here first? I'm here now, aren't I? And I didn't kick you out.'

'But I got here first and bagged it with my pack. I had to go and find the rest of my Mess.'

'My dear old boy, there must be roughly a hundred packs littered all over this floor at the moment. How is one to know which is keeping a place and which isn't? No, sorry, the only thing that keeps a place here is a body, and that's why mine is staying here.'

I waited with Michael and Mark on the fringe of this dispute, hoping for a favourable result. By the time Tom had given it up as hopeless almost the whole of the rest of the floor had been occupied and we had to be content with a little puddle of linoleum in the centre. It was a large class-room from which all desks and chairs had been removed, leaving only the floor and the high walls and the white ceiling. We were grateful enough to be there. It was dry except where the snow from overcoats and boots had melted into slush but that was soon mopped up by the mass of human bodies who only wanted somewhere to sit, and we had soon generated an appreciable animal warmth. My body began to glow as I leant back against my kit-bag staring over the sea of legs and packs of faces heaving all round me.

'My God!' said Mark suddenly, 'look over there.'

He pointed to the other end of the room. There was a long blackboard set into the wall there and on it was a lot of writing in chalk. The electric light made the board shiny for me so that I couldn't read it. I leant over to where Mark was sitting.

It was written in English, in a strong round hand:

221

'To be or not to be, that is the question . . .'

I read on and on. The whole of the soliloquy was there, covering almost every inch of the board.

'To die: to sleep,
No more; and by a sleep to say we end
The heart ache and the thousand natural shocks
That flesh is heir to, 'tis a consummation
Devoutly to be wished . . .'

The words came from far, far away, like a voice heard in a dream, an old familiar voice that had made the world and watched it still.

I believe there is a harp which men hang up in trees so that it plays wild tunes when the wind blows through it. So it was now with this music which was not mine and yet seemed to come from deep inside me.

'. . . The undiscovered country from whose bourn
No traveller returns . . .'

The disorder of that crowded room, the voices and the smell of steaming clothes grew round me again. I had to say something which would fit into it.

'Extraordinary! Absolutely extraordinary!'

'How on earth do you think it got there?' asked Mark.

'I suppose someone's been giving an English lesson in here.'

'It seems pretty advanced for an English lesson.'

'Yes, I suppose it does. You think . . .?'

Mark was a romantic.

'Yes, I do. I think that someone heard that we were coming and wrote it up to encourage us.'

It was a pleasant thought, but I didn't think it very likely. I noticed that some of the more obscure words like 'fardels' and 'bodkin' had been underlined in chalk. But I didn't draw Mark's attention to this. I was afraid it might spoil it for him and it was important for me that it should not be spoilt for anyone.

The S.B.O. was standing in the doorway, looking helplessly at the babbling confusion which stretched all over the floor in front of him.

'Quiet, please,' screamed the voice of Limpet cracking suddenly so that it slid hopelessly like a pencil on a slate. Everyone roared with laughter. Still it had the effect of making us pay attention. 'Quiet please,' he said again, deep down, 'the S.B.O. wants to make a speech.'

The S.B.O. said:

'Well done, chaps . . . an excellent day's march . . . showing the Huns a thing or two . . . no issue of food from the Huns, I'm afraid, for some time . . . One last thing,' he concluded, 'I had a great deal of difficulty in getting the Hun Hauptmann to let us into this place. Apparently the local schoolmaster resented having his school defiled by what he called terror murderers . . .' There was a routine jeer at this. 'So don't smash up the place too badly or it may not be so easy to do the trick another time.'

Everyone felt better for the S.B.O.'s speech. It had not told us much, but it gave us something to talk about and made us feel that we were in the know.

'We'll have to start being careful with the food.'

'We'll get down to trading in earnest tomorrow.'

I thought about the objections of the nationalist schoolmaster.

'. . . For who would bear the whips and scorns of time,
The oppressor's wrong, the proud man's contumely . . .'

But of course he was quite right, in a way. We had murdered men, women and children, hundreds of thousands of them.

'What's the time, dear boy?' asked Tom Jelliss.

'Twenty past ten. My God . . .'

'Yes,' he said, nodding pompously, 'do you remember? Seems a long time ago, doesn't it?'

To me it didn't even seem to have any connection at all. This was a new life altogether.

'It's going to be bloody awkward if anyone wants to go to the lavatory in the middle of the night,' said Michael, eyeing the mass of prostrate bodies that stretched between us and the door.

6

The days conformed to a regular pattern. We would set out in the early morning with the light still grey over the snow, marching with a long eager stride if we were near the end of the column or if at the head a short compressed tramp. The pace at the head of the column always had to be controlled because the slightest speed exaggerated itself quickly down half a mile of marching men. In fact, however slowly those at the front marched those behind had to run to keep up. As this was impossible they lagged, so that at the end of the day the column was often spread out over two or three miles of road. Those in front would have found their fuel and lit their fires by the time the end of the column arrived, tired, irritable and hungry.

But every morning the cold air and the prospect of new scenes and new events refreshed us after the cramped exhaustion of the night. We would pull determinedly on the ropes of the sledges, enjoying the changing countryside and wondering what we would see during the day. Certain features of the march which had emerged tentatively on the first day hardened and were accepted as a routine part of existence. Bartering turned from a sport into a necessity. The Germans gave us only half a loaf of bread each for the week, and though each man had originally brought a fair supply of tinned food it was not possible to live by this alone. As the cold and the exercise made us hungry even this disappeared rapidly. Unlike many less fortunate camps we were never starving on this march, although we always wanted more to eat than we had. What was particularly galling was the fact that because there is a limit to the amount of neat cheese, margarine or sardines which the stomach will take we were often unable to eat even what we had. All this made bartering an earnest necessity, and every time we approached a town or a village, Michael and I, who were the only two of our four who spoke German easily, would stuff our pockets full of cigarettes and range round the outskirts of the column approaching bystanders for bread or potatoes.

'Would you exchange bread for cigarettes?'

'How many cigarettes?'

The inhabitants of these towns and villages had seen other columns of prisoners marching through and by the time we arrived they were usually wise to the procedure. Sometimes the women and the old men would be standing ready by the side of the road with loaves of bread under their arms, and if excessive bargaining was necessary they would run alongside the column to complete the exchange. For though the guards did not interfere with any of this they would never let us stop. All bargaining had to be done on the move.

It was possible to pick up two or three loaves a day in this way if one worked hard. Sometimes we would be unlucky. A column of prisoners who were richer in cigarettes than we were had been through a town before us. The market had been spoilt and no German would then part with his bread except for an exorbitant price. This happened invariably after a column of Americans had been through ahead of us. On the rare occasions when we found a village that had seen no prisoners it was possible to obtain a loaf for as little as twenty cigarettes, but prisoners of all nationalities were streaming westwards down almost all the roads of eastern Germany at this time and prices rose steadily throughout the march. By the end one often had to pay a hundred cigarettes for a loaf. Thus prices rose as we had less and less to meet them with and bartering became more and more of a serious business.

It was on about the second day that we began to meet the refugees. There were whole families of them, sitting huddled among the bedsteads and the clothing on their long peasant's carts, with the men driving the horses or leading them by the bit.

Most of the Germans were neither friendly nor antagonistic when we spoke to them. The men seemed completely absorbed in the immediate realities of their experience, intent on getting their carts and horses over the next few miles. The women, sitting numbed and silent at the back of the carts were sometimes scarcely distinguishable from the bundles of household goods all round them and might have been thinking of anything or nothing. The animation of our column and the silence of these caravans contrasted sharply like fast and sluggish currents in the same stream.

'Where are you from?'

'Posen.'

'East Prussia.'

'Breslau.'

'Where are you going to?'

'God knows.'

One of the drivers was a Frenchman still wearing his boat-shaped French Army hat.

'What are you doing?'

'Driving my master.'

'What do you mean – your master?'

'I've been working for him for five years now.'

'Where are you from?'

'Silesia.'

'The war's nearly over!'

'Yes, thank God. Dirty Boche.'

225

There was a cry from somewhere inside the waggon:

'Look after that off-side horse. He's not doing any work.'

'Ja, ja.'

The Frenchman bustled servilely with the reins, whipped the horse and clattered past me.

'What are most of them like?' Mark asked me. 'Friendly or hostile?'

'Oh, pretty friendly.'

He went up to a cart and started talking to the driver in heavy, elementary German. The man paid no attention to him for about a half minute and then turned on him yelling and shaking his fist.

'Swine! Terror bombers! Murderers!'

Mark withdrew.

'Definitely hostile,' he said.

The guards became milder and milder until at the end I was feeling quite sorry for them. They experienced all the gloom and discomfort of the march and none of the expectation. There was no sense of something ending for them. They knew that whatever it was was only just beginning.

One day we stopped for lunch on an exposed strip of road. Flat snow-deep fields stretched away on either side to the grey horizon. A thin row of spiky trees in the middle distance stood hopeless and forlorn in the wind. It seemed a bad place to stop, but someone suggested that the head of the column was probably in a village. We sat down on the road and unpacked some food. We had no more bread left so we ate margarine by itself, hacking it out of the frozen tin in chunks with our knives. A guard, who had just unwrapped his bread and sausage from the *Völkischer Beobachter*, came over to us and said:

'Haven't you got any bread?'

'No.'

He looked distressed.

'Oh, that is bad,' he said, 'they should at least give you some bread.'

He glanced furtively up and down the road.

'Here,' he said, 'have some of this.'

He cut us a slice each off his own loaf. It only left him with a small crust.

'No, you really mustn't do that. You won't have any left for yourself.'

We were embarrassed.

'Ah, that doesn't matter. I'm better off than you.'

We made him share our margarine in return.

After we had eaten Tom went and squatted a little distance away by the side of the road.

'This is most distasteful, I know,' he said, 'but as you will see there is no decent cover anywhere around for about three miles.'

The guard who had given us his bread said, interested:

'Ah, that is most remarkable. He squats the Jewish way.'

In every town and village, in addition to the traders, there were the women who stood by the side of the road with jugs and buckets, giving us water and sometimes hot coffee or soup. They were doing this, not with a self conscious or charitable air, but in a grim everyday fashion as if it were part of their house-work. They took it so much as a matter of course that I often wondered if they knew who they were giving it to. When I asked one of the women, I got the same answer as I had had before.

'I don't care who you are. You're men aren't you?'

Once when we stopped outside a butcher's shop, Michael persuaded the butcher to bring out a bucket of broth. A crowd collected round him, jostling and pushing forward their cups, and the bucket was soon empty. Twice he went back for more.

Michael took him on one side and gave him forty cigarettes.

'That was wonderful soup, Mr. Butcher.'

'It's the best that I can do, but you should have come yesterday really. It was better then.'

Meanwhile Tom had just closed a bargain over their heads with a man at the second floor window of the house. The man threw down a loaf and Tom gave the butcher some cigarettes to hand on to him.

'What, that crook?' said the butcher looking up at the window. 'Oh, all right.'

But the best drink of all came from a little bunch of Ukrainian women while we were on the march. It seemed a fairly large town as we entered it, but we were not going to stop there. The Ukrainians were waiting on a corner at the bottom of a hill. It was a thick meaty brown soup and it was so good that several of us stopped to drink it so that we could fill up our mugs again before moving on. There were tears of pleasure in the eyes of the women.

'Drink! Drink!' they cried happily, ladling the heavy liquid out of the bucket.

The Hauptmann was on top of us without any warning.

'March! March! March! Damn you!'

We scattered.

He stopped and yelled at the women.

I looked back.

'Bloody Bolshevik swine!'

He kicked at the bucket. The women cowered backwards and the brown liquid spread in a wide stain over the snow.

It was towards the end of the day, when we were tired and becoming anxious about where we were going to spend the night, that the march was most unpleasant. Always after each halt it became more and more of an effort to get going again. People became irritable. Thighs ached and feet were sore. And yet the sledges had to be pulled and the shambling column ahead had to be followed, on and on and on through woods and villages and towns, and down vast bleak stretches of road until it seemed that the day would never end. At such moments I found myself surrendering more and more to a sullen despair which alone kept me going. I would walk purposely a little ahead or behind the others so that I didn't have to talk to them. So that I could contain all my tiredness and resentment within myself.

It was at such a moment of one day, a little before dusk, that we passed a column of Russian prisoners coming from the other direction. They had no packs and no sledges, but they staggered as they walked. Their clothes were so ragged that it was impossible to tell what colour or shape or even what garment they had been originally. Many were not even wearing boots, but had rags bound round their feet. Their white starved faces contrasted horribly with the black unshaven growth of beard which covered them. Only their eyes shone out as something human, distressed and furtive but human all the same, flashing a last desperate S.O.S. from the person trapped inside. We emptied our pockets of cigarettes and soap and threw them across to them as they passed. Such things could give them little comfort, but one had to do something in protest.

One of the cigarette packets fell short and a Russian stooped and grovelled for it in the roadway. One of their guards, a civilian carrying a shot gun and wearing the arm band of the Volksturm on his coat, saw him and ran at him, stamping on his fingers, kicking him and striking him over and over again in the face and chest with the butt of his gun. The Russian collapsed and lay on the ice-hard

228

road whimpering like a dog that had been run over.

There was a wild roar of rage from every part of our column that had seen this. The guard stopped beating the Russian and looked up astonished. He had obviously become so hardened to brutality that it no longer occurred to him that human beings had any right to protest. He was at a loss for a moment. Then he started shouting at us and waving his gun. It was the only thing he knew how to do, and if he had not found himself faced by so many he would not have confined himself to the threats. But for once in his life even his threats were drowned by the roaring and jeering from two or three hundred angry voices. Some of our own guards came running up the side of the column. When they saw what was happening they went over and talked to the man, tapping him on the shoulder and shooing him after his own prisoners. Meanwhile the Russian in the roadway had recovered. He staggered after the others and rejoined them, even remembering to pick up the packet of cigarettes on the way.

'My God!' said Michael, 'I'll forgive the Russians absolutely anything they do to this country when they arrive. Absolutely anything.'

After I had seen this I didn't feel sorry for myself any more. During the next few months self-pity often crept easily into the mind, a secreted antidote to pain, but always I had only to look at the pathetic weak figures of the Russians who struggled for life all round me to exchange it for the depths of shame. Day after day for three or four years they had lived through extremes of hunger and misery which we had never known, and yet they smiled or said 'Good Morning' or winked behind the back of a guard as they ran their fingers eagerly round the tins which we had thrown away into the incinerator. Sometimes even human hope would flicker for a moment in their sunken glassy eyes.

7

Thus the days of the march shared a common pattern and even before it was over they had merged easily into one another. It quickly became difficult to remember on what day such and such an incident had occurred.

The nights however were different. Every night we stopped in a place with a personality of its own, and there was time for this personality to establish itself. So it is the nights which peg out the march coherently in memory.

The night in the Church with Tom sleeping high up among the cushions on the fantastic rococo pulpit, and Michael playing poker in the pews.

The night in the second school, more dilapidated and less comfortable than the first, with the German family in the basement who gave us hot water.

'Have you always lived here?' I asked the woman.

'Oh, no, we're evacuees. We live in East Prussia.'

'Oh, I see.'

'We didn't come straight here. We went to live with my mother's family near Breslau first of all. Then when the Russians came we had to move again. This is the second time we've had to move.'

'When do you think the war will be over?'

'I don't know,' she said. 'What does it matter so long as we win in the end?'

'But you don't really still believe in victory, do you?'

'Of course. The Führer knows what he's doing.'

I found this conversation unsettling. I had heard people talk exactly like that in England during the Battle of Britain. Perhaps the war would last for years yet.

It was in this school, after we had settled down for the night, adjusting ourselves as amicably as possible among the bodies that overlaid us ('I hope you're not a restless sleeper, old boy' – 'Well, I'll try not to turn over more than once or twice') and feeling the wind as it blew straw and dust from the crannies of the attic into our faces, that Michael said:

'I've only been in one bloodier place than this for the night, and that was when I was reporting the Spanish Civil War. It was a place exactly like this only there were machine gun bullets coming through the roof and three-quarters of the Spaniards lying all round and on top of me were dying. Still, I did know that if I survived the night I should be back in England in a couple of days and I can't say the same thing now.'

Then there was the night in the glass factory. No-one who experienced that will ever forget it. Not that it was uncomfortable: it was in fact the most luxurious place we found. But it was also the weirdest and certainly for those who slept near the blast furnace the most macabre. An unearthly blue light beat down on us as we settled our packs and sledges all over the warm brick floor. Faces turned a livid green and the hum and throb of machinery soothed the atmosphere. At the vast round bowl of the furnace, peeping white hot from chinks in the fittings, we hung our soaking boots and socks to dry or boiled bucketfuls of water in a few minutes. And all the time the glass blowers, patient and unconcerned, pursued their peculiar trade.

We had washed and were beginning to make preparations for a meal, deciding whether we could afford one or two tins of stew and one or two slices of bread, when Tom said:

'I shall go mad if I have to spend the whole night in here. Couldn't we go and look for somewhere else?'

We thought about it. We were free to move anywhere we liked in the factory, and although the heat from the furnace was an advantage the noise of the machinery and the ghastly light were unsettling. We decided to search for other quarters. As we came out into the darkness Mark said:

'That's funny, it's quite warm out here too. I hope it's not going to thaw.'

There was a man standing in the shadows. He was a civilian and had a promising furtive air about him.

'I'll catch you up,' I shouted to the others.

'What have you got?' I asked the man.

'Potatoes – cooked and hot. They're lovely.' He spoke German like a Pole.

I looked inside the paper bag.

'I'll give you twenty cigarettes for them.'

'All right.'

He handed them over.

'Are you a Pole?'

'Yes.'

'Heard any news?'

'The Russians are still advancing.'

'How do you feel about the Russians?'

'They're all right. I've worked in Russia. It's a wonderful country.'

It was a change to talk to a Pole who had something good to say for the Russians.

I went after the others. I found them just inside the packing shed. All round the walls were stacks of paper and cardboard, and, waiting to be packed, all types of glass-manufactured goods: bowls, ash

231

trays, glasses, cigarette-holders and hideous ornamental horses and fawns. Other groups of prisoners had already settled there, tearing down great quantities of paper and cardboard for bedding.

'This doesn't look too bad,' said Mark, putting down his pack.

I noticed that Michael wasn't there.

'Where's Michael?'

'Outside, talking to some goon in a hat.'

There were some French prisoners in the shed, workers in the factory. They were helping people to tear the packing to bits, and seemed to be in very good spirits.

'Les chars soviétiques sont déjà à Küstrin.'

'Si vous voudriez une femme . . .'

Michael came in.

'Come on, chaps,' he said, 'I've got just the place for us.'

'Who's that goon you were talking to?'

'The Works Manager. He's going to let us into his office.'

So in the end we had a room of our own. Admittedly its furniture was strange, consisting mostly of lathes and machine saws and lone loose straps connecting wheels, but when we shut the door the peace was wonderful. In an attempt to strengthen our hold on the place we asked the Works Manager to share our supper with us. It was a good move. He refused the supper, but gave us a key of our own.

Later in the evening there came a knock at the window. We had finished our supper and I was lying on a work bench, enjoying the prospect of being able to stretch and turn in my sleep as much as I liked for the first time since the march had begun. Tom and Michael were playing a sort of double patience on the floor and Mark was dreamily reading aloud to himself from a book propped against a vice:

'If there be any beauty, and if there be any truth, think on these things . . .'

The knock came again, louder. It rattled the glass in the frame.

Mark went over and unlocked the door. It was Jack Nopps.

'Nice little place you've got for yourselves here,' he said grudgingly.

'Yes.'

He went over to an electric fitting in the wall.

'I just wanted to see if you'd got the right sort of plug, because if you have . . . Yes, just what I was looking for. You don't mind if I

232

bring the boys along for the night do you, and we fit up the set in here?'

So that night we listened to a complacent well-fed voice which said:

'This is the B.B.C. Home Service . . .'

and told us about the Russian advance into Silesia as if it was something that was going on in a drawing room, and how the prisoners of war moving westwards down the roads of Germany made a picturesque sight dragging their little sledges behind them.

It thawed the next day.

The first thing I knew of it was when I was awakened by the scream of the machine saw and the slap and rustle of the driving belts. A little German in a square peaked cap was at work. Jack Nopps was up and dressed, talking to him.

'Hey, what the hell's going on?' I asked.

'It's raining,' said Jack, 'raining hard. I'm just getting this goon to make some wheels for a trolley for the S.B.O.' He paused. 'Actually, I'm getting him to make some for me too. I think he'd even make some for you if you asked him nicely.'

It was a sudden unmistakable thaw and though some people persisted in ignoring it by starting out with sledges they had to admit defeat by midday when the snow was already lying about in dirty isolated lumps like newspapers left on the stands after a race meeting. The road was soon lined with discarded sledges which only the day before had been their owners' most valuable possessions.

But though wheels now replaced runners the pattern of the day's march was little altered. There was just something else to be bartered for now, although reliable carts and trolleys were not easy to get. The best one we saw was being used by an old woman to whom we offered everything we could think of: margarine, cheese, cigarettes, soap – in vain. For a moment her eyes lit up with excitement at the thought of it all. Then they dulled again and she shook her head.

'It is a long time since I have had such things, but how would I fetch my coal if I had no cart?'

Just before we left, the German workman had made little wooden wheels for our sledge. These looked precarious from the very beginning and sagged and wobbled ominously. But they lasted until the middle of the afternoon when they finally split and collapsed as we were passing over a level crossing. Our food and clothes spilt all over the road, the tins rolling under the feet of those following and the clothes being splashed with slimy muddy scars. We grovelled panic-stricken in the road for a few minutes, but picked most of it up again and stuffed it into our packs. For the first time we had to carry all our possessions. But as we had already eaten a large part of them this was no longer impossible as it would have been at the start. A little later Tom bought a rickety pram from some children for a few lumps of sugar. It looked as if it would collapse in the first five minutes, but actually lasted the rest of the march.

That night we slept in a barn. The fight to secure sufficient space in which to sleep was worse than ever because no lights were allowed for fear of setting fire to the straw. We plunged with our packs and pram straight from the moonless gloom of the night into the black unknown interior of the barn. There were already about five hundred men inside it fighting their way through the straw and bodies for space they could only feel. Tempers ran high. It was the hopelessness caused by being unable to see which made the confusion so distressing.

'For Christ's sake, look out, can't you?'

'I've got to find somewhere.'

'Damn your eyes, you're treading on my hand.'

'Get on, can't you?'

'No, I can't. There's no room here.'

The voices came out of blackness.

With hands and feet I felt the bodies lying on the ground or standing helplessly in front of me, but I could see nothing. There was a continuous rustling and stamping in the straw as if it were alive with a legion of enormous maggots. Blindly following the overcoat of the man in front I found myself with one foot on the bottom rung of a ladder. When I had gone half way up the overcoat stopped.

'It's no good. There's no room up here.'

I tried to go down, but I was wedged.

'Go on up, damn you. What are you waiting for?'

'I can't. There's no room.'

A new sensation started inside my head. First, there was the despair, overwhelming and complete. This was what life really was. This was all — confusion, hate, helplessness, indifference and misery. Then on top of the despair came the tantalizing prodding of a stick on the raw brain. Life would not let me stop and admit defeat. I could not just give up. I had to go on living, knowing this despair and yet

234

never being able to accept it.

This feeling now became a physical pain in my head. Because I was a human being I could not just leave the ladder and stop, as one sometimes stops in a dream. I had to go on shouting against the frustration above and below me until in the end I found a place where I could collapse into the straw.

In the morning sleep had made me feel better. I remembered my thoughts of the previous evening clearly as I laced up my boots and put on my pack for the day's march, but I had recovered hope as well. Now I thought: it is only a matter of enduring this for a little longer. It will not always be like this. I must brace myself to hang on to hope until the end of the war. That will bring the end of all this.

And the march, revealing new places and new possibilities every day helped to keep this hope alive. The march was leading us all towards a climax which amongst other things would contain the end.

So I was glad when at the end of the sixth day we trudged into a marshalling yard and halted alongside a train of cattle trucks. The Hauptmann ran up and down shouting at everybody, trying to decide how many men to allot to each truck and at the same time trying to make his guards stop the civilians from trading with us. The S.B.O. followed him with a gentle smile of patience and satisfaction. We sat down by the railway line, lit fires and cooked stew, traded and wondered where the train would take us to.

In the end we lay on the filthy floor in the darkness, sixty men to a truck. This was civilization compared with the crowding which the Germans usually enforced on prisoners and slave workers when moving them by cattle truck. Even so one had to accept slightly more of the next door man's arms and legs on top of one than during the previous nights. And it must have been unpleasant for the man who slept with his face close to the slit by the door which the Germans, unusually, allowed for sanitation. But the slow bump of the wheels which after a few hours started underneath us made discomfort unimportant. We were moving with the train towards the end of it all.

A day of bumping. And squeaking to a standstill after a few hours. And bumping on again.

At one halt the S.B.O. persuaded the Hauptmann to let us out of the trucks for exercise and fresh air. An armoured train from the other direction came to rest alongside us. There was some brisk trading for bread in and out of the guns and the tanks. The soldiers seemed very glad to get cigarettes before they rolled on again towards the East.

Once an astonishing rumour seeped into the truck.

'Have you heard?'

'No, what?'

'A deputation from the German Foreign Office met the train at that last halt and had a talk with the S.B.O.'

'Perhaps it's a peace move.'

'Perhaps they're going to send us to a neutral country.'

Another night, more irritating than the one before. I felt suffocated by a whole day of everyone's familiar jokes and complaints. We had not expected to spend two nights in the train. A guard had said that we were only going a hundred kilometres.

In the middle of the second day an unusually long halt. Three hours. Four hours.

There was a tiny grilled window at one corner of the truck and we knew that we were in a marshalling yard. We were not allowed to get out of the trucks.

I could hear Jack Nopps' voice growling away at the other end of the truck.

'I expect this place is down on "Butch" Harris' list for tonight and the goons are saving the treat for us. I could just imagine a few four thousand pounders coming down among this lot.'

He looked contemptuously round the carriage as if he thought it would do us all a lot of good.

Tom was standing by the grille, looking out of it.

'Perhaps this is our destination,' he said.

'What's it look like, Tom?'

'The arse-piece of the world.'

It was dusk when they let us out onto the platform. I asked one of the guards if we had arrived.

'Yes, I think there's a camp here somewhere.'

The word camp rang like an alarm bell. Of course I had known that our destination would be a camp of some sort, but always at the back of my mind there had been a feeling that it would not be a camp in the old sense. Something might even happen before we got to it, but if not, it would be only a sort of transit camp, the last stage before the final release. But when I heard the guard talking of a camp in this dull matter-of-fact tone the word suggested once again the old timeless backwater.

It was dark before we finally marched off again. We moved fast, carrying everything we had. We had had to leave all carts and trolleys behind when we entrained.

It was good to be able to stretch out again after the cramped conditions in the train. Through the blacked-out town we went, marching for the first time almost in step and whistling in unison, not patriotic songs but cowboy and Walt Disney tunes which we had whistled when in England. They echoed shrilly through the empty streets. The town beat with the sound of our marching. The inhabitants sat behind their blacked-out windows wondering perhaps who would be marching through their town next.

'. . . singing yi, yi, yippy, yippy, yi,
Singing yi, yi, yippy, yippy, yi . . .'

We swung up the hill. There was a mist of light coming up from behind it, like the headlights of some car in the distance. Only this light was not moving. The whistling died down. We reached the top. The familiar pattern of a prisoner of war camp at night lay before us in the hollow. We weren't marching in step any more.

Outside the gates we stopped and waited. There was a lot of congestion at the front of the column, and voices were shouting in English and German. Apparently there was some sort of count going on. We sat down on our packs. It began to rain.

After a bit we became too cold and wet to be able to go on sitting down, so we walked about asking each other questions, hopelessly trying to find out from each other what the camp was like.

'I've heard that our part of the camp's quite comfortable.'

'Do you know if they've got any parcels?'

Inevitably people were again beginning to think in terms of settling down.

There was still a lot of shouting in the distance ahead, and every now and again there would be a surge forward and we would pick up our bags only to come to rest ten yards further on.

Someone found a German who belonged to the camp. He was

237

wearing the green uniform of the Army and kept on saying that he couldn't answer any more questions because he had to get away to a date in the town. But the crowd round him wouldn't let him out so he had to go on answering.

'Yes, it's a big camp. Officers and men.'

'Yes, a lot of British — mostly other ranks.'

'Yes, a lot of other nationalities — Norwegian, Americans, Poles, Jugoslavs, French, Russians . . . Oh, all nationalities.'

'No, there are no rooms for the officers. Just barracks.'

'No, I don't think there are any Red Cross parcels just at the moment.'

It was raining harder now and we were all soaked. Very gradually we moved forward until we arrived at the gate. Torches and search-lights revealed the rain driving millions of steel needles down through the darkness. The Germans were collecting us into tens and then sending us through the gate. Limpet was there, running back-wards and forwards like a sheep dog trying to get us through the gate as quickly as possible.

'There'll be a bath and a hot meal when you get inside, chaps. The goons have promised it.'

'A hot meal. Did you hear?'

'Hot baths when we get inside!'

Our longing for such things dulled all sense of reality. We repeated the words amongst ourselves.

Mark came up to me. A searchlight caught his face for a moment, tired and glistening with rain.

'Thank God for that,' he said, 'a hot meal and a bath when we get inside. Sounds too good to be true, doesn't it?'

It was. They got us as far as an annexe to the shower room and there we stuck.

Duckboards covered the floor. We set down our packs and waited. The room filled. Every few minutes we had to squash closer up against each other. Soon it was impossible to sit down any more. Voices were raised in protest, but still people forced their way in.

'Move over, can't you?'

'No, I bloody well can't. I'm right up against a wall as it is.'

Outside in the darkness could be heard the continuous shouting of Germans. The rain came down so hard on the tin roof that it sounded like gravel. But it made one grateful for cover, even under these conditions. I just managed to squeeze my hand into an overcoat

238

pocket and pulled out my battered anthology.

'The blessed Damozel leaned out
From the gold bar of heaven . . .'

For a few moments the confusion and the pressure of bodies all round me faded.

'When round his head the aureole clings,
And he is clothed in white,
I'll take his hand and go with him
To the deep wells of light,
And we will step down as to a stream
And bathe there in God's sight.'

'Bah!' I said in disgust and stuffed the book into my pocket.
'What's the matter, dear boy?' asked Tom with mock concern, 'Something paining you?'
Then the air raid siren blew and the lights went out.

Several hours later the showers started. They were cold by the time our turn came, but it was pleasant to be able to take off one's clothes for the first time for a week.

Afterwards I talked to the German who was supervising the two Russians who turned the taps on and off.

'All right,' he said, 'I'll admit we've lost, but what's that got to do with it? We've been fighting for decent things and it doesn't make them any less decent just because we've lost. I'd rather go down fighting.'

He sucked comfortably at his pipe.

'How long have you been here?'

'Three years.'

M_____ _____ over his wireless _____ contacting the Russians and had search. _____ parts to them until after the

It was about four o'clock in the morning when the search started. The Germans seemed almost as tired as we were. It was a pointless search because everything of any value had been deposited with the French or the Russians beforehand. The Germans looked as if they knew this, but they went through with what they had been told to do, laboriously and politely like customs officers.

I was very tired. My brain was drugged with exhaustion. In spite of all my clothes and the stuffiness of the hut I was beginning to shiver as I left it.

A guard was taking parties of twenty at a time to the officers' compound. Somehow I had got separated from Mark and the others. Perhaps because I was so tired this struck me as a great calamity. Miserably I shuffled with nineteen strangers through the rows of barbed wire. It seemed an enormous camp.

Bleak grey silhouettes of huts and barbed wire stretched on all sides to the horizon. As I looked streaks of yellow appeared on the distant edges, the first signs of the dawn.

We were counted through another gate. It was locked behind us. We stood still for a moment, staring at the mud round our feet and at the yellow brick huts which lay ahead of us like disused uncared-for public lavatories.

'Well,' said someone, picking up the pack which he had dumped for a moment in the mud, 'here we are.'

As I searched for a vacant bed through the damp evil-smelling barrack blocks, filled with row after row of triple tiered bunks on which hundreds of exhausted men lay sleeping, the old feeling of complete despair returned. This was truth. This was what life really was: something foul and heartless, something with no good in it whatsoever. However much men might look the other way and pretend that this was not so, they lied. I too had once had my absurd hopes and beliefs, my dreams of escape and liberation. Now I knew that though of course I should be released one day, there could be no real escape or liberation from this, ever.

In a last minute revolt against this despair I tried to think of everything that I had once held dear.

Those I had loved. For me they had all died more than three years ago. And had I ever really loved them?

Beauty. Where was it now?

I thought of the anthology in my pocket. Once I had believed that the beauty which it contained could never . . . . I had believed that whole of life. Now the idea was absurd. I thought of the . . . . . in the book and they were worthless.

I had been through all the barrack blocks except one. I should have to lie down somewhere in the next one even if it was full. Just before I went into it I pulled the book from my pocket and dropped it onto the ground. It lay there for a moment, its leaves turning slowly in the wind which blew over the mud, the breath of a new day. Then it was trampled out of sight by the boots of the man behind me.